J.M. SYNGE
TRAVELLING
IRELAND

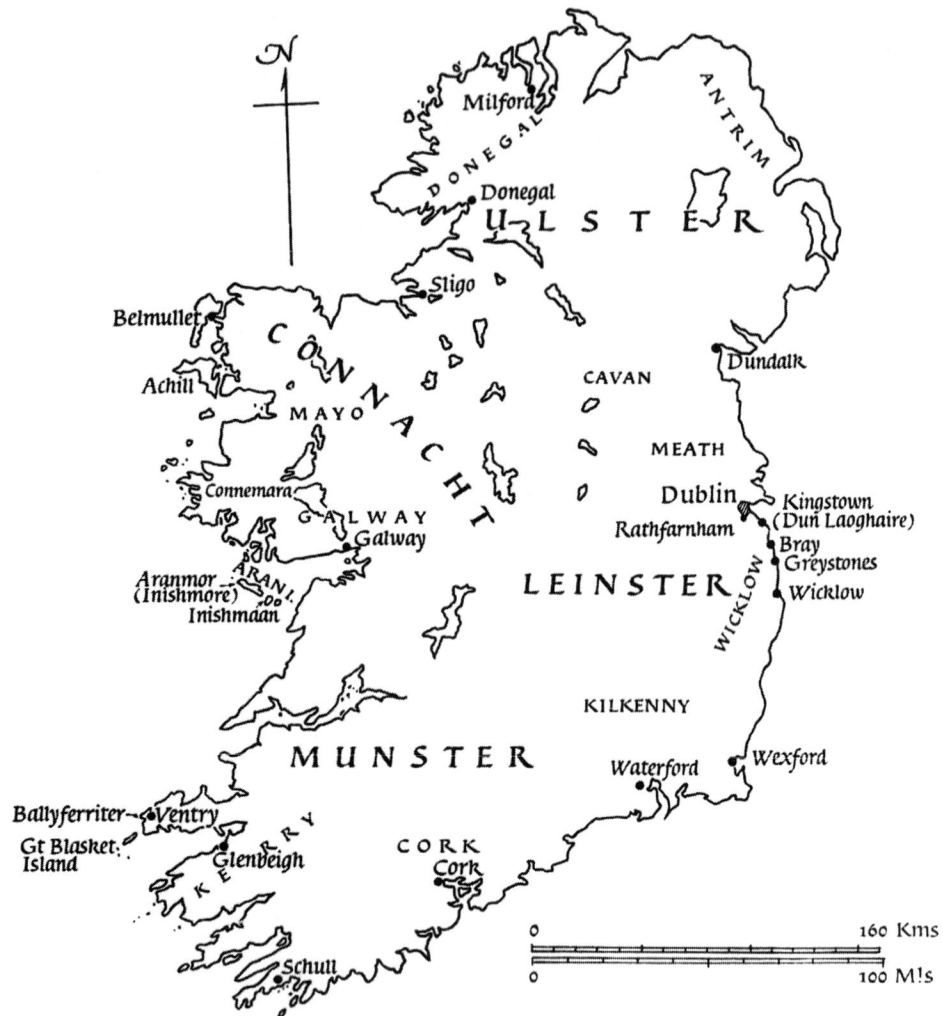

Map of Ireland

J.M. SYNGE
TRAVELLING IRELAND

ESSAYS 1898–1908 *Edited by Nicholas Grene*

THE LILLIPUT PRESS
DUBLIN

First published 2009 by
THE LILLIPUT PRESS
62–63 Sitric Road, Arbour Hill
Dublin 7, Ireland
www.lilliputpress.ie

Copyright © The Lilliput Press and Nicholas Grene, 2009

ISBN 978 1 84351 157 1

1 3 5 7 9 10 8 6 4 2

All rights reserved. No part of this publication may
be reproduced in any form or by any means
without the prior permission of the publisher.

A CIP record for this title is available
from The British Library.

Set in 13 on 16pt Jensen by Marsha Swan
Printed by MPG Books Group, Bodmin, Cornwall, UK

Contents

Illustrations — vii
Acknowledgments — ix
Abbreviations — xi
Introduction — xiii
Note on the Text — li

ESSAYS

'A Story from Inishmaan' (1898) — 3
'The Last Fortress of the Celt' (1901) — 10
'An Autumn Night in the Hills' (1903) — 22
'A Dream of Inishmaan' (1903) — 29
'An Impression of Aran' (1905) — 31
'The Oppression of the Hills' (1905) — 36
'In the "Congested Districts": From Galway to Gorumna' (1905) — 40
'In the "Congested Districts": Between the Bays of Carraroe' (1905) — 45
'In the "Congested Districts": Among the Relief Works' (1905) — 50

CONTENTS

'In the "Congested Districts": The Ferryman of Dinish Island' (1905)   55

'In the "Congested Districts": The Kelp Makers' (1905)   60

'In the "Congested Districts": The Boat-Builders' (1905)   65

'In the "Congested Districts": The Homes of the Harvestmen' (1905)   70

In the "Congested Districts": The Smaller Peasant Proprietors' (1905)   75

'In the "Congested Districts": Erris' (1905)   80

'In the "Congested Districts": The Inner Lands of Mayo – The Village Shop' (1905)   85

'In the "Congested Districts": The Small Town' (1905)   90

'In the "Congested Districts": Possible Remedies – Concluding Article' (1905)   95

'The Vagrants of Wicklow' (1906)   100

'The People of the Glens' (1907)   107

'At a Wicklow Fair: the Place and the People' (1907)   117

'A Landlord's Garden in County Wicklow' (1907)   122

'In West Kerry' (1907)   126

'In West Kerry: the Blasket Islands' (1907)   138

'In West Kerry: to Puck Fair' (1907)   152

['In West Kerry: at the Races' (1910)]   165

'In Wicklow: On the Road' (1908)   178

Bibliography   183

Illustrations

Map of Ireland (Photographic Centre, Trinity College Dublin) — ii

Map of Wicklow (reproduced from Ann Saddlemyer (ed.), *Letters to Molly: John Millington Synge to Maire O'Neill* (Cambridge: Harvard University Press, 1971) — xvi

Margaret and Pegeen Harris, Coolnaharrigle, Mountain Stage, Co. Kerry (photo by Synge) — xx

Map of Connemara (reproduced from *Mecredy's Road Map of Connemara for Tourists and Cyclists*, Glucksman Map Library, Trinity College Dublin) — xxv

Rail map of Ireland (reproduced from Michael Baker, *Irish Railways Past and Present*, Volume I (Peterborough: Past and Present Publishing, 1995)) — xxviii

Map of Kerry railways (reproduced from John O'Donoghue, *The Sunny Side of Ireland, as Viewed from the Great Southern and Western Railways* (Dublin: Alex Thom, [1898])) — xxix

Title-page of *The Gael*. — xxxv

'The Last Fortress of the Celt', *The Gael*, April 1901. — xxxvii

Title-page of *The Green Sheaf*. — xxxix

ILLUSTRATIONS

Title-page of *The Shanachie*.	xliii
Spinning girls (photo by Synge, Paris)	13
Launching the curraghs (photo by Synge, Paris)	14
The fishermen's return (photo by Synge, Paris)	16
Going for turf (photo by Synge, Paris)	18
'You've come on a bad day', said the old woman (M. O'Flaherty)	24
Near Castelloe, Co. Galway, (Jack B. Yeats)*	40
[The Poorest Parish]: Connemara Mare and Foal (Jack B. Yeats)	45
A Man of Carraroe (Jack B. Yeats)	49
Relief Work (Jack B. Yeats)	50
The Causeway of Lettermore (Jack B. Yeats)	54
The Dinish Ferryman (Jack B. Yeats)	55
Gathering Seaweed for Kelp (Jack B. Yeats)	60
Kelp-Burning (Jack B. Yeats)	64
Boat Building at Carna (Jack B. Yeats)	65
A Cottage on Mullet Peninsula (Jack B. Yeats)	70
Outside Belmullet (Jack B. Yeats)	75
Belmullet (Jack B. Yeats)	80
The Village Shop (Jack B. Yeats)	85
Mayo Fair (Jack B. Yeats)	90
The Emigrant (Jack B. Yeats)	95
The Tinker (Jack B. Yeats)	106

* The titles given for the Jack B. Yeats drawings here are taken from the definitive catalogue in Hilary Pyle, *The Different Worlds of Jack B. Yeats* (Dublin: Irish Academic Press, 1994), pp. 129–33. The illustrations to the *Manchester Guardian* articles were without captions.

Acknowledgments

The drawings of Jack B. Yeats used as illustrations for the essays 'In the Congested Districts' and 'The Vagrants of Wicklow' appear by permission of DACS on behalf of the Estate of Jack B. Yeats; the photographs by Synge are reproduced courtesy of the Board of Trinity College Dublin. The book would not have been possible without the financial support of the School of English, Trinity College, The Provost's Academic Development Fund, and the Trinity Association and Trust, which is gratefully acknowledged.

    I owe a special debt of thanks to Emilie Pine, who typed the whole text, and to Sophia Grene, who provided copies of the original articles from *The Manchester Guardian*. In the sourcing and preparation of the illustrations, I acknowledge gratefully the help of the staff of the National Library of Ireland; within Trinity College I have to thank the Library staff of the Manuscripts and Early Printed Books Departments, Paul Ferguson of the Glucksman Map Library, Brendan Dempsey and Brian McGovern of the Photographic Centre, and, for the recovery of otherwise inaccessible audiotaped material, Martin Murphy of Audio-Visual and Media Services. Elaine Maddock of the School of English gave endless and endlessly patient technical support. For the provision of all sorts of information which I could have found in no other way, I want to thank Aidan Arrowsmith, Angela Bourke, David Fitzpatrick, Muiris Mac Conghail, Cormac Ó Gráda and Hilary Pyle. I am especially grateful to Eamon Ó Fiachán

ACKNOWLEDGMENTS

and Pat O'Shea, grandson and great-grandson of Philly and Margaret Harris, Synge's hosts in Mountain Stage, for the benefit of family memories of his visits. I owe an enormous debt of gratitude to my colleague Paul Delaney for his generosity and care in reading my whole manuscript so meticulously. The mistakes that remain are none of his fault. As always, I have benefited from the advice, judgment and help of my wife Eleanor, not to mention the pleasure of her company on our joint tour of Synge sites in the West of Ireland. I am grateful to Antony Farrell of Lilliput Press for agreeing to publish the book and seeing it through to completion.

Abbreviations

CL I-II John Millington Synge, *Collected Letters*, ed. Ann Saddlemyer (Oxford: Clarendon Press, 1983), 2 vols.
CW I-IV J.M. Synge, *Collected Works*, general editor Robin Skelton (London: Oxford University Press, 1962–8) 4 vols:
    I *Poems*, ed. Robin Skelton (1962)
    II *Prose*, ed. Alan Price (1966)
    III *Plays*: Book 1, ed. Ann Saddlemyer (1968)
    IV *Plays*: Book 2, ed. Ann Saddlemyer (1968)
Greene & Stephens David H. Greene and Edward M. Stephens, *J.M. Synge 1871–1909* (New York: Collier, 1961 [1959])
Hannigan & Nolan Ken Hannigan and William Nolan (eds), *Wicklow: History and Society* (Dublin: Geography Publications, 1994)
Interpreting Synge Nicholas Grene (ed.), *Interpreting Synge: Essays from the Synge Summer School 1991–2000* (Dublin: Lilliput, 2000)
Mc Cormack W.J. Mc Cormack, *Fool of the Family: A Life of J.M. Synge* (London: Weidenfeld & Nicolson, 2000)
Micks W.L. Micks, *An Account of the Constitution, Administration and Dissolution of the Congested Districts Board for Ireland from 1891 to 1923* (Dublin: Easons, 1925)
Ó Muirithe Diarmaid Ó Muirithe, *A Dictionary of Anglo-Irish* (Dublin: Four Courts, 1996)

Introduction

In the 'Preface' to *Synge and the Ireland of His Time*, W.B. Yeats tells how he consoled himself during his friend's final illness with the thought that at least Synge 'would leave to the world nothing to be wished away – nothing that was not beautiful or powerful in itself, or necessary as an expression of his life and thought'.[1] The Preface goes on to explain why *Synge and the Ireland of His Time* was appearing as a separate pamphlet rather than as the Introduction to the four-volume *Works of John M. Synge*, published by Maunsel in 1910. Yeats had quarelled bitterly with the publisher George Roberts over the decision to include in the *Works* the twelve essays, 'In the "Congested Districts"', published in the *Manchester Guardian* in 1905. For Yeats this inferior journalistic writing was not worthy of the Synge canon, but something to 'be wished away'.

With the authority of Synge's executors apparently behind him, Roberts had won the day in this argument. The fourth volume of the 1910 *Works* had duly appeared with the somewhat awkward subtitle: 'In Wicklow, In West Kerry, In the Congested Districts and Under Ether,' the latter a previously unpublished piece Synge had written about his experience of undergoing his first operation under general anaesthesia. In 1911, however, the topographical essays were collected as *In Wicklow,*

---

1. W.B. Yeats, *Synge and the Ireland of His Time* (Dundrum: Cuala, 1911), n.p.

INTRODUCTION

West Kerry and Connemara with eight newly commissioned drawings by Jack Yeats, to match those that illustrated *The Aran Islands* as originally published in 1907, and this was to become the received form of Synge's travel writings. Although Roberts and Yeats were initially at odds over the issue of literary standards, they were both concerned to compose Synge's work into a monumental completed *oeuvre*. The invented title *In Wicklow, West Kerry and Connemara* brings together three picturesque areas of rural Ireland into a resonantly rhythmic and alliterative cadence. North Mayo, one of the less famously scenic of the Congested Districts observed is omitted, as is the term 'congested districts' itself, with all its associations of political and social issues. The travel writings are aestheticized and removed from their historical contexts.

The aim of this edition is to re-historicize them. Yeats wanted within the *Works* nothing that was not 'beautiful or powerful in itself'; Roberts in publishing *In Wicklow, West Kerry and Connemara* sought to produce another book to complement *The Aran Islands* and the plays by which Synge had won his fame. My aim, by contrast, is to return to the original writings of the literary journalist who was still struggling to get published, who wrote and re-wrote his reflections in Ireland for whatever journals or newspapers could be persuaded to take them. In place of a travel book organized by area,[2] the original texts of the essays published in his lifetime are here arranged in the chronological order of their publication. *Synge and the Ireland of His Time* was an attempt by Yeats to conjure up a specifically Yeatsian vision of the Ireland of Synge's time. This edition looks to situate the travel essays within an Edwardian Ireland rather different from that of the Yeatsian or even the Syngean imagination. I want to include some of the features of that period which Synge may have chosen to omit or occlude. This is not done out of either pedantry or perversity. Rather, I

---

2. Synge had planned but did not live to complete what he refers to in his notes as a 'Wicklow and Kerry book', TCD MS 4334, f. 172v: see *The Synge Manuscripts in the Library of Trinity College Dublin* (Dublin: Dolmen, 1971), p. 24. All further references to manuscript material in this collection are cited by TCD MS number. In the posthumously collected versions of the travel writings, Roberts drew on Synge's manuscript revisions: see the 'Note on the Text' below.

hope to provide a context for Synge's travel essays – the places he went to, the forms of transport he used to get there, the journals and newspapers in which he published – that may help us better to understand both Synge and the Ireland of his time.

Destinations

John Millington Synge was a city-dweller. Born in Rathfarnham near Dublin in 1871, the son of a barrister who died when he was only a baby, he lived almost all his life with his widowed mother in one Dublin suburb or another, apart from some time in Germany (1893–5) shortly after graduating from Trinity College, and a series of winters in Paris (1895–1902). When he became a founding Director of the Abbey Theatre in 1905, he was the only one of the theatre's ruling triumvirate actually resident in Dublin: Lady Gregory lived in Coole Park, County Galway, W.B. Yeats was based in London. The Synge family, however, was only one generation removed from land and landownership. Synge's grandfather had held large estates in Wicklow, and when the writer was a boy, his uncle, Francis Synge, still occupied the grand Georgian castle of Glanmore. Synge was thinking of his own family situation when, contemplating 'A Landlord's Garden in County Wicklow', he remarked that 'many of the descendents of these people have … drifted in professional life into Dublin, or have gone abroad'. One of John's older brothers was a landagent, another an engineer working in Argentina, a third a medical missionary in China; his sister had married a lawyer. To some extent, still, they thought of themselves as the Synges of Wicklow, and it was close to Glanmore and the village of Annamoe that Mrs Synge, the playwright's mother, rented holiday homes for the months of summer from 1890 on.

For Synge to travel to Wicklow each summer was to return to familiar territory, but also to escape from the city. He participated in the country pastimes of his family, typical enough of their class; he fished, walked and cycled with his brothers. If he did not shoot with his brother-in-law Harry Stephens, he accompanied him on the outing to retrieve a

INTRODUCTION

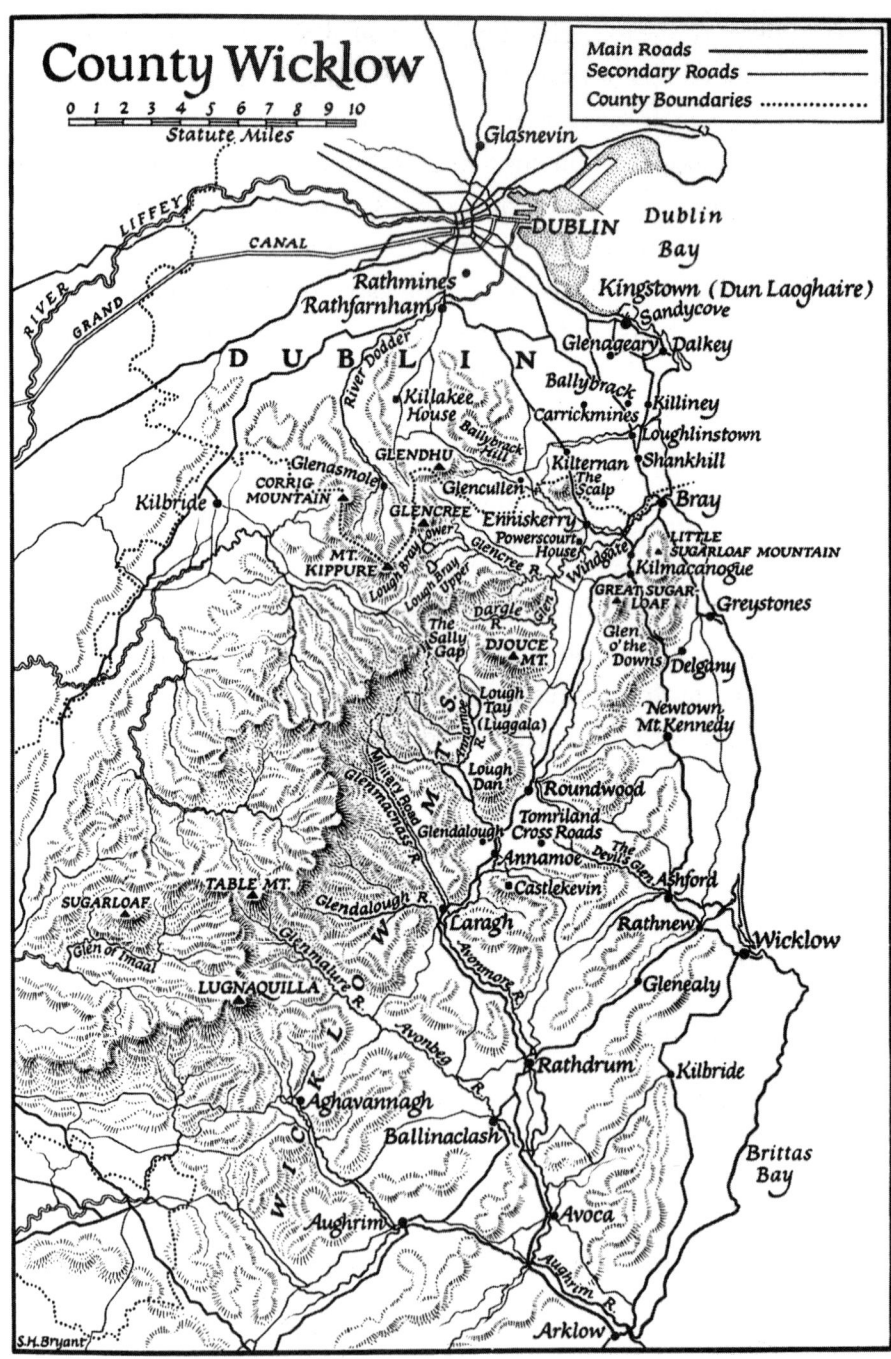

Map of Wicklow

wounded gun-dog, the incident that provided the basis for 'An Autumn Night in the Hills'. It is noticeable, however, that in the essay the brother-in-law is suppressed altogether, and the journey to Glenmalure (which was actually a family affair involving two outside cars, Synge's mother, sister, niece and nephews) is turned into a solitary walking expedition into the mountains.³ Instead of the sinister return alone through the darkening valley portrayed in the essay, Synge had ended the actual day in question fishing with Stephens, and taking *table d'hôte* in the Glenmalure Hotel.⁴ Synge, as family dissident, nationalist in politics, freethinker in religion, saw Wicklow differently from the people of his class and background. His self-consciously Wordsworthian poem 'Prelude', for instance, has no place for social setting. It represents instead a flight from human contact towards an unmediated intercourse with nature:

> Still south I went and west and south again,
> Through Wicklow from the morning till the night,
> And far from cities, and the sites of men,
> Lived with the sunshine and the moon's delight.
>
> I knew the stars, the flowers, and the birds,
> The grey and wintry skies of many glens,
> And did but half remember human words,
> In converse with the mountains, moors, and fens. (CW I 32)

The push in Synge's travels was towards edges, peripheries, away not only from Dublin but from the socio-political contexts in which he, by virtue of being one of the Synges of Wicklow, was implicated. He sought those least modernized, least Anglicized remotenesses of Ireland in which people lived on frontiers of the natural world.

---

3. See E.M. Stephens, *Life of J.M. Synge*, TCD MS 6191, f. 1262. Edward Stephens' enormous manuscript *Life* of his uncle has never been published in its entirety but has been used as the basis for two books: David H. Greene and E.M. Stephens, *J.M. Synge 1871–1909* (New York: Collier, 1961 [1959]) and Andrew Carpenter (ed.), *My Uncle John: Edward Stephens's Life of J.M. Synge* (London: Oxford University Press, 1974).

4. Ibid, f. 1264.

INTRODUCTION

Wicklow itself was curiously anomalous in this. Its wild mountainous terrain made it one of the last strongholds of native Irish resistance to English rule. Still in the late sixteenth century a traditional chieftain like Feagh MacHugh O'Byrne could hold out against the colonial forces of the English, and inflict repeated defeat on the forces of Lord Deputy Gray, to the indignation of Spenser in his *View of the State of Ireland*.[5] Wicklow, known throughout this period only as the 'O'Byrne country', was the last county to be assimilated into the standard English administrative system when it was shired in 1606.[6] But, so close as it was to Dublin, by the eighteenth century it had become a favourite site for gentleman's residences, landed estates with fine houses and picturesque views owned by aristocrats such as the Fitzwilliams, who had huge properties elsewhere, or people, like the Synges themselves, who had made their money in the city and invested in land as a sign of status. This upper-class recreational aspect to Wicklow became a mass phenomenon in the nineteenth century when its beauty-spots, Glendalough, the Meeting of the Waters – made famous by one of Thomas Moore's 'Irish Melodies'–drew regular crowds of day-trippers from Dublin. It is from this time that the county acquired its tourist soubriquet of the 'Garden of Ireland'. Yet still there were mountains and wild glens beyond the tourist trail, and it is to these empty spaces and the sparse population that inhabited them that Synge was drawn. In the Wicklow essays it is such a territory that he contemplates, a territory beyond the tenanted social landscape of his own family, a natural world on the margins of the processes of history.

If Wicklow was one sort of marginal space for Synge, in spite of its proximity to Dublin, Aran as islands off the west coast of the western island of Ireland represented some sort of ultimate extremity. 'It gave me a moment of exquisite satisfaction,' commented Synge in *The Aran Islands* on his first curragh journey from Aranmore, the largest of the islands, to Inishmaan, 'to find myself moving away from civilisation in this rude

5. See Edmund Spenser, *A View of the State of Ireland*, ed. Andrew Hadfield and Willy Maley (Oxford: Blackwell, 1997), pp. 112–13.

6. See *The Last County: the Emergence of Wicklow as a County 1606–1845* (County Wicklow Heritage Project, 1993).

canvas canoe of a model that has served primitive races since men first went on the sea' (CW II 57). He was not by any means the first to have made this trip. The McDonagh cottage on Inishmaan had provided lodgings for many previous visitors when they went to Aran to learn Irish, including Patrick Pearse in 1898, the year of Synge's own first visit. Antiquarians, anthropologists, folklorists and Celtic scholars had all found materials to interest them in Aran. Yeats and his friend Arthur Symons had visited in 1896, a visit described by Symons in an essay in *The Savoy*. Yeats was still full of the enthusiasm of that visit when he met Synge for the first time in Paris in December 1896, though it may not have been at this first meeting that he gave the famous advice:

> 'Give up Paris … Go to the Aran Islands. Live there as if you were one of the people themselves; express a life that has never found expression'. (CW III 64)

The remote islands of Aran, as a primitive westernmost place, did stand for Synge as some sort of polar opposite to the cultural cosmopolitanism of Paris. And yet they were connected also. Commenting on the story of the Lady O'Connor, told him by the old shanachie Pat Dirane, which provided the basis for his first Aran essay 'A Story from Inishmaan', Synge remarked: 'I listened with a strange feeling of wonder while this illiterate native of a wet rock in the Atlantic, told the same tales that had charmed the Florentines by the Arno.' To go to these Irish-speaking islands at the very edge of Europe was to return to origins, not only to a pre-colonized Irish culture but to the folk matrix from which European culture itself evolved.

Synge remained faithful to Aran for five years, with month-long visits every summer or autumn from 1898 to 1902, almost always to his favoured Inishmaan. And then in 1903 came a change to Kerry. It was to his brother Robert that he owed the suggestion of staying with Philly and Margaret Harris in Mountain Stage, near Glenbeigh in the south-western county of Kerry: Robert had stayed there when fishing. Again this is a detail that Synge suppresses in his West Kerry essays. No more than in Wicklow does he want his own class persona, his associations with a family that shot and fished, to obtrude into the scenes he is evoking. Kerry became

INTRODUCTION

Synge's holiday destination for successive years from 1903 to 1906. If it was the primitive austerity of Aran that attracted him, it was the colour and strangeness of the county known in Ireland as the 'Kingdom'. It was here that he gathered many of the experiences that were to enrich *The Playboy of the Western World*: the vivid language of Michael James and the other inhabitants of his Mayo shebeen; the races on the strand, modelled on the races Synge witnessed in Rossbeigh on 3 September 1906 (CL I 201). For Synge Kerry was a place not only of great natural beauty but of conviviality and of the carnivalesque atmosphere evoked in the races and in Puck Fair, the centre piece of his third 'In West Kerry' essay.

Margaret and Pegeen Harris, Coolnaharrigle, Mountain Stage, Co. Kerry

INTRODUCTION

Yet even in Kerry, the remoteness of the islands had a special importance. A disproportionate amount of the West Kerry essays is devoted to the Dingle peninsula, north of Dingle Bay, where he spent time in 1905 and, very briefly and unhappily again in 1907, when he was too ill to stay long. And it is the visit to the Blasket Islands, off the extreme tip of the Dingle peninsula, to which the whole of the second West Kerry essay is devoted. It was a renewal of the feeling he had had in Aran. He wrote in the original *Shanachie* essay, in a passage omitted from the revised *In Wicklow, West Kerry and Connemara* text, of the emotions he felt on landing on the Great Blasket – 'the sharp qualm of excitement I always feel when setting foot on one of these little islands where I am to stay for weeks'. It is excitement, but it is also a qualm in the sense of the separation from the ordinary. The stay in the Blaskets was significant as the most intimate experience Synge had of the lives of the people. In the McDonagh cottage where he stayed on Inishmaan and in the Harrises in Mountain Stage also, he had at least his own room. Staying with Pádraig Ó Catháin, the so-called King of the Great Blasket Island, he shared a bedroom with the other men of the house, had to wash and shave in the kitchen, surrounded by the family. This degree of intimacy, his awareness of the physical proximity of Máire Ní Catháin, the young married daughter of the widowed King, whom he calls the 'little hostess', and her daily activity running the household, inspired his admiring poem 'On an Island':

> You've plucked a curlew, drawn a hen,
> Washed the shirts of seven men,
> You've stuffed my pillow, stretched the sheet,
> And filled the pan to wash your feet,
> You've cooped the pullets, wound the clock,
> And rinsed the young men's drinking crock;
> And now we'll dance to jigs and reels,
> Nailed boots chasing girls' naked heels,
> Until your father'll start to snore,
> And Jude, now you're married, will stretch on the floor. (CW I 35)

Synge was never to get closer than this to the sense of an Irish domestic interior at its most basic.

Yeats had instructed Synge to go to Aran, 'to live there as if if you were one of the people themselves'. Someone of Synge's class and background could never do that: for all his admiration and affection for the people, the self-conscious sense of strangeness permeates all his writing about them. But Synge's visits to Aran and the Blaskets may have indirectly led on to the islanders themselves coming to 'express a life that has never found expression'. Only five years after Synge, the Celticist Robin Flower paid his first visit to the Blaskets, the experience he was to evoke in *The Western Island*.[7] Later the classical scholar George Thomson went there also. Between them Flower and Thomson helped to stimulate the production of the island autobiographies of the 1930s which together form some of the most important writing in Irish of the period: Tomás Ó Criomhthain, *An tOileánach* (*The Islandman*), 1929, Muiris Ó Súilleabháin, *Fiche Blian ag Fás* (*Twenty Years a'Growing*), 1933, and Peig Sayers, *Peig*, 1936. Synge's sympathetic vision of the islands from outside provided encouragement to testimony from within those communities, and in the language to which he had at best only partial access.

For students of Irish, for Gaelic revivalists, for national enthusiasts, the western seaboard of Ireland and its remote extremities represented the true spirit of the nation to be visited from the modernized east coast as pilgrimage or retun to origin. From the point of view of the British colonial administration of Ireland, this same area was a chronic and at times acute social and political problem. This was a region of high crime, and common agrarian disturbances. It was in the northwestern county of Mayo that the Land League was formed in 1879 as a concerted grassroots movement to oppose landlord power. The western counties, not coincidentally, were also some of the very poorest in Ireland. In 1891, the year of the fall of Parnell, there was established the Congested Districts Board (CDB) to provide support for the improvement of those areas where the resources available were not sufficient to support the population. In spite of the name, already

---

7. Robin Flower, *The Western Island, or The Great Blasket* (Oxford: Clarendon Press, 1944).

many of these districts were rapidly being decongested through emigration, and that was one of the issues that the Board was intended to address: how to enable the people to support themselves adequately without having to leave. The CDB invested in the infrastructure of the region, building bridges, harbours and piers, and improved communications. It assisted local fishermen in buying or building boats, and set up local or home industries such as lace-making and knitting. And for the areas over which it had jurisdiction (eventually the whole western seaboard) it was assigned responsibility for land purchase and re-distribution. Instituted by a Conservative administration, it was associated with the politics of constructive unionism by which the government of the time sought to reconcile Irish people to the Union by an amelioration in their social condition.

It is in this context that Synge's commission to write about the Congested Districts for the *Manchester Guardian* needs to be placed. He would have seen something of Connemara before on his way to the Aran Islands; he had visited North Mayo in 1904. But the perspective he brought to these areas in June-July 1905 when he visited them with Jack Yeats, who was to act as illustrator for the articles, was bound to be conditioned by the nature of the commission. He was there to investigate conditions in the Congested Districts, to report on what he found: the degree of poverty and deprivation of the people; the success or otherwise of the CDB in the enterprises they had sponsored; the social and demographic trends. While circumspect in his criticism of the CDB, Synge was clearly not in sympathy with its centralized planning strategies, pursued, as he saw it, mechanically and without sensitivity to local conditions. He found Mayo, in particular, disheartening, a desolate landscape of demoralized people, though he tried hard to keep an upbeat tone in at least some of the articles. His overall reaction, in a letter to his friend Stephen McKenna, was suggestive of his mixed feelings:

> we pushed into out-of-the-way corners in Mayo and Galway that were more strange and marvellous than anything I've dreamed of. Unluckily my commission was to write on the 'Distress' so I couldn't do any thing like what I would have wished to do as an interpretation of the whole thing.

Still, he was exultant at having been paid more than he had ever had before for any journalism, and 'I'm off to spend my £25.4.0 on the same ground' (CL I 116) – not in fact, Galway or Mayo but his still preferred Kerry. That impulse to push into out-of-the-way corners, that desire to find there the strange and marvellous in a reality beyond dreaming, this is the spirit that animated Synge's travelling throughout.

Transport and communications

Synge's self-image through most of the travel essays is of the lone walker, wandering in desolate places, meeting and talking with the people of communities remote from the modern urban world. There are here conscious elisions, giving a very partial view of the realities on the ground. Synge was in fact very much a man of his own time, taking easily to the new technologies as they became available to him. He bought his first camera from a fellow visitor to Aran in 1898, and later acquired a plate changing Klito, made by Houghtons of London.[8] A camera accompanied him throughout his travels, his photographs often used as an important ice-breaker in his meetings with local people, as on the Blaskets, where in fact he may have been the first person to take photographs.[9] Synge must also have been among the earliest professional writers to compose directly on a typewriter, a Blickensderfer that he acquired in 1900. Most importantly for his travels in Ireland, he was very much up to date in his use of a bicycle. The 1890s was the great era of cycling, with writers as distant and unlike as Bernard Shaw and Leo Tolstoy learning how to bicycle. By 1895, Synge was already on to his second bicycle, a chain-driven machine with pneumatic tyres, replacing his previous older heavier model. This was a mere seven years after the Irish-based veterinary surgeon John Dunlop had patented the pneumatic tyre, five years since commercial production had begun in Belfast. His cycling is mentioned occasionally in the essays, but Synge rarely alludes to the fact that he brought his bicycle with him on his

---

8. See J.M. Synge, *My Wallet of Photographs* (Dublin: Dolmen, 1971), frontispiece.
9. See Muiris Mac Conghail, *The Blaskets* (Dublin: Town House, 1987), p. 120.

travels. So, for example, at the opening of his first 'In West Kerry' essay, he remarks that at Tralee station 'I found a boy who carried my bag a couple of hundred yards along the road to an open yard where the light railway starts for the west'. Why would he have needed a boy to carry his bag? Because he would have been pushing his bicycle, recovered from the guard's van of the Dublin-Tralee train. The bicycle shows up unannounced later in the essay when he is trying to cycle back to Ballyferriter after a night out at the circus in Dingle. This is an anomaly that Synge removed when he revised the text of the *Shanachie* essay; there is no reference whatsoever to him cycling in the version eventually published in the 1910 *Works*.

Through the islands and inlets of Connemara there was no way to travel but by hired outside car.

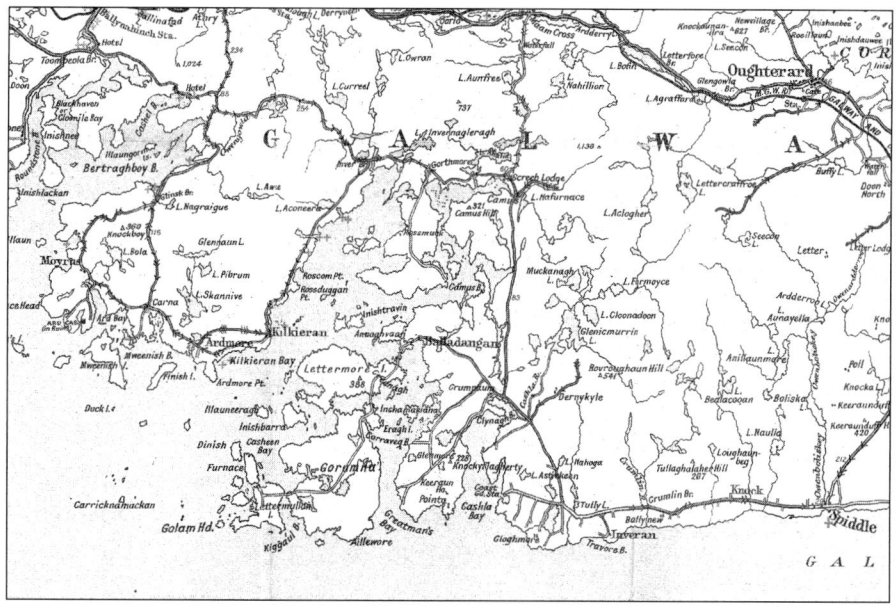

Map of Connemara

This was how Synge and Jack Yeats journeyed through the Congested Districts: a charming Yeats vignette as tailpiece to 'Among the Relief Works' shows the two of them sitting behind the driver on the car, as they cross the bridge from Gorumna to Lettermullan. This was such a standard way of observing the countryside that Synge felt called upon to warn in one of the articles against the distorting effect of relying on the carman for information: 'The car drivers that take one round to isolated places in Ireland seem to be the cause of many of the misleading views that chance visitors take up about the country and the real temperament of the people'. Here, of course, he is claiming the authority of the insider, someone who knows 'the real temperament of the people' and is not reliant on the prejudices of the car driver, early twentieth-century equivalent of the cabbie, stand-by of later lazy journalists. The journey from the first part of the Congested Districts tour in Connemara to North Mayo was a real odyssey, as Synge reported to his mother from Belmullet (acknowledging the safe arrival of the parcel she had sent him 'with pyjamas, and cigarettes'):

> We started for here [from Carna] at 11 a.m. with a two hours' drive to the Clifden line, then we had to train all the way back to *Athlone* and wait there 5 hours to get the connection for Ballina, so that in the end we reached Ballina at 3 o'clock this morning, then drove here the 40 miles on the long car, in a downpour most of the way, and got here at 10.30. (CL I 113–4)

The two hours on the outside car from Carna on the Galway coast would have taken them inland to Recess, where they could catch the Clifden to Galway train, with a connection at Galway for the main Dublin line to Athlone. They there were able to transfer to the westward line that ran from Athlone out to Killala, getting off at Ballina. The 'long car' would have been a descendant of the service originally established by Charles Bianconi to connect first the canal stations and then the railheads with more remote parts of the country.[10] This uncovered vehicle, drawn by up to four horses, delivered the post and also carried passengers with six or eight people seated on either side facing outwards with the luggage stacked in between. In 'The Homes of the Harvestmen' Synge gives a graphic account of the forty mile journey that took six and a half hours in the pouring rain, delivering the post on the way, changing horses every fifteen miles, though he leaves out the fact that Jack Yeats 'was so sleepy he had to tie himself on

---

10. See Constantia Maxwell, 'Bianconi and his Irish cars', *Country Life*, 16 April 1948, 776–7.

to the car', as Yeats reported in a letter to John Masefield: 'When the driver saw me apparently pitching off head foremost he roared with horror but when he saw the rope held he roared with pleasure.'[11]

It was thus not always easy, and certainly not comfortable, travelling around the more remote parts of Ireland in 1905. All the same, the country had an extended public transport system at that time to which one can only look back with envy from a century later. Steamboat services, subsidized by the CDB, had been introduced in the 1890s from Galway to the Aran Islands, and from Sligo to Belmullet. Railway lines, run by a series of competing companies, crisscrossed the whole country. The connections might not have been too convenient on the Midland Great Western that took Synge and Yeats from Recess to Ballina, but still it was possible to make that journey by train. And the Tralee and Dingle three foot gauge light railway carried Synge on the precipitous thirty-two mile trip across the spine of the Dingle peninsula, with a branch line to the seaside resort of Castle Gregory on the north coast.

The railroads had already developed an advanced tourist industry: this is the fact that Synge most obviously leaves out of his account of the west coast. So, for example, he begins his third West Kerry essay, 'To Puck Fair', with a description of the cottage of the Harrises in Mountain Stage: 'After a long day's wandering I reached, towards the twilight, a little cottage on the south side of Dingle Bay, where I have often lived. There is no village near it … this cottage is not on the road anywhere – the main road passes a few hundred yards to the west.' What you would never guess from this is that the cottage was within a very few yards of a railway station, as Margaret Harris explained to him when he first wrote to ask for lodgings with them in 1903.[12] Mountain Stage acquired its name because

---

11. Quoted in Bruce Arnold, *Jack Yeats* (New Haven and London: Yale University Press, 1998), p. 142. This form of primitive seat-belt was not uncommon on the cars; *Murray's Guide* for 1878 recommends that 'the traveller should obtain a strap by which he may buckle himself to the seat during the night journeys and thus go safely to sleep without fear of being jerked forward'. Cited in Peter Somervillle-Large, *The Grand Irish Tour* (Harmondsworth: Penguin, 1985 [1982]), p. 182.

12. See letter of 24 August 1903, TCD MS 4424–26, 131.

INTRODUCTION

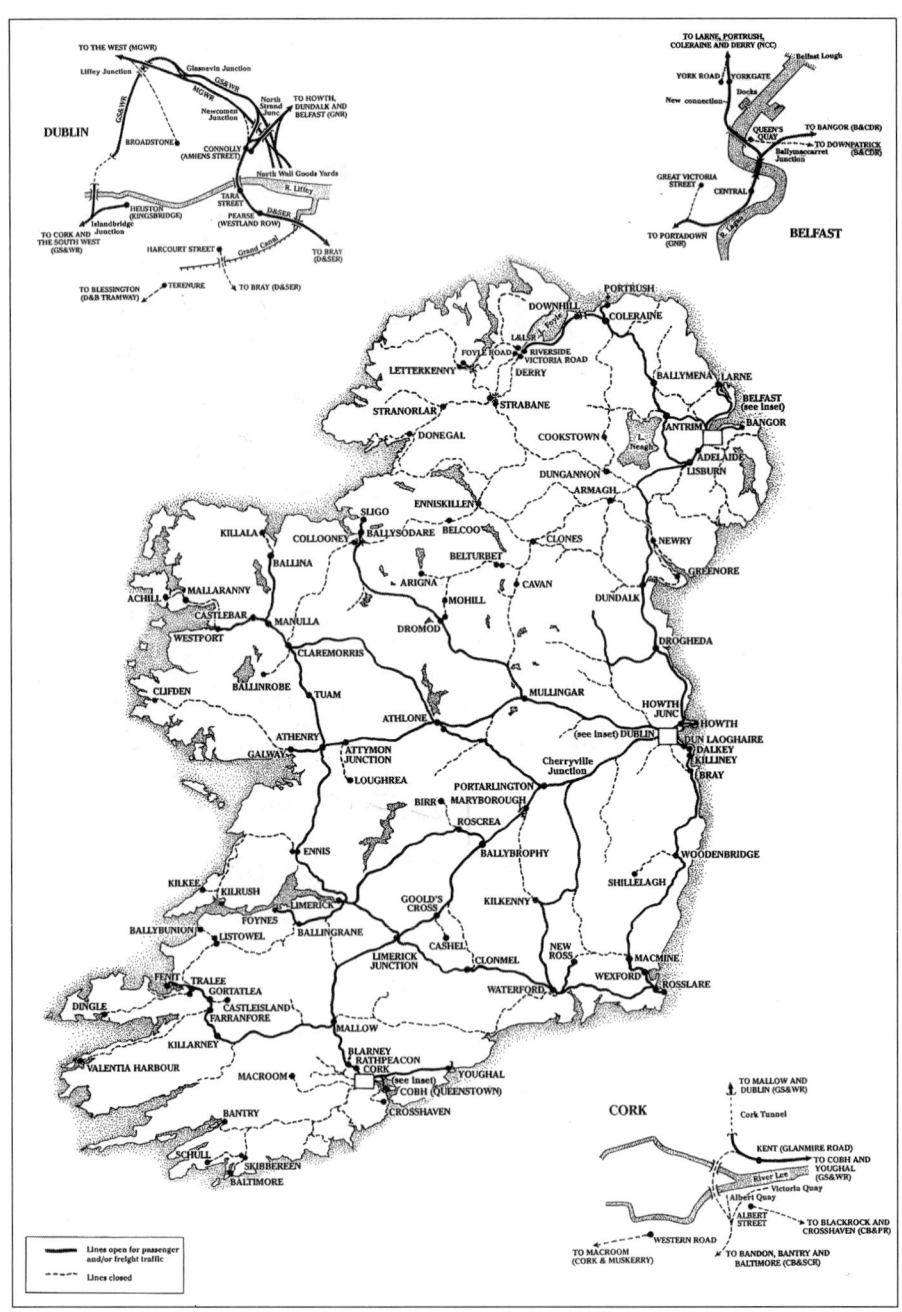

Rail map of Ireland

INTRODUCTION

it was a staging post of the old coach road, but from 1891, when the Great Southern and Western had extended its line from Faranfore to Killorglin on to Valentia Harbour, it had its own railway station.

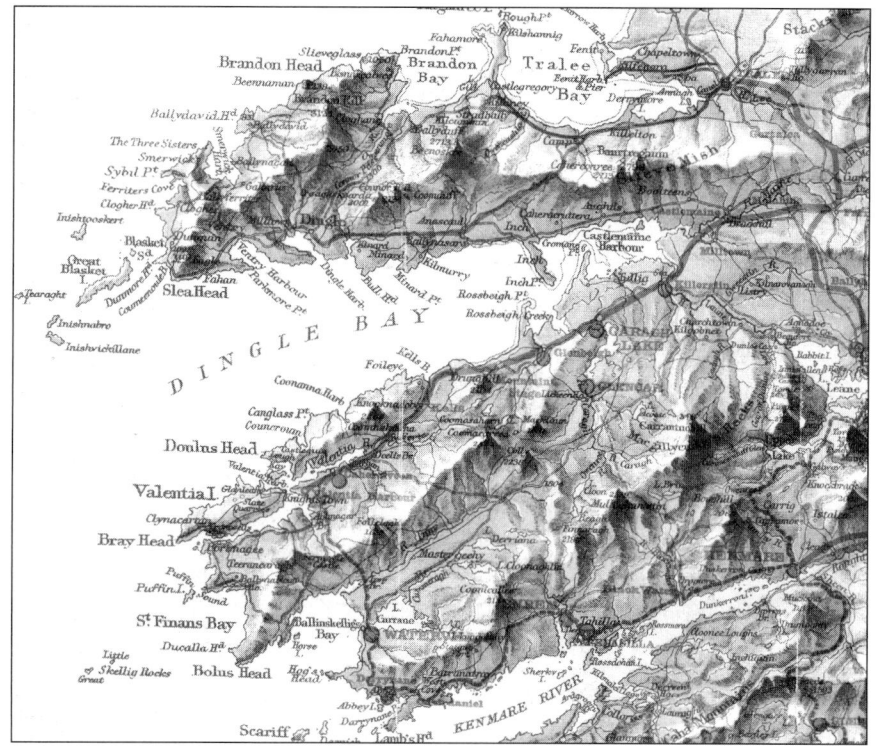

Map of Kerry railways

What is more, just two stops short of Mountain Stage, Synge could have alighted at Caragh Lake, marked in block capitals on the map as the station for the Great Southern's sumptuous hotel with all the amenities the fisherman, sportsman or just 'common or garden tourist' could want.[13] The view of the area given by John O'Donoghue in *The Sunny Side of Ireland, as Viewed from the Great Southern and Western Railways* is necessarily unlike Synge's; though the rail tour promoter and the essayist recount the same local mythology of Diarmuid and Grania, it is in markedly different prose

---

13. John O'Donoghue, *The Sunny Side of Ireland* (Dublin: Alex Thom, n.d. [1898]), p. 163.

styles.[14] Synge in his concentration on the traditional lives of the people simply writes out the developed modern infrastructure that had turned such districts into recreational commodities for the urban middle classes.

Synge frequently stressed the isolation of the communities he visits, and this was one of the attractions both of Inishmaan and the Blaskets for him. Yet in both islands he lodged with the postmaster, Patrick McDonagh in Aran, the King Pádraig Ó Catháin on the Great Blasket, and he was never out of reach of the postal service. In one post, he comments in a notebook, letters reached him on the Blaskets from 'Berlin, the Argentine, Gort, Dublin, and Rathdrum'.[15] On that tiny western island, therefore, he could still be in touch with his German translator Max Meyerfeld, his fellow Abbey Director Lady Gregory in Galway, his brother Robert in South America and other family members in Dublin and Wicklow.

Synge tended to stress the disconnection of the island communities from mainstream culture, particularly in the Aran essay 'The Last Fortress of the Celt': 'As a child sees the world only in relation to its own home, so these islanders see everything in relation to their island. Without some such link as Lipton's Teas, the matters of the outside world do not interest them.' But the very examples he gives in this passage suggests the opposite. Immediately before this he has commented on the level of concern shown on Aran with the Spanish-American War of 1898, being fought out in Cuba and the Philippines. And their awareness of Lipton's Teas, alluded to here, that led them to take a partisan interest in the 1899 yachting race for the America's Cup, in which Sir Thomas Lipton was the British challenger, was not a wholly trivial one either. Within a generation of this time, Lipton had been responsible for transforming tea from a luxury drink to one cheap enough to reach ordinary consumers and thus – for better or worse – producing a radical change in Irish diet. By the 1890s in some areas of the Congested Districts, tea accounted for over 10 per cent

---

14. 'All who have read the fine old Finnian romance "The Pursuit of Diurmuid and Grannie" which tells the iliad of their flight across ancient Erin, will remember that here on the shores of Kerry he met his enemies and discomfited them'. Ibid, p. 160. Compare this with Synge's version of the same folklore below p. 165–6.

15. MS 4404, f. 20v.

of annual household income.¹⁶ The old man Synge meets in Gorumna, complaining of the pay on the relief works, puts in significant order the necessaries of life: 'A shilling a day ... would hardly keep a man in tea and sugar and tobacco and a bit of bread to eat.' It is hardly surprising that the Scottish merchant Lipton, who had so popularized tea by mass advertising as well as cutting its price, and who was sufficiently proud of his Irish roots to call all his racing yachts Shamrock, should have been well known on Aran.

For Synge what made the island communities so significant was their difference. Built in to the legendary advice of Yeats was a contrast between literariness – 'Give up Paris. You will never create anything by reading Racine' – and an orality that remained unrepresented in literature – 'Go to the Aran Islands ... express a life that has never found expression' (CW III 63). But that separateness of the traditional pre-literate society of oral folk culture from the print culture of the outside world turned out to be illusory, as Synge was to find out when he published 'The Last Fortress of the Celt' in *The Gael* in April 1901. After the article appeared Synge was initially hesitant about returning to Inishmaan, for reasons Mrs Synge explained in a letter to her older son Samuel:

> he heard ... Martin McDonough [*sic*], his chief friend on the island ... is offended with him because he put a version of a letter he got from McDonough in an article he sent to an American paper. John thought that he would be quite safe, but someone sent Martin the paper and he is offended. The letter was written in Irish to John and he put in a free translation I fancy.¹⁷

In the event, Synge did go back to the island and had no difficulty in persuading Martin to forgive him. What is striking here is Synge's presupposition that an essay published in a journal in New York would not find its way back to Inishmaan. In fact, communications between Aran and the Irish diaspora would have been excellent, and something written about

---

16. See Ciara Breathnach, *Congested Districts Board of Ireland, 1891–1923* (Dublin: Four Courts, 2005), p. 114.

17. Quoted in Greene and Stephens, 125.

the islands in an Irish-American publication would hardly have escaped notice. Similar offence was taken, apparently, at Synge's representation of his visit to the Blaskets. Máire Ní Catháin, the 'little hostess', was not pleased at being described as having made tea for the visitors on arrival 'without asking if we were hungry', nor yet at having taken off her apron to use as a curtain for Synge's bedroom (a detail to be used in *The Playboy*). Muiris Mac Conghail, who reports this, assumes that the people would have read the essays in *The Shanachie*, but points out that 'their relatives in Boston and New York were also a factor in the view of Synge; there was constant correspondence between the Islanders at home and in America'.[18]

Implicit throughout many of the travel essays, in some sense endemic in the form itself, is a contrast between the traveller observer, cosmopolitan, mobile, literate, and the culture he observes, oral, stable, more or less unaffected by modernity. Again and again, however, especially in the Congested Districts essays, Synge reveals the unreality of that contrast. The men and women of Mayo and Sligo travel regularly, every year, for seasonal work in England and Scotland. 'The Homes of the Harvestmen' reports on the hundreds going in the months of June and July on the boat from Belmullet to Sligo and from there on to Glasgow. Emigration to America is one of the central issues of the *Manchester Guardian* articles, viewed as the key social problem; the lace and knitting schools set up by the CDB to provide home industries only provide girls the money to emigrate. However, 'returned Americans' are also commented on a number of times, and there is a whole economy by which young women can work in the United States long enough to earn a dowry to marry advantageously back home. Differences of class, education and background, of course, remain between Synge and the people he meets and describes; but they live within a single modern world of trains and boats, the circulation of post and print.

---

18. Mac Conghail, *The Blaskets* p. 133.

Publications

It is widely and rightly accepted that the visit to Aran in May 1898 was to transform Synge's career and make a writer of him. It is hard not to back project, therefore, and see the emergent playwright from that point on, regarding the travel essays largely as quarry for the great plays to come. But who knew in 1898 what sort of writer Synge was to be? After that first visit to Aran, Yeats reported proprietorially to William Sharp from Coole Park: 'Synge a new man ... I have started in folklore has been here on his way from the Arran islands where he has been seven weeks perfecting his gaelic and getting stories.'[19] Nine months later, Yeats was still thinking of him primarily in these terms, commenting from Paris to Lady Gregory: 'He works very hard & is learning Breton. He will be a very useful scholour.'[20] Certainly a scholarly folklorist is what Synge looks to be in the first Aran essay, 'A Story from Inishmaan', which he published in November 1898 in the *New Ireland Review*.

The *New Ireland Review* was established in March 1894 by Father T.A. Finlay, the Jesuit priest and economist, as successor to *The Lyceum*, which he had also founded. Finlay was an active partner in Horace Plunkett's Irish Agricultural Organisation, dedicated to promoting the principles of co-operation among Irish farmers. The *New Ireland Review* might be placed politically as moderately reformist, publishing articles and reviews on contemporary social and political questions as well as historical and cultural matters. So, for instance, in the November 1898 edition in which Synge's essay appeared, there was a review-article by Finlay himself on the co-operative movement in Ireland and Britain, pieces promoting temperance, and a comparative study of Gladstone (very respectfully treated) and Bismarck, both of whom had recently died. In other issues of the time there was a running series of Irish religious songs, with texts in Irish and English, poems by Æ, an article on 'West of Ireland Distress 1898', and a polemic essay arguing for Irish language revival from D.P. Moran, later

---

19. W.B. Yeats, *Collected Letters*, II: *1896–1900*, ed. Warwick Gould, John Kelly, and Deirdre Toomey (Oxford: Clarendon Press, 1997), pp. 250–1.

20. Ibid, p. 359.

editor of *The Leader*. Synge's 'A Story from Inishmaan' was collected from Pat Dirane on the island on his first visit in May 1898, a combination of narrative motifs used both in the *Merchant of Venice* (the pound of flesh) and *Cymbeline* (the wager on the wife's fidelity). Synge's comments on the tale-type and its analogues are almost ostentatiously scholarly, and his conclusion suggests that he regarded the article as a contribution to the study of comparative folklore.

There is little doubt that our heroic tales which show so often their kinship with Grecian myths, date from the pre-ethnic period of the Aryans, and it is easy to believe that some purely secular narratives share their antiquity. Further, a comparison of all the versions will show that we have here one of the rudest and therefore, it may be, most ancient settings of the material.

He claims that Dirane himself translated it for him from the original, 'as my Celtic would not carry me through extended tales' and adds, 'I have kept closely to his language'. By the time this material is re-worked in *The Aran Islands*, however, the scholarly commentary is cut back, and the language of the story is substantially changed. The rather awkward standard English, with occasional constructions borrowed from Irish, has been revised into something very like Synge's stage Hiberno-English.[21]

From his first visit to Aran Synge had hoped to write a book about his experiences there, and he worked away to that end over the years 1898 to 1902. It was to prove difficult to find a publisher for the manuscript, however, and he sought to place individual essays drawn from the material in periodicals. He found an outlet for 'The Last Fortress of the Celt', an account of Inishmaan, with *The Gael* where it appeared in April 1901. The paper obviously thought well of the essay because it was featured in large block letters at the head of the title-page. *The Gael*, with its alternative Irish title *An Gaodhal*, was billed as 'a monthly bi-lingual magazine devoted to the promotion of the language, literature, music and art of Ireland', and had been published in Brooklyn since 1882. Its nationalist political commitment had been even clearer in its original self-description

---

21. For a full analysis, see Nicholas Grene, 'Synge's Creative Development in *The Aran Islands*', *Long Room*, 10 (1974), 30–36.

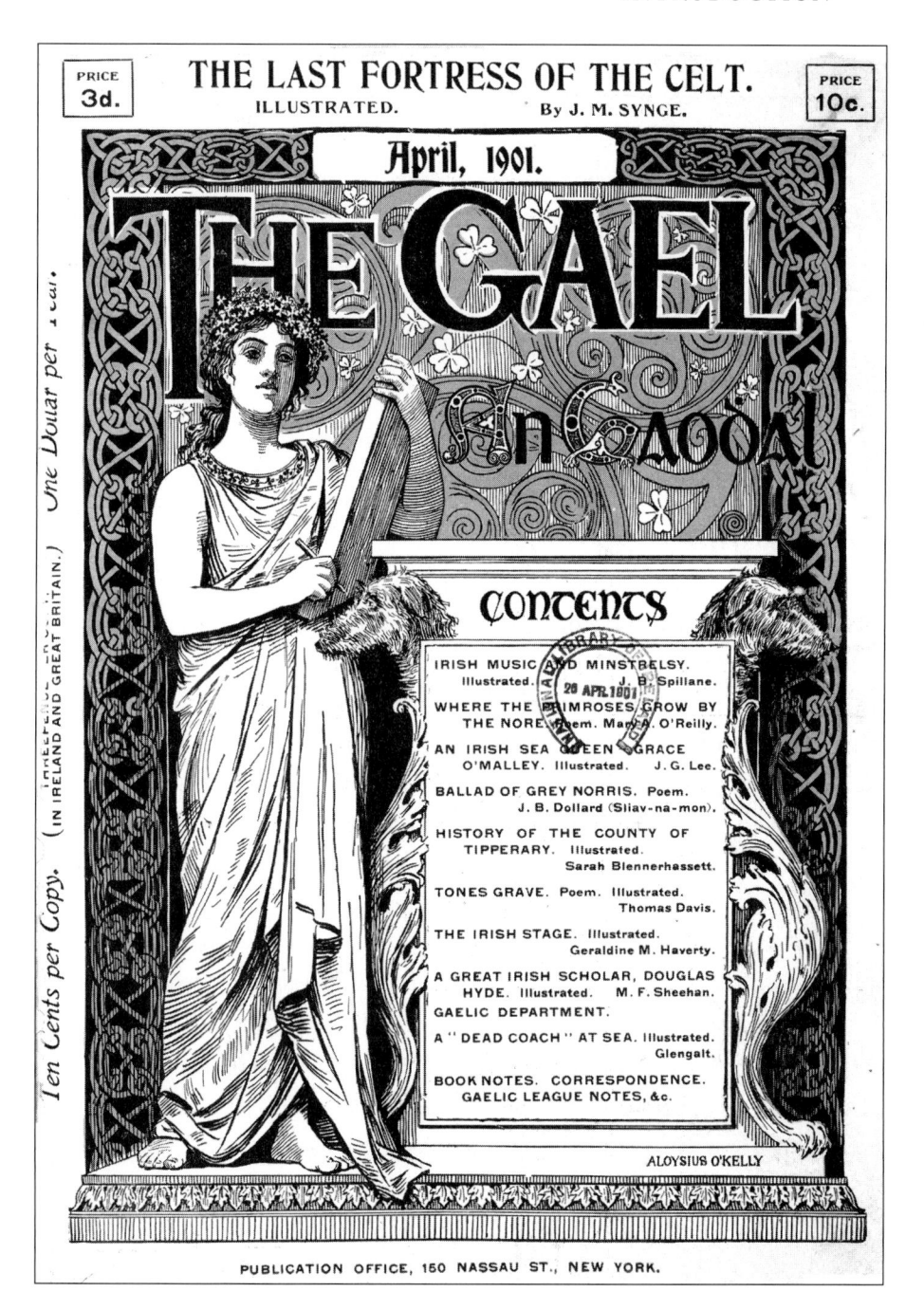

Title-page of The Gael

as 'a monthly journal devoted to the preservation and cultivation of the Irish language and the autonomy of the Irish nation'. It did publish other Irish literary writers; the April 1903 issue in which Synge's 'An Autumn Night in the Hills' appeared also included a story by Katharine Tynan (long-time friend of Yeats), and George Moore's sharply ironic short story 'Home-Sickness', as well as a letter from John Quinn defending the principles of the literary revival. 'The Last Fortress of the Celt', with a title drawing showing an Edenic naked youth on what looked more like a South Sea island than Inishmaan, stressed the primal character of Aran culture:

> On an island in the Atlantic, within a day's journey from Dublin, there is still a people who live in conditions older than the Middle Ages, and have preserved in an extraordinary degree the charm of primitive man.

Much of the material of this essay was to be re-used in *The Aran Islands*, but there were adjustments made for the periodical publication. So, for instance, the description of the keen was without the sceptical conclusion Synge gave it in the later text:

> Before they covered the coffin an old man kneeled down by the grave and repeated a simple prayer for the dead.
> There was an irony in these words of atonement and Catholic belief spoken by voices that were still hoarse with the cries of pagan desperation. (CW II 75)

Given the title of the essay and the likely sympathies of the readers of *The Gael*, the account of the eviction would have had a sharper political significance in the essay than in the book; even this last fortress of the Celt, it is implied, the dispossessing English have invaded.

Synge had been drafting essays based on his experiences in Wicklow as well as Aran at this time before his talent as a playwright declared itself with the writing of his first one-act plays in the summer of 1902. But these reflective pieces combining individual anecdote and scenic description with sociological and psychological generalization were hard to place. Drafts of 'The Oppression of the Hills' and what was to become 'The Vagrants of Wicklow', on which he was working in the winter and spring of 1902,

April, 1901.   THE GAEL.   109

The Last Fortress of the Celt.

By J. M. Synge.

ON an island in the Atlantic, within a day's journey from Dublin, there is still a people who live in conditions older than the Middle Ages, and have preserved in an extraordinary degree the charm of primitive man.

Innishmaan, the middle, and least sophisticated island of the Aran group off County Galway, has no harbor worthy of the name, no real roads, no carts, no post office, and, what is rare in Ireland, no police barrack. The population, of about three hundred and fifty, depend for their meagre livelihood on net and line fishing, which they carry on in curraghs, or canvas canoes, with the greatest enterprise and daring.

The visitor usually reaches this lonely rock from Kilronan, the principal village in the great Aran Island, whence he is borne to his destination in the stern of a long eight-oared curragh. The sound is not much more than a mile wide at the narrowest part, yet the voyage from Kilronan takes almost an hour, and the unfamiliar company of lithe islanders dressed in gray homespun flannels, together with the leaping oscillation of the canoe, gives one a strange sense of novelty. A landing is effected at a small pier and after half an hour's walk between flat sheets of naked limestone, where a few goats nibble a repast of blue gentian and maiden-hair, one reaches a straggling settlement of about seventy cottages. It is only when one has spent months in one of these, and grown, so to speak, into one's place in the chimney-corner, that the full charm of the people can be realized.

Lodgings in the ordinary sense are not, of course, to be had, but I was fortunate enough to find a room, sometimes used by Gaelic scholars, which was tolerably comfortable. My hostess was an elderly woman who wore the short red petticoat, indescribable shawl, and raw cow-skin shoes, which form the national costume. Like most of the older women she was quite ignorant of English, but her daughter could both read and understand it, though she never used a Saxon word except when speaking to her pigs, a curious habit which is common in the island, and may be explained in more ways than one. This girl was dressed exactly as her mother, except that when she went out on Sunday she put an elaborate shawl over her head, while the older women, indeed all the married women, are satisfied with an extra red petticoat, worn with the waistband round the face.

Their cottage was one of the most important in the island, and there were numerous visitors from early morning till bedtime. All were received with the usual Gaelic salutation, "That God may bless thee," given a stool by the fire, and drawn into the conversation with unconscious yet admirable courtesy. Shoes and stockings are still regarded as a thing put on, an extra, and when the day's work was done the women generally laid them aside, showing finely formed feet and ankles under their short petticoats, while they did the honors of their kitchen.

At first the men spoke English for my convenience expressing themselves more correctly than the ordinary peasant, though some used the Gaelic idioms continually, and substituted "he" or "she" for "it," as the neuter pronoun is not found in modern Irish. Their vocabulary was, of course, very limited, which gave rise at times to curious nomenclature. Thus one evening when my comb had been mislaid, my old host came to me and asked if I had found my "little rake!"

The faces of the men were somewhat unlike the Irish type, and showed traces of the Pre-Celtic blood, which has lingered in the west of Europe, while among the women were some curiously Mongolian features, rather resembling the Bigoudennes of the south coast of Brittany.

The kitchen where we sat was a marvel of unconscious decoration. The deep glow from the red garments of the women who clustered round the fire on their stools lent a color of almost oriental richness, and the whitewashed walls were toned by the turf smoke to a delicate brown which harmonized as if by design with the hard earthen floor. On one side of the fire stood the spinning wheel, on the other a large pot of indigo for dying wool. Round the walls, or among the open rafters, one could see many sorts of fishing tackle, with the oilskins of the men, and right over head, under the thatch, a whole red cowskin destined for the primitive shoes, or pampooties, as they are called in English.

Of all the topics which we touched on, war was

'The Last Fortress of the Celt', The Gael, April 1901

were turned down by *The Gael* and the *Cornhill Magazine*.[22] *The Gael* did eventually take 'An Autumn Night in the Hills', the heavily fictionalized version of Synge's outing to Glenmalure to collect his brother-in-law's wounded pointer dog Ben. From that starting point Synge assembled a vivid mood picture of the lonely cottage at the end of Glenmalure, and his encounter with the girl who lavished her love on the dog for want of any other object.[23] After an atmospheric rain-soaked lone walk down the glen, Synge ends his essay with the sight of the coffin of Mary Kinsella, the young married woman who has died mad in the Richmond Asylum. This Gothic conclusion – Synge originally entitled the essay 'The Body of Mary Kinsella' – gives the essay a narrative shape unlike some of the more loosely structured Wicklow pieces and may have been what disposed *The Gael* to accept it, though the accompanying drawing, with its fashionably dressed young lady serving tea to the dapper Synge figure looks anything but Gothic.[24]

The Gael took one more piece of Synge's, the very brief 'A Dream of Inishmaan', but this had already appeared in the second issue of Pamela Colman Smith's *The Green Sheaf* in 1903. Colman Smith was an American artist, book illustrator and stage designer, who performed in plays of Yeats and was later to produce stage designs for Synge's *The Well of the Saints*. She had worked for a time with Jack Yeats on his monthly illustrated magazine *A Broad Sheet*, and *A Green Sheaf* was conceived on very much the same lines: a handcoloured little gathering of poems, prose pieces and paintings, on handmade paper, edited, printed and published by Colman Smith herself and distributed by Elkin Matthews, later co-publisher of *The Aran Islands*. It had a strong Irish dimension, featuring a translation of the poet Raftery by Lady Gregory in the first issue, contributions from both Yeats brothers and a painting by Æ, with the emphasis on the occult, mystical and fey side of Celticism. So, for example, Synge's 'A Dream in

---

22. Diary entries for 26 March and 2 April 1902, MS 4421.

23. For details, see *Interpreting Synge*, pp. 33–4.

24. This appears to have been the standard style of the illustrator M. O'Flaherty, who supplied a similar drawing for Katharine Tynan's story in the same issue of *The Gael*.

No. 2.

The Green Sheaf

1903

LONDON
SOLD BY ELKIN MATHEWS, VIGO STREET, W.

Title-page of *The Green Sheaf*

Inishmaan' appeared in the second issue in a sequence entirely devoted to dreams placed between 'A Dream of the World's End', a half satiric, half apocalyptic vignette by W.B. Yeats, and 'Jan A Dreams' by John Masefield, with a supplement including a spectral painting by Æ called 'A Million Years Hence'. In its eventual setting in *The Aran Islands*, Synge's dream of the irresistible music that leads him into the dance that is both a terror and an ecstasy looks anomalous in a book that is otherwise so austere, all but impersonal in tone. But in *The Green Sheaf* it falls as it were naturally into place, assimilated into the aestheticism of its arthouse surroundings.

John Masefield, Synge's fellow *Green Sheaf* contributor, to whom he had been introduced in London in January 1903, was to prove important, also, in giving him an entrée to the *Manchester Guardian*, which was to be the main publisher of his travel essays. Masefield, who was responsible for the paper's 'Miscellany' at the time, wrote to Synge on 15 December 1904 asking him if he would be interested in 'reviewing, paragraph or article writing – or indeed any kind of newspaper work', adding in a postscript that 'Aran articles would be welcomed I should think'.[25] They were, and 'An Impression of Aran' appeared on 24 January 1905, to be followed the next month by the Wicklow essay 'The Oppression of the Hills' that Synge had been unable to place elsewhere.

The *Manchester Guardian*, under its long-term editor C.P. Scott, had a special commitment to Ireland. Scott had played a leading role in the political crisis of 1886, when he had championed Gladstone's policy of Home Rule in the paper, against the faction in the party that broke away as the Liberal Unionists.[26] It was Scott himself who suggested Synge write a series of articles on the Congested Districts. Synge accepted the proposition with alacrity, though he was firm in establishing his own political terms: 'In my letters I could work on the lines you suggest, but I would deal with the problem independently, rather than from the point of view of the strictly orthodox Nationalist.'[27] Scott replied reassuringly:

---

25. MS 4424–25, 156.

26. See J.L. Hammond, *C.P. Scott of the Manchester Guardian* (London: Bell, 1934), pp. 63–8.

27. Letter from J.M. Synge to C. p. Scott, 22 May 1905, John Rylands University Library,

> I should like you to take time to do the thing comfortably and thoroughly – three weeks to a month would seem a quite reasonable time, working at the thing in the way you would, intimately, and trying to give the reader a sympathetic understanding of the people and the way their life is lived, and to let the political lesson emerge out of that. Certainly I should wish you to deal with the problem independently and entirely in your own manner.[28]

Having gained that important free hand, and with the inspired addition of Jack Yeats as illustrator, Synge set off for Connemara in June 1905.

Jack Yeats set the tone for the series as a whole in the illustration for the first article, 'From Galway to Gorumna', with a witty double portrait of himself and Synge looking like two countrymen near the village of Castelloe, the taller, heavy-set author with face shaded, beside the slighter thin-faced artist in his boater. This camouflaged appearance chimes with the self-effacing point of view of the articles throughout in which Synge rarely refers to himself or his own feelings, almost never to his companion. They are there to observe and record. Yeats' drawings, though, are acute at pinpointing the tone of Synge's text. The illustration to 'Among the Relief Works' brings before us vividly the 'sight of a dozen or more men and women working hurriedly and doggedly … with a ganger swaggering among them and directing their work'. Both article and drawing express a protest against the system of relief, with miserable pay for the workers and oppressive authority by the bosses. Synge tries hard to be scrupulously fair to the work of the CDB, praising particularly their re-distribution of land on the (often huge) estates they bought up. He engages carefully with the economic issues, the help represented by CDB investment in an improved infrastructure and their contribution to the building of boats and houses for the local people. But his final article, in which he wrestles with 'Possible Remedies', makes his own political view clear. He reminds his readers that 'the whole moral and economic

---

University of Manchester: *Guardian* (formerly *Manchester Guardian*) Archive, Scott General Correspondence, MS 126/64. I am most grateful to Aidan Arrowsmith for transcribing this letter for me.

28. Quoted in Hammond, *C.P. Scott*, p 53.

condition of Ireland has been brought into a diseased state by prolonged misgovernment' and concludes

> the only real remedy for emigration is the restoration of some national life to the people. It is this conviction that makes most Irish politicians scorn all merely economic or agricultural reforms, for if Home Rule would not of itself make a national life it would do more to make such a life possible than half a million creameries.

He worked hard on this passage as we can see from numerous versions of it in his notebook,[29] and it is unlikely that it was a mere gesture towards the *Manchester Guardian*'s Home Rule politics. This is Synge's nationalist declaration against the constructive unionism of the CDB, for all his cautious praise of their work.

Scott was extremely pleased with the articles and was later to publish several more of Synge's Wicklow essays, and to suggest a series on 'various "Types" of Irishmen, which need not be entirely imaginary, but could be reinforced by personal touches and anecdotes' (CL II 43 n1). This Synge never succeeded in undertaking, though it remained a notional project until within months of his death. However, he found an Irish publication to take his travel essays with the establishment of *The Shanachie* in 1906. *The Shanachie*, subtitled 'An Illustrated Irish Miscellany' was set up by the newly-founded Dublin publisher Maunsel, 'as a Magazine primarily for Irish writers, Irish artists and an Irish public'.[30] True to its principles, it contained a substantial number of illustrations by Irish artists, including Jack Yeats and William Orpen, and a cover design by Beatrice Elvery. George Roberts, co-owner of Maunsel, tried to enlist Synge as a contributor from the first planning of *The Shanachie* (CL I 135), and in the event he was to appear in all but one of the magazine's six issues, beginning with 'The Vagrants of Wicklow'. The advantage of *The Shanachie* for Synge was the fact that it was prepared to take substantially longer essays than the *Manchester Guardian*. His series of essays 'In West Kerry' that appeared in the Spring, Summer and Winter 1907 issues of the magazine

---

29. See MS 4398, f. 45r.
30. *The Shanachie*, flyer at the end of Vol 1 (1906).

Title-page of The Shanachie

were all in excess of 4000 words whereas the *Manchester Guardian* articles had been limited to 1750. This allowed for a much more discursive, impressionistic style, a day to day reflective travel journal. It was Synge's inside understanding of a hidden Ireland that was pre-advertised for this 'series of articles on the Blasquet [sic] Islands and the south-west coast of Kerry. The life in these parts, and especially in the Islands themselves, is exceedingly primitive and distinct, and little is known of it except to a very occasional traveller. Mr. Synge, however, writes from intimate knowledge, having spent much time amongst the people of these districts.'[31]

By the time the essays appeared in 1907, in the wake of the *Playboy* controversy, Synge stood much in need of support for the authenticity of his portrayal of the Irish country people. His own policy, on the whole, was not to respond to the attacks upon him. But there is a defiant fight back in the concluding paragraph of his *Shanachie* essay 'The People of the Glens', a passage he cut from the text of his projected Wicklow book. He protests against

> the fashion in Dublin, quite recently, to reject a fundamental doctrine of theology, and to exalt the Irish peasant into a type of almost absolute virtue, frugal, self-sacrificing, valiant, and I know not what. There is some truth in this estimate, yet it is safer to hold with the theologians that, even west of the Shannon, the heart of man is not spotless, for though the Irish peasant has many beautiful virtues, it is idle to assert that he is totally unacquainted with the deadly sins, or with any minor rogueries. He has, however, it should never be forgotten, a fine sense of humour, and the greatest courtesy. When a benevolent visitor comes to his cottage, seeking a sort of holy family, the man of the house, his wife, and all their infants, too courteous to disappoint him, play their parts with delight. When the amiable visitor, however, is once more in the boreen, a storm of good-tempered irony breaks out behind him that would surprise him could he hear it. This irony I have heard many times in places where I have been intimate with the people, and I have always been overjoyed to hear it. It shows that, in spite of relief-works, commissions, and patronizing philanthropy – that sickly thing – the Irish peasant, in his own mind, is neither abject nor servile.

---

31. Ibid.

George Roberts buttressed this attack on the critics of the *Playboy* with an essay, in the same number of *The Shanachie* in which 'The People of the Glens' appeared, pugnaciously entitled 'A National Dramatist'. Roberts adroitly played the Irish card in making the case for Synge as interpreter of the national life. The love scene in Act III of the *Playboy*, he claimed, 'can be compared with nothing hitherto seen on the stage; so characteristically Gaelic is it in thought, feeling, and expression, that we must go to "The Love Songs of Connaught" for a parallel'.[32] In the culture wars that followed the production of the *Playboy*, *The Shanachie* was an important ally for Synge, and it is likely that it was only its discontinuation at the end of 1907 that prevented him from publishing a fourth 'In West Kerry' essay which he had drafted as 'At the Races'.[33]

The Synge travel essays, thus, are not homogeneous as Yeats wanted them to be by excluding the articles on the Congested Districts, nor even the integrated travel book that George Roberts created by collecting them as *In Wicklow, West Kerry and Connemara*. They bear the marks of Synge's own uncertain development as a writer and their origins in different sorts of publication. The first Aran essays show how little he yet knew quite where he was going, whether as semi-scholarly folklorist in *The New Ireland Review*, or romantic reporter from 'the last fortress of the Celt' for the Irish-American readership of *The Gael*. He found his voice by degrees, gaining confidence particularly as he completed *The Aran Islands* and his first staged plays. But that voice is heard quite differently in the various publications in which the essays appeared. The mystical 'Dream in Inishmaan' takes its colouring from the arts and crafts *Green Sheaf*, the sober social commentary of the Congested Districts articles from the concerned Liberal *Manchester Guardian*. And these are different again from the more leisurely and meditative series on West Kerry in *The Shanachie* where observation is filtered through the mood of the observer. Synge never wrote to order; even in the case of the *Manchester Guardian* series, which was commissioned, he was scrupulous in establishing his own terms of reference for the articles.

---

32. *The Shanachie*, II.3 (March 1907), 57–60 [59].

33. See MS 4334, ff. 156r–172r.

INTRODUCTION

In fact, in most cases he was trying to place material that he had already written in one form or another. But the essays need to be seen in relation to the diverse vehicles available to him in the Irish, British and American press, and the political and cultural constituencies they served.

Conclusion

In many respects Synge shared, even embodied the values of the Irish literary revival. Yeats' much mythologized story of his first meeting with Synge in Paris dramatizes the revivalist urge to go westward, to re-discover an all but lost native Irish culture and to find there a fresh inspiration for literature. And the visit to Aran in 1898 did provide a conversion experience for Synge, turning him away from the aesthetics of the decadent authors, Huysmans and Maeterlinck, which had attracted him up to that point, teaching him to see the world anew. Thereafter, in his travels he sought out marginal communities in the least modernized parts of Ireland, the western seaboard and its islands, the remoter valleys of Wicklow. Within those communities, also, he was attracted by the unintegrated figures, with a degree of self-identification made obvious in 'The Vagrants of Wicklow':

> wherever the labourer of a country has preserved his vitality, and begets an occasional temperament of distinction, a certain number of vagrants are to be looked for. In the middle classes the gifted son of a family is always the poorest – usually a writer or artist with no sense for speculation – and in a family of peasants, where the average comfort is just over penury, the gifted son sinks also, and is soon a tramp on the roadside.

Synge, the would-be writer and musician, with his three older brothers settled in middle-class professions, sees the tramp as his surrogate.

'All wild sights appealed to Synge', wrote Jack Yeats, 'he did not care whether they were typical of anything else or had any symbolical meaning at all.'[34] That is true, but once again his background was a conditioning factor. As the repressed child of a severely evangelical family, Synge found

---

34. Jack B. Yeats, 'With Synge in Connemara' in Yeats, *Synge and the Ireland of His Time*, p. 43.

an imaginative exhilaration in the spectacle of the carnivalesque, the anarchic and disreputable sights of fair, circus and race-meeting. One can sense his disappointment when Pádraig Ó Cadháin, King of the Blaskets, rules that he should not go to the sports on the mainland:

> you'd do better to stay quiet in this place where you are. The men will be all drunk coming back, fighting and kicking in the canoes, and a man the like of you who aren't used to us would be frightened out of his life. Then if you went the people would be taking you into one public-house, and then into another, till you'd maybe get drunk yourself, and that wouldn't be a nice thing for a gentleman. Stay where you are in this island, and you'll be safest so.

Synge stayed safely on the island as became the gentleman he was, but his imagination throughout the essays goes out to the spirit of carnival from which his upbringing inhibits him. This may even be psychologically coded into the 'Dream in Inishmaan', the terror of self-annihilation combating the almost overwhelming impulse to follow the music and join in the dance.

The travel essays are romantic in their descriptions of picturesque scenes, their cult of loneliness and desolation, their attraction to the exoticism of peasant life: one notices how often people and customs are described as 'almost oriental'. Yet this is rarely sentimental or self-indulgent, worked up for effect. The feeling for the people is sincere and unaffected. He knew that differences of class, religion and education represented permanent barriers between himself and the men and women of Aran, West Kerry or the Blaskets, but he genuinely enjoyed being with them, felt excluded when he had to leave. The best proof of this is simply the amount of time – and money – he spent there. No sooner has he finished the tour of the Congested Districts, than he is off to spend his earnings 'on the same ground', in a six-week stay in Kerry. It cannot have been comfortable for Synge living with the McDonaghs in Inishmaan, the Harrises in Mountain Stage, or the Ó Catháins on the Great Blasket. He suffered from asthma all his life, and in fact his last visit to Ballyferriter in 1907 (yielding material partly used in 'At the Races') was miserably cut short by asthma attacks. But whatever the discomforts, being there fed the life of his spirit and imagination as nothing else did.

Synge went to Aran at first at least partly to revive his Irish, learned originally in Trinity College, and in his 1905 visit to Kerry he was determined to work at the Munster dialect of the language. He was obviously pleased with his success with an old man he met near Ballinskelligs: 'He had little English, but when I tried him in Irish we got on well, though he didn't follow any Connaught forms I let slip by accident.' Although his spoken Irish was obviously never completely fluent, the command of the language was important to him. In Wicklow, in particular, his educated English speech was inclined to mark out his class difference. Patrick Kehoe, the octogenarian encountered in 'The People of the Glens', initially thinks he is foreign: 'you don't speak the same as we do; so I was thinking maybe you were from another country'. Increasingly in the essays, Synge masks this difference by rendering his own speech as well as those of the people he meets in something like the Hiberno-English of his plays. His greatest moment of triumph comes when the man on the train to Dingle in 'At the Races' takes him for a Kerry fish-dealer.

If Synge was not 'by nature unfitted to think a political thought', as Yeats claimed,[35] he took care not to obtrude his political views into his writings. He was wary of movements and parties, resigning from Maud Gonne's revolutionary Association Irlandaise within months of joining, declaring that 'I wish to work in my own way for the cause of Ireland' (CL I 47). As committed as he was himself to the Irish language, he reacted against the zeal of the Gaelic League, and while crediting the work the League had done in the Congested Districts of Mayo coolly assumed that their 'hope of restoring a lost language is a vain one'. He was clear-eyed, however, in the analysis of the failure of his own Anglo-Irish class. There may be a touch of the characteristic nostalgia for the eighteenth-century Ascendancy culture of the Big House in 'A Landlord's Garden in County Wicklow', but it is measured and qualified:

> Everyone is used in Ireland to the tragedy that is bound up with the lives of farmers and fishing people, but in this garden one seemed to feel the

---

35. W.B. Yeats, *Essays and Introductions* (London: Macmillan, 1961), p. 319.

tragedy of the landlord class also, and of the innumerable old families that are quickly dwindling away. These owners of the land are not much pitied at the present day, or much deserving of pity, and yet one cannot quite forget that they are the descendants of what was at one time, in the eighteenth century, a high-spirited and highly cultivated aristocracy.

They are landlords only now, not 'much deserving of pity' and Synge concludes 'The Oppression of the Hills' with the triumphant doggerel celebrating their enforced exile.

The most striking feature of Synge's travel writing is its honesty and integrity of thought and feeling. In his Congested Districts essays – for all Yeats' disparagement by no means mere routine journalism – he engages seriously with the social problems of the people. It is evident that he is not really sympathetic to the 'improving' spirit of the modernizing CDB, feels how such 'improvements' may be made at the expense of just those qualities in the people's lives he most admires. But he accepts that they are improvements, and can only regret that the colourful and picturesque in Irish life are bound up with a poverty that is intolerable. He yearns towards integration with communities from which he knows himself ultimately excluded. A passage from his first West Kerry essay catches this poignantly:

> As far as I could see there were little groups of people – mostly women and children – on their way to the chapel in Ballyferriter. A few of the women wore round blue cloaks; but the larger number had simply black or blue shawls over their heads. This procession along the olive bog between the mountains and the sea, on this grey day of autumn, seemed to wring me with the pang of emotion one feels everywhere in Ireland – an emotion that is partly local and patriotic, and partly a share of the desolation that is mixed everywhere with the supreme beauty of the world.

The strength of Synge's travel essays lies in this capacity to render vividly from the viewpoint of an alienated observer, scenes and people to which he feels nonetheless intensely committed.

Nicholas Grene
September 2008

Note on the Text

This edition is the first collection of Synge's travel essays to use the texts published in his lifetime in newspapers and journals. The Aran essays are here reprinted for the first time, although material from them was re-used in *The Aran Islands* (London: Elkin Matthews; Dublin: Maunsel, 1907). The Wicklow and West Kerry essays, somewhat revised by Synge before his death in his efforts to gather them together for a book, are reprinted as they originally appeared in the *Manchester Guardian* and *The Shanachie*. The articles on the Congested Districts, commissioned by the *Manchester Guardian*, with their accompanying illustrations by Jack Yeats are also included. The only essay that was not published in Synge's lifetime in this edition is 'At the Races', the fourth in the West Kerry series. This was printed first in Volume IV of the posthumous *Works* of Synge brought out by Maunsel in 1910, as the final section of what is there arranged as a single undifferentiated 'In West Kerry' essay. However, the title 'At the Races' is to be found in Synge's typescript draft, and it seems to have been planned as another essay that would have continued the series in *The Shanachie* if the magazine had not ceased publication after 1907.

The non-Aran travel essays were collected in the 1910 *Works* without illustrations, and then again, with newly commissioned drawings by Jack Yeats, but without the original Congested Districts illustrations, in *In Wicklow, West Kerry and Connemara* (Dublin: Maunsel, 1911). This latter volume has formed the basis for a number of popular reprints, the most recent being *Travels in Wicklow, West Kerry and Connemara* (London: Serif, 2005). The fullest edition of these essays to date is that edited by Alan Price in the Synge *Collected Works*, Vol. II: *Prose* (London: Oxford University Press, 1966). Unfortunately the editorial principles adopted in that volume seem to have been very loose and confused. So, for example, it includes both the Jack Yeats illustrations from the original *Manchester Guardian* articles and the *In Wicklow, West Kerry and Connemara* collection without discriminating between them, often displacing the drawings from the essays they illustrated. Passages from unpublished manuscripts are arbitrarily introduced into the printed text, and in the case of one piece, 'People and Places', a synthetic essay is created as a collage of passages from a number of different manuscripts. Annotation is helpful in supplying relevant material from manuscript notebooks and drafts, but is erratic and provides no information on the actual events, places and people to which Synge refers in the essays.

In preparing this edition, I have corrected obvious mistakes in the text and regularized spelling. I have noted significant differences between the newspaper and periodical versions here reprinted and later revisions, though I have not attempted a full and systematic collation. I have included all the illustrations from the first publication texts in as near as possible the original form and placing.

When writing his travel essays, Synge deliberately withheld the actual names of the people he met or used pseudonyms for them. I have tried to identify them where possible in my notes. The best source of information here is the 1901 Census, which gives only the English form of names, so in most cases this is the form in which they are referred to in the notes, though I have given their Irish equivalent where this is known, as in the case of the Blasket Islanders. Place names in the period often had many variant forms; I have retained Synge's anglicized spelling – Inishmaan for Inis Meáin – throughout.

J.M. SYNGE
TRAVELLING
IRELAND

'A Story from Inishmaan'[1]

The following story and others were told to me in Inishmaan[2], middle island of the Aran group, by an old man[3] who came every day and sat with me by the kitchen fire, in the cottage where I lodged. As the stories went on, the family would draw round on their stools. Some of the near neighbours came in to listen also, while the mother or her daughter, in their wonderful red garments, sat at their wheel by the door. The old man had some knowledge of English, and translated for my convenience[4], as my Celtic would not carry me through extended tales. I have kept closely to his language.

There were two farmers in County Clare with farms not far apart. The one had a son, and the other, who was richer, a daughter.

One day the son said to his father that he wished to marry his neighbour's daughter.

'Well', said the father whose name was O'Conor, 'try, if you think it good; but there is not gold enough with us to win her'.

---

1. The story is included in *The Aran Islands* (CW II 61–4) in revised form.

2. Anglicized form of Inis Méain, which literally means 'middle island'. The story was told to Synge during his first visit to Aran, 10 May-25 June 1898.

3. Pat Dirane, who died in 1899.

4. In *The Aran Islands*, Synge in fact says that the story was told him in English (CW II 60). On the changes in the story between essay and published book, see Introduction p. xxiv.

'I will try,' said the son.

He put all his gold into a bag, and going over to the other farm he opened the door and threw in the bag before him.

'Is that all gold?' said the father of the girl.

'All gold,' said O'Conor.

'It will not weigh down my daughter,' said the father.

'Let us try,' said O'Conor.

Then they put them in the scales, the daughter in one side and the gold in the other, but the girl went down against the ground, so O'Conor took up his bag and went away.

As he was going along the road he came to where there was a little man standing with his back against the wall.

'Where are you going with your bag?' said the man.

'Going back home,' said O'Conor.

'Is it gold you might be wanting?' said the man.

'It is,' said O'Conor.

'I will give what you need,' said the man, 'and we can bargain in this way – you will pay me back in a year, the gold I give you, or five pounds of your own flesh'.

So that bargain was made between them, and O'Conor went back with the gold from the man, and married the daughter of his neighbour.

They were rich, and he built her a grand castle on the cliffs of Clare, with a window that looked out straight over the wild ocean. One day when he went with his wife to look out over the wild ocean they saw a ship coming in straight upon the rocks, and there were no sails on her at all, and the ship was wrecked upon the rocks, and her load was tea and coffee and silk.

O'Conor and his wife went down to look at the wreck, and when Lady O'Conor saw the silk, she said she wished a dress of it.

'You shall have it,' said her husband.

They got the silk from the sailors, and when the captain came up to get the money for it, O'Conor asked him to come to them again, and have dinner with them; and they had a grand dinner, and they drank after they had dined till the captain had more drink than was good. While they were still drinking a letter was brought to O'Conor to tell him that a friend of his had died, and he would have to go away on a long journey.

As he made ready to go away, the captain came to him and said:

'Are you fond of your wife?'

'I am fond of her,' said O'Conor.

'Will you make me a bet of twenty guineas, no man visits her while you make your journey?' said the captain.

'I will bet it,' said O'Conor, and he went away on his journey.

There was an old hag near the castle who sold trinkets to all who passed on that way, and Lady O'Conor allowed her to sleep up in a big box in her own room. The Captain came down on the road to the old hag, and said:

'For how much will you let me sleep one night in your box?'

'For no sum would I do such a deed,' said the hag.

'For ten guineas?' said the captain.

'Not for ten guineas,' said the hag.

'For twelve guineas?' said the captain.

'Not for twelve guineas,' said the hag.

'For fifteen guineas?' said the captain.

'For fifteen guineas I will do it,' said the hag.

Then she took him up, and hid him in the box. When night began the Lady O'Conor came up into her room, and the captain watched through a hole that was in the box. He saw her take off her two rings, and put them up on a sort of board that was over her head like a chimney-piece, and take off her clothes, and blow out the candle as she went up into her bed. As soon as she slept the captain came out of the box, and he had some means of making light, for he lit the candle. He went to the bed where she was sleeping, and without disturbing her took the two rings off the board, and, blowing out the light, got down again into his box.

When O'Conor came back the captain met him, and told him he had been a night in his wife's room, and gave him the two rings. O'Conor gave him the twenty guineas of the bet. Going up to his castle he took his wife to the window to look out over the wild ocean. While she was in the window he pushed her from behind, and she fell down over the cliff into the sea.

An old woman was on the shore, and saw her falling, so she brought her out, and took the wet clothes off her, and put on some old rags belonging to herself. When O'Conor had pushed his wife from the window he went away into the land. After a few days Lady O'Conor went out after him to find him, and after much wandering she heard that he was reaping in a field with sixty men. She came to the field, and would have gone in, but the gate-man would not open the gate to her. Then the owner of the field came down, and she told him her story, and he made them to open the gate, and brought her in. Her husband was there reaping, but he never gave any sign of knowing her, and she pointed him out to the owner, and the owner made him come out and go with his wife. She brought him down to where her horses were, and made him get up, and she got up behind him and rode away. When they came to the part of the road where O'Conor had met the little man, he was there on the road before them.

'Have you my gold on you?' said the man.

'I have not,' said O'Conor.

'Pay me then the flesh,' said the man.

So they went into a house, and a knife was brought, and a clean white cloth was put upon a table, and O'Conor was put upon the cloth.

The little man was just striking the lancet into his flesh when, says Lady O'Conor:

'Have you bargained for five pounds of flesh?'

'For five pounds of flesh,' said the man.

'Have you bargained for any drop of blood?' said Lady O'Conor.

'For no blood,' said the man.

'Cut out your five pounds of flesh,' said Lady O'Conor, 'but if you take one drop of his blood I'll put that through you,' and she put a pistol to his head.

Then the little man went away, and they saw him no more.

When they came home to their castle they made a great supper, and invited the captain, and the old hag, and the old woman who had pulled Lady O'Conor from the sea.

After they had eaten well, Lady O'Conor began, and said, they would all tell their stories, and she told how she had been saved from the sea, and found her husband.

Then the old woman told her story, how she had found Lady O'Conor wet, and in great disorder, and how she had brought her in, and put on her old rags of her own.

Lady O'Conor asked the captain for his story, but the captain said they would get no story from him. Then Lady O'Conor took her pistol and put it on the edge of the table and said, anyone who refused to tell his story would get a bullet into him. So the captain told how he had got into the box, and come over to her bed, without disturbing her at all, and had taken away the rings. Then Lady O'Conor took up her pistol and shot the hag through the body, and they threw her corpse over the cliff into the sea. That is my story.

Readers will recognize here two motives used by Shakespeare, one in the *Merchant of Venice*, the other in *Cymbeline*. The pistol is of course a modern substitution. The story of the wager occurs in Boccaccio (Decamerone II, 9), in several French romances of early date: the 'Roman de la Violette', 'Dou roi Flore et de la belle Jehanne' (Dunlop, *History of Fiction*),[5] and in a German tale of 'The Two Merchants and the Faithful Wife of Ruprecht von Würzburg.'[6]

The other portion, dealing with the pound of flesh, is even more widely distributed, occurring in Persian and Egyptian forms; in the *Gesta Romanorum*,[7] in *Il Pecorone* of Ser Giovanni, a Florentine Notary,[8] and in the ballad of Cernutus.[9]

---

5. John Colin Dunlop, *History of Fiction*, revised H. Wilson, 2 vols (London: Bell, 1888).

6. Fourteenth-century verse tale in German.

7. Medieval collection of tales and anecdotes in Latin, first translated into English in the sixteenth century.

8. Ser Giovanni's collection of stories, *Il Pecorone* (*The Dunce*), 1558, was one of Shakespeare's sources for *The Merchant of Venice*.

9. An old English ballad, telling the story of the pound of flesh, sometimes thought to be a source for Shakespeare.

Returning to the British Isles we find in Campbell's *Popular Tales from the Western Highlands*, a story which unites the two elements.[10] A comparison with this version is not without interest. In it the hero is not a farmer, but a king's son who sets out with fifty pounds to seek a wife. He stops at an inn for the night and, making no secret of his mission, the innkeeper informs him that there are three fair daughters in the house over the way, of whom the eldest may be known by a mole upon her body, and lends him a further fifty pounds, needful for her purchase, on condition that he shall be repaid within the year, or shall take a strip of skin from the crown of the head, to the sole of the foot, from the king's son.

Here it is curious to note the mole upon the heroine which plays an important, though different part, in the French and Italian versions. The strip of skin occurs in other Highland tales, and is believed by Campbell to be a Scandinavian mode of torture.

The prince marries the eldest daughter, and all goes well till the ship comes with a load of silk. It is not wrecked, as in the Aran tale, and the captain wagers it against the kingdom. He then bribes the henwife of the castle, who pretends that her sister is dying – compare the friend of O'Conor's who dies in the Aran version – and goes off on a journey, getting her valuables carried up to the king's room, in a chest, in which the captain is confined.

He wins the wager and is made king. The queen dresses in man's clothes – as in the Italian version – and goes to seek her husband who has disappeared. She finds him and takes him into her service, saving him from the innkeeper by Portia's device. Finally, the king is put upon the stairs to listen while the queen sits with the captain and induces him to explain how he came to possess the kingdom. The usurper is then handed over to justice, and all ends well. It is hard to assert at what date such stories as these reached the west. There is little doubt that our heroic tales which show so often their kinship with Grecian myths, date from the pre-ethnic period of the Aryans, and it is easy to believe that some purely

---

10. The story is 'The Chest' in J.F. Campbell, *Popular Tales of the West Highlands* (Edinburgh: Birlinn, 1994 [1860]), pp. 379–90; Campbell's collection of folk-tales were orally collected in Scots Gallic and printed with translations.

secular narratives share their antiquity. Further, a comparison of all the versions will show that we have here one of the rudest and therefore, it may be, most ancient settings of the material.

New Ireland Review (November 1898)

'The Last Fortress of the Celt'[11]

On an island in the Atlantic, within a day's journey from Dublin, there is still a people who live in conditions older than the Middle Ages, and have preserved in an extraordinary degree the charm of primitive man.

Innishmaan, the middle, and least sophisticated island of the Aran group off County Galway, has no harbour worthy of the name, no real roads, no carts, no post office, and, what is rare in Ireland, no police barrack. The population, of about three hundred and fifty, depend for their meagre livelihood on net and line fishing, which they carry on in curraghs, or canvas canoes, with the greatest enterprise and daring.

The visitor usually reaches this lonely rock from Kilronan, the principal village in the great Aran island,[12] whence he is borne to his destination in the stern of a long eight-oared curragh. The sound is not much more than a mile wide at the narrowest part, yet the voyage from Kilronan takes almost an hour, and the unfamiliar company of lithe islanders dressed in gray homespun flannels, together with the leaping oscillation of the canoe, gives one a strange sense of novelty. A landing is effected at a small pier

---

11. Most of the material in this essay derives from Synge's experiences during his first visit to Inishmaan in May-June 1898 and was re-used in *The Aran Islands* I (CW II 49–104).

12. Inis Mór known in English either as Inishmore or Aranmore.

and after half an hour's walk between flat sheets of naked limestone, where a few goats nibble a repast of blue gentian and maiden-hair, one reaches a straggling settlement of about seventy cottages. It is only when one has spent months in one of these, and grown, so to speak, into one's place in the chimney-corner, that the full charm of the people can be realized.

Lodgings in the ordinary sense are not, of course, to be had, but I was fortunate enough to find a room, sometimes used by Gaelic scholars, which was tolerably comfortable. My hostess[13] was an elderly woman who wore the short red petticoat, indescribable shawl and raw cow-skin shoes, which form the national costume. Like most of the older women she was quite ignorant of English, but her daughter[14] could both read and understand it, though she never used a Saxon word except when speaking to her pigs, a curious habit which is common in the island, and may be explained in more ways than one. This girl was dressed exactly as her mother, except that when she went out on Sunday she put an elaborate shawl over her head, while the older women, indeed all the married women, are satisfied with an extra red petticoat, worn with the waistband round the face.

Their cottage was one of the most important in the island, and there were numerous visitors from early morning till bedtime. All were received with the usual Gaelic salutation, 'That God may bless thee', given a stool by the fire, and drawn into the conversation with unconscious yet admirable courtesy. Shoes and stockings are still regarded as a thing put on, an extra, and when the day's work was done the women generally laid them aside, showing finely formed feet and ankles under their short petticoats, while they did the honours of their kitchen.

At first the men spoke English for my convenience expressing themselves more correctly than the ordinary peasant, though some used the Gaelic idioms continually, and substituted 'he' or 'she' for 'it,' as the neuter pronoun is not found in modern Irish. Their vocabulary was, of course, very limited, which gave rise at times to curious nomenclature. Thus one

---

13. Bridget McDonagh, who unlike her husband Patrick, could only speak Irish and could not read or write. Though described here by Synge as 'elderly' she was only 47 in 1901.

14. Mary McDonagh.

evening when my comb had been mislaid, my old host came to me and asked if I had found my 'little rake'!

The faces of the men were somewhat unlike the Irish type, and showed traces of the Pre-Celtic blood, which has lingered in the west of Europe, while among the women were some curiously Mongolian features, rather resembling the Bigoudennes of the south coast of Brittany.[15]

The kitchen where we sat was a marvel of unconscious decoration. The deep glow from the red garments of the women who clustered round the fire on their stools lent a colour of almost oriental richness, and the whitewashed walls were toned by the turf smoke to a delicate brown which harmonized as if by design with the hard earthen floor. On one side of the fire stood the spinning wheel, on the other a large pot of indigo for dying wool. Round the walls, or among the open rafters, one could see many sorts of fishing tackle, with the oilskins of the men, and right over head, under the thatch, a whole red cowskin destined for the primitive shoes, or pampooties, as they are called in English.

Of all the topics which we touched on, war was perhaps their favourite. The contest between Spain and America was in progress when I first went to the island, and caused much excitement.[16]

Nearly all the families have relations beyond the Atlantic, and all eat of the flour and bacon of the United States, hence they have a vague feeling that 'if anything happened to America' their own island would be no longer habitable. On a subsequent occasion the great International Yacht Race was the all engrossing topic, partly because it was a nautical event, partly because 'Lipton's Teas' stand high in their esteem.[17] As a child

---

15. Synge was interested in Breton culture and language, and had visited Quimper in Brittany for two weeks in April 1899.

16. The Spanish-American War of April-August 1898 was ended by the Treaty of Paris, giving independence to Cuba and possession of the Philippines and Puerto Rico to the United States.

17. Sir Thomas Lipton (1850-1931), highly successful Glasgow merchant of Irish origins, first brought tea, originally a luxury drink, within the reach of ordinary consumers and by this time it was widely drunk even in the poorest areas of the West of Ireland. Lipton's yacht *Shamrock I*, was beaten by the American *Columbia* in the America's Cup 16-20 October 1899, just after the end of Synge's second visit to Aran, 12 September-7 October 1899.

sees the world only in relation to its own home, so these islanders see everything in relation to their island. Without some such link as Lipton's Teas, the matters of the outside world do not interest them, even the politics of Ireland being regarded with indifference.

Spinning girls (photo by Synge, Paris)

When they talk with strangers, language is a favourite subject. As all outsiders who spend any time upon the island are philologists, the islanders have concluded that linguistic studies – particularly Gaelic studies – are the chief object in a life of moneyed leisure.

'We have seen', said one of my visitors, 'Frenchmen, Danes and Germans, and there was not one of them without books of Irish, which they could read better than ourselves. Believe me there are no rich men now in the world who are not studying the Irish.'

They think little of the stranger who cannot claim mastery over five or six idioms, and, as they are themselves bi-lingual, they realize in a way the ordinary peasant cannot do what it means to think and speak in several languages. In spite of their simplicity they are not easy to deceive, weighing what is told them with much deliberation. One day I heard a heated discussion under my door as to whether I had written with my own hand the Irish letters I had sent them in my absence; the doubt, of course, was raised because I write the language more correctly than I speak it. The schoolmaster has an ingenious test for his philological visitors. When a newcomer is announced, he invites him into his parlour, and pours out a glass of the national beverage. Then he leads the conversation to linguistic matters, and when the foreigner has committed himself to a not always modest statement of his learning, he produces an advertisement of some patent medicine, printed in about twenty different tongues, and requests the visitor to demonstrate his attainments.

Launching the curraghs (photo by Synge, Paris)

'THE LAST FORTRESS OF THE CELT'

The youngest son of the household where I lodged was appointed as my teacher and guide,[18] and whenever he was not at work, he led me about the island or took me out fishing, in a curragh, teaching me Irish all the time. The rough fossiliferous limestone which abounds in some places soon destroyed my shoes, so I was compelled to adopt the pampooties of the natives. They consist simply of a piece of cow-skin laced round the heel and toe, with the hair outside. In the evening when they are taken off, they are placed in a basin of water – as the rough hide cuts the foot and stocking if it is allowed to harden – then about mid-day, if occasion offers, the wearer steps into the surf, up to his ankles, so that the feet are continually moist. At first I threw my weight upon my heels, as is done naturally in a boot, and was a good deal bruised, but, after a day or two, I learned the natural elastic walk of primitive man, and could follow my companion in any portion of the island. Sometimes one goes for a mile or more jumping from rock to rock without a single ordinary step. This exercise soon taught me that toes have a definite employment, for I found myself jumping by instinct on to any tiny crevice in the rock before me, and clinging with an eager grip in which ten separate muscles ached with their unusual exertion.

One day a steamer came out from Galway with a party of police and land agents, who had long been expected, as evictions were impending on the island.[19] Till then no islander had consented to act as bailiff, so it had been impossible to find, or identify, the cattle of the defaulters. On this occasion, however, a man undertook the dishonorable office, and many lean cows fell into the hands of the law. In the evening, when the last policeman had embarked, an old woman came forward from the crowd, and, mounting on a rock near the boatslip, began a fierce rhapsody in Gaelic, waving her withered arms with extraordinary passion.

'This man', she said, 'is my own son. It is I that ought to know him. He is the first ruffian in the whole big world.'

---

18. Martin McDonagh, whom Synge calls 'Michael' in *The Aran Islands*. He was 19 in 1901.

19. Two previous attempts at carrying out these evictions had been made in January and May 1898. These evictions, which took place on 11 June 1898, may in fact have been the last carried out in Aran. For the full details, see J.M. Synge, *The Aran Islands*, ed. Tim Robinson (Harmondsworth: Penguin, 1992), p. 143.

The fishermen's return (photo by Synge, Paris)

During my first visit to the island an old man used to come up every day to tell me stories in the kitchen and was generally followed by some of the neighbours who knew his custom and came in to listen also. One story he told was of peculiar interest: the old folk tale which unites the 'Pound of Flesh' theme, used by Shakespeare in the 'Merchant of Venice,' and the 'Wager on the Faithful Wife,' given by Boccaccio, and again by Shakespeare in 'Cymbeline.' These stories are, of course, very widely distributed, yet I listened with a strange feeling of wonder while this illiterate native of a wet rock in the Atlantic, told the same tales that had charmed the Florentines by the Arno. Once or twice his stories were so Boccaccian in their flavour that I blushed to hear them in the company of girls and women. He gave me also a very full account of the fairies and their proceedings. He had often seen them, he said, playing ball in the evening by the boatslip, and they were about a yard high, with caps like the peelers (policemen).

Once he saw a woman who was 'away' with them, looking over a wall toward the north, but she did not speak to him. Another night he heard a voice crying out in Irish, 'Oh mother, I'm killed,' and in the morning there was blood upon the wall, and a child in a house not far away was dead. He advised me earnestly not to linger in certain portions of the island after nightfall, for fear 'the good people' might 'do me a mischief'. When I knew him better he took me aside and said he would tell me a secret he had never yet told to living man. 'Take a sharp needle,' he said, 'and stick it in under the collar of your coat, and not one of them will be able to have power on you.' Iron is a common talisman with barbarians, but in this case the idea of exquisite sharpness was also present, and, perhaps, the traditional sanctity of the instrument of toil, a belief which is common in Brittany. He shed tears when I went to his hovel to see him before my departure, as he said he would never see me again. Then, with a curious change of thought, he urged me to 'put insurance on him,' as his death was certainly approaching, and I might win five hundred pounds. He was buried between the following Christmas and the new year.

An old woman died in the cottage next mine while I was on the island, and I was enabled to witness the curious lamentations for the dead. I did not go to the wake, as I feared my presence might jar upon the mourners, but all the evening before the funeral I could hear the strokes of a hammer in the yard, where the next of kin laboured at the coffin. Next day, a few minutes before the start, poteen – the illicit whiskey of western Ireland – was served liberally to the men who stood about upon the road, and a portion was brought to me in my room. Then the coffin was carried out, and the procession, composed for the most part of old men and women, moved off to the graveyard, in the low eastern district of the island. While the grave was being opened all the women sat down among the flat tombstones bordered by a pale fringe of early bracken and began the wild keene,[20] or lamentation. Each aged crone, as she took her turn of the leading recitative, seemed possessed for the moment with a profound ecstacy of grief, swaying to and fro, and bowing her withered forehead to

---

20. Irish *caoineadh*, lamentation for the dead, more usually anglicized as 'keen'.

the stone before her, while she called out to the dead with a perpetually recurring chant of sobs. All round the graveyard old wrinkled women, looking out from under their deep red petticoats, rocked themselves with the same rhythm, and intoned the half articulate wail which is sustained as an accompaniment. The morning had been beautifully fine, but as they lowered the coffin into the grave thunder rumbled overhead, and hailstones hissed among the bracken.

Going for turf (photo by Synge, Paris)

The tendency to drink is the only vice upon the island, and it cannot be severely censured. When storm and fog come up from the Atlantic, and beat for weeks upon the cliffs, the sense of desolation that grows on one is indescribable. Nothing can be seen but a mass of wet rock, a strip of surf, and then a tumult of grey waves. The inhabitants do not seem at first to pay much attention to the dismal fury that is around them, but after a few days they begin to talk about their pigs, or cattle, with the voice of men telling stories in a haunted house, and the bottle of poteen is drawn from its hiding-place. In some circumstances an anaesthetic is needful, and a storm in Innishmaan is one of these.

One day during my second visit, a letter was brought to me from my former teacher, who had gone out into the world to seek his fortune.[21] I will translate it literally.

'Dear noble one,

I write this letter to thee with joy and pride, that thou foundest the way to the house of my father the day thou wast on the steamship. I am thinking there will not be loneliness on thee, for there will be the fine, beautiful Gaelic League every Sunday, and thou wilt be learning powerfully.

I am thinking there is no one in life walking with thee now from morning till the night, but thine own self, and great is the pity. What way are my mother, and sister, and Martin, and do not forget white Michael, and the poor little child, and the old grey woman, and Rory.

I am getting a forgetfulness on all my friends and kindred.

I am your friend,

-----------------------'[22]

It is curious how he accuses himself of forgetfulness, after inquiring for all his family by name. I suppose his first homesickness was wearing away, and he looked on his recovery as a treason toward his kindred. One evening soon afterwards a young poet of the Island, a former comrade of

---

21. Martin McDonagh moved to Galway in July 1899 to work for Mrs Monica McDonagh and in 1900 was managing a lime works: see MS 4424–6, 84 and 89.

22. For the Irish original of this letter, dated 22 September 1899, see MS 4424–6, 85. For the offence caused by its publication without permission, see Introduction, p. xxxi. Synge reproduced the letter again in *The Aran Islands* (CW II 111–2), but he changed the archaic sounding attempt to render the second person singulars of Irish throughout: 'thou foundest the way' becomes 'you found the way'.

my correspondent's,[23] came up to talk to me in the kitchen. I showed him the letter, and, by old Martin's[24] request, he read it aloud. When he reached the last sentence he hesitated an instant, and then, with rare tact, omitted it altogether.

The material life of the people is beset with many difficulties. Turf is not found on the island, and has to be brought from the mainland at considerable expense. Again, the horses can find no grass in the summer, and are sent over to graze on the mountains. When they return, they are thrown into the sea, about a hundred yards from land, and swim ashore. The shipping of the young cattle for Galway fair is another serious undertaking. When the hooker, or fishing smack, which is used for their transport, is made fast by the pier, the cattle are slung down by a rope from the mast head, with much struggling and confusion. Sometimes the tide becomes too low in the middle of this tedious process, in which case the unfortunate animals are dragged out through the surf, towed for a hundred yards by a curragh, and finally hoisted on board the hooker, more drowned than living. The agility and courage shown by the men in capturing these half-wild bullocks on the sand, is worthy of remark, and causes much amusement to the girls, who lie along the summit of the cliffs, shouting down a running comment of satire or approbation.

It is curious to observe how the setting of this simple life where all art is unknown, becomes as beautiful as any organized pageant in its direct union with a specialized yet natural existence.

Every article in Inishmaan has an almost personal character. The curraghs, the spinning wheels, the miniature wooden barrels which still replace earthenware to a large extent, the home-made cradles, churns and baskets are all full of individuality; and, again, the simple events of the year, the drawing of the nets, the shipment of the cattle, the gathering and burning of the seaweed, the marriages and funerals, are all primitive dramas of much interest and beauty, in which every inhabitant plays in turn all the parts.

23. Probably Peter Concannon; at the bottom of Martin McDonagh's letter in Irish is added in English 'Peter Concannon will read this letter to you if you are not able.'

24. Presumably Synge's pseudonym for Martin's father, Patrick McDonagh, who was 60 in 1901.

It is vain to seek for a people like this in civilisation; the type is disappearing from Ireland and not from Ireland only but from the world.

The Gael (April 1901)

'An Autumn Night in the Hills'[25]

A few years ago a pointer dog of my acquaintance was wounded by accident in a wild glen on the western slope of County Wicklow.[26] He was left at the cottage of an under-keeper, or bailiff – the last cottage on the edge of two ranges of mountains that stretch on the north and west to the plain of Kildare – and a few weeks later I made my way there to bring him down to his master.[27]

It was an afternoon of September, and some heavy rain of the night before had made the road which led up to the cottage through the middle of the glen as smooth as a fine beach, while the clearness of the air gave the granite that ran up on either side of the way a peculiar tinge that was nearly luminous against the shadow of the hills. Every cottage that I passed had a group of rowan trees beside it covered with scarlet berries that gave brilliant points of colour of curious effect.

Just as I came to the cottage the road turned across a swollen river which I had to cross on a range of slippery stones.[28] Then, when I had

---

25. Based on an incident in August 1897; Synge was in fact accompanied by his brother-in-law Harry Stephens who owned the pointer dog. See Introduction p. xvi–xvii.

26. Glenmalure, setting also for *The Shadow of the Glen*.

27. The cottage was that of Michael Harney, his sister Esther and his brother James, at Baravore at the head of Glenmalure. See *Interpreting Synge*, p. 33.

28. Baravore Ford across the river Avonbeg.

gone a few yards further, I heard a bark of welcome, and the dog ran down to meet me. The noise he made brought two women to the door of the cottage, one a finely made girl, with an exquisitely open and graceful manner, the other a very old woman. A sudden shower had come up without any warning over the rim of the valley, so I went into the cottage and sat down on a sort of bench in the chimney-corner, at the end of a long low room with open rafters.

'You've come on a bad day,' said the old woman, 'for you won't see any of the lads or men about the place.'

'I suppose they went out to cut their oats,' I said, 'this morning while the weather was fine.'

'They did not,' she answered, 'but they're after going down to Aughrim for the body of Mary Kinsella, that is to be brought this night from the station. There will be a wake then at the last cottage you're after passing, where you saw all them trees with the red berries on them.'

She stopped for a moment while the girl gave me a drink of milk.

'I'm afraid it's a lot of trouble I'm giving you,' I said as I took it, 'and you busy, with no men in the place.'

'No trouble at all in the world,' said the girl, 'and if it was itself, wouldn't any one be glad of it in the lonesome place we're in.'

The old woman began talking again.

'You saw no sign or trace on the road of the people coming with the body?'

'No sign,' I said, 'and who was she at all?'

'She was a fine young woman with two children,' she went on, 'and a year and a half ago she went wrong in her head, and they had to send her away. And then up there in the Richmond asylum maybe they thought the sooner they were shut of her the better, for she died two days ago this morning, and now they're bringing her up to have a wake, and they'll bury her beyond at the church, far as it is, for it's there are all the people of the two families.'

While we talked I had been examining a wound in the dog's side near the end of his lung.

'He'll do rightly now,' said the girl who had come in again and was putting tea-things on the table. 'He'll do rightly now. You wouldn't know he'd been hurted at all only for a kind of a cough he'll give now and again. Did they ever tell you the way he was hit?' she added, going down on her knees in the chimney-corner with some dry twigs in her hand and making a little fire on the flag-stone a few inches from the turf.

I told her I had heard nothing but the fact of his wound.

'Well,' she said, 'a great darkness and storm came down that night and they all out on the hill. The rivers rose, and they were there groping along by the turf track not minding the dogs. Then an old rabbit got up and run before them, and a man put up his gun and shot across it. When he fired that dog run out from behind a rock, and one grain of the shot cut the scruff off his nose, and another went in there where you were looking, at the butt of his ribs. He dropped down bleeding and howling, and they thought he was killed. The night was falling and they had no way they could carry him, so they made a kind of a shelter for him with sticks and turf, and they left him while they would be going for a sack.'

'You've come on a bad day,' said the old woman (M. O'Flaherty)

She stopped for a moment to knead some dough and put down a dozen hot cakes – cut out with the mouth of a tumbler – in a frying pan on the little fire she had made with the twigs. While she was doing so, the old woman took up the talk.

'Ah,' she said, 'there do be queer things them nights out on the mountains and in the lakes among them. I was reared beyond in the valley where the mines used to be, in the valley of the Lough Nahanagan,[29] and it's many a queer story I've heard of the spirit does be in that lake.'

'I have sometimes been there fishing till it was dark,' I said when she paused, 'and heard strange noises in the cliff.'

'There was an uncle of mine,' she continued, 'and he was there the same way as yourself, fishing with a big fly in the darkness of the night, and the spirit came down out of the clouds and rifted the waters asunder. He was afeared then and he run down to the houses trembling and shaking. There was another time', she went on, 'a man came round to this county who was after swimming through the water of every lake in Ireland. He went up to swim in that lake, and a brother of my own went up along with him. The gentleman had heard tell of the spirit but not a bit would he believe in it. He went down on the bank, and he had a big black dog with him, and he took off his clothes.

"For the love of God," said my brother, "put that dog in before you go in yourself, the way you'll see if he ever comes out of it." The gentleman said he would do that and they threw in a stick or a stone and the dog leapt in and swam out to it. Then he turned round again and he swam and he swam, and not a bit nearer did he come.

"He's a long time swimming back," said the gentleman.

"I'm thinking your honor'll have a grey beard before he comes back," said my brother, and before the word was out of his mouth the dog went down out of their sight, and the inside out of him came up on the top of the water.'

By this time the cakes were ready and the girl put them on a plate for me at the table, and poured out a cup of tea from the tea-pot, putting

---

29. Mountain lake in the valley of Glendasan on the road from Glendalough to the Wicklow Gap, close to the Luganure lead mines, which were no longer being worked by the late nineteenth century.

the milk and sugar herself into my cup as is the custom with the cottage people of Wicklow. Then she put the tea-pot down in the embers of the turf and sat down in the place I had left.

'Well,' she said, 'I was telling you the story of that night. When they got back here they sent up two lads for the dog, with a sack to carry him on if he was alive and a spade to bury him if he was dead. When they came to the turf where they left him they saw him near twenty yards down the path. The crathur thought they were after leaving him there to die, and he got that lonesome he dragged himself along like a Christian till he got too weak with the bleeding. James, the big lad, walked up again him first with the spade in his hand. When he seen the spade he let a kind of a groan out of him.

'That dog's as wise as a child, and he knew right well it was to bury him they brought the spade. Then Mike went up and laid down the sack on the ground, and the minute he seen it he jumped up and tumbled in on it himself. Then they carried him down, and the crathur getting his death with the cold and the great rain was falling. When they brought him in here you'd have thought he was dead. We put up a settle bed before the fire, and we put him into it. The heat roused him a bit, and he stretched out his legs and gave two groans out of him like an old man. Mike thought he'd drink some milk so we heated a cup of it over the fire. When he put down his tongue into it he began to cough and bleed, then he turned himself over in the settle bed and looked up at me like an old man. I sat up with him that night and it raining and blowing. At four in the morning I gave him a sup more of the milk and he was able to drink it.

'The next day he was stronger, and we gave him a little new milk every now and again. We couldn't keep him here all day in the kitchen so we put him in the little room beyond by the door and an armful of hay in along with him. In the afternoon the boys were out on the mountain and the old woman was gone somewhere else, and I was chopping sticks in the lane. I heard a sort of a noise and there he was with his head out through the window looking out on me in the lane. I was afraid he was lonesome in there all by himself, so I put in one of our old dogs to keep him company. Then I stuffed an old hat into the window and I thought they'd be quiet together.

'But what did they do but begin to fight in there all in the dark as they were. I opened the door and out runs that lad before I could stop him. Not a bit would he go in again, so I had to leave him running about beside me. He's that loyal to me now you wouldn't believe it. When I go for the cow he comes along with me, and when I go to make up a bit of hay on the hill he'll come and make a sort of bed for himself under a haycock, and not a bit of him will look at Mike or the boys.'

'Ah,' said the old woman, as the girl got up to pour me out another cup from the tea-pot, 'it's herself will be lonesome when that dog is gone, he's never out of her sight, and you'd do right to send her down a little dog all for herself.'

'You would so,' said the girl, 'but maybe he wouldn't be loyal to me, and I wouldn't give a thraneen[30] for a dog as wasn't loyal.'

'Would you believe it,' said the old woman again, 'when the gentleman wrote down about that dog Mike went out to where she was in the haggard, and says, "They're after sending me the prescription for that dog", says he, "to put on his tombstone." And she went down quite simple, and told the boys below in the bog, and it wasn't till they began making game of her that she seen the way she'd been humbugged.'

'That's the truth,' said the girl, 'I went down quite simple, and indeed it's a small wonder, that dog's as fit for a decent burial as many that gets it.'

Meanwhile the shower had turned to a dense torrent of mountain rain, and although the evening was hardly coming on, it was so dark that the girl lighted a lamp and hung it at the corner of the chimney. The kitchen was longer than most that I have met with and had a skeleton staircase at the far end that looked vague and shadowy in the dim light from the lamp. The old woman wore one of the old-fashioned caps with a white frill round the face, and entered with great fitness into the general scheme of the kitchen. I did not like leaving them to go into the raw night for a long walk on the mountains, and I sat down and talked to them for a long time, till the old woman thought I would be benighted.

'Go out now,' she said at last to the girl, 'go out now and see what water is coming over the fall above, for with this rain the water'll rise fast, and

---

30. From Irish *tráithnín*, a straw, and so, anything worthless: O Muirithe, p. 200.

maybe he'll have to walk down to the bridge, a rough walk when the night is coming on.'

The girl came back in a moment.

'It's riz already,' she said. 'He'll want to go down to the bridge.' Then turning to me: 'If you'll come now I'll show you the way you have to go, and I'll wait below for the boys; it won't be long now till they come with the body of Mary Kinsella.'

We went out at once and she walked quickly before me through a maze of small fields and pieces of bog, where I would have soon lost the track if I had been alone.

The bridge, when we reached it, was a narrow wooden structure fastened up on iron bars which pierced large boulders in the bed of the river. An immense grey flood was struggling among the stones, looking dangerous and desolate in the half-light of the evening, while the wind was so great that the bridge wailed and quivered and whistled under our feet. A few paces further on we came to a cottage where the girl wished me a good journey and went in to wait for her brothers.

The daylight still lingered but the heavy rain and a thick white cloud that had come down made everything unreal and dismal to an extraordinary degree. I went up a road where on one side I could see the trunks of beech trees reaching up wet and motionless – with odd sighs and movements when a gust caught the valley – into a greyness overhead, where nothing could be distinguished. Between them there were masses of shadow, and masses of half luminous fog with black branches across them. On the other side of the road flocks of sheep I could not see coughed and choked with sad guttural noises in the shelter of the hedge, or rushed away through a gap when they felt the dog was near them. Above everything my ears were haunted by the dead heavy swish of the rain. When I came near the first village I had to pass I heard noise and commotion. Many cars and gigs were collected at the door of the public-house, and the bar was filled with men who were drinking and making a noise. Everything was dark and confused yet on one car I was able to make out the shadow of a coffin, strapped in the rain, with the body of Mary Kinsella.

The Gael (April 1903)

'A Dream of Inishmaan'[31]

Some dreams I have had in a cottage near the Dun of Conchubar,[32] on the middle Island of Aran, seem to give strength to the opinion that there is a psychic memory attached to certain neighbourhoods.

One night after moving among buildings with strangely intense light upon them, I heard a faint rhythm of music beginning far away from me on some stringed instrument.

It came closer to me, gradually increasing in quickness and volume with an irresistibly definite progression. When it was quite near the sounds began to move in my nerves and blood, and to urge me to dance with them,

I knew, even in my dreams, that if I yielded to the sounds I would be carried away to some moment of terrible agony, so I struggled to remain quiet, holding my knees together with my hands.

The music increased again, sounding like the strings of harps tuned to a forgotten scale, and having a resonance as searching as the strings of the Cello.

---

31. The text here follows that in *The Green Sheaf* published a year earlier than that in *The Gael*, even though they are nearly identical. It was included also in *The Aran Islands* I (CW II 99–100).

32. Dún Chonchúir (Dun Conor), a large prehistoric fort in the centre of Inishmaan, very close to the McDonaghs' house where Synge stayed.

Then the luring excitement became more powerful than my will, and my limbs moved in spite of me.

In a moment I was swept away in a whirlwind of notes. My breath and my thoughts and every impulse of my body became a form of the dance, till I could not distinguish any more between the instruments and the rhythm, and my own person or consciousness.

For a while it seemed an excitement that was filled with joy: then it grew into an ecstasy where all existence was lost in a vortex of movement.

I could not think there had ever been a life beyond the whirling of the dance.

At last, with a sudden movement, the ecstasy turned to an agony and rage. I struggled to free myself, but seemed only to increase the passion of the steps I moved to. When I shrieked I could only echo the notes of the rhythm.

Then, with a moment of incontrollable frenzy, I broke back to consciousness, and awoke.

* * *

I dragged myself, trembling, to the window of the cottage and looked out. The moon was glittering across the bay, and there was no sound anywhere on the island.

The Green Sheaf, no. 2 (1903); *The Gael* (March 1904)

'An Impression of Aran'[33]

I am on Aranmore, sitting over a turf fire, listening to a murmur of Gaelic that is rising from a little public-house under my room.[34]

The steamer which comes to Aran sails according to the tide,[35] and it was six o'clock this morning when we left the quay of Galway in a dense shroud of mist. A low line of shore was visible at first on the right between the movement of the waves and fog, but when we came further it was lost sight of, and nothing could be seen but the mist curling in the rigging and a small circle of foam. There were few passengers – a couple of men going out with young pigs tied loosely in sacking, three or four young girls who sat in the cabin with their heads completely twisted in their shawls, and a builder on his way to repair the pier at Kilronan, who walked up and down and talked to me. In about three hours Aran came in sight. A dreary rock appeared at first sloping up from the sea into the fog; then, as we drew nearer, a coastguard station and the village.

A little later I was wandering out along the one good roadway of

---

33. This is an edited version of what was to become the opening of *The Aran Islands* I (CW II 49–53).

34. Synge was staying at the Atlantic Hotel: see Greene and Stephens, 85.

35. From 1892 the Congested Districts Board had paid an annual subsidy of £700 to the Galway Bay Steamboat Company to support a thrice-weekly steamer service from Galway to Kilronan.

the island, looking over low walls on either side into small, flat fields of naked rock. I have seen nothing so desolate. Grey currents of water were sweeping everywhere upon the limestone, making at times a wild torrent of the road, which itself twined continually over low hills and cavities in the rock, or passed between small fields of grass or potatoes hidden away in corners that had shelter. Whenever the cloud lifted I could see the edge of the sea below me on the right and the naked ridge of the island above me on the other side. Occasionally I passed a lonely chapel or schoolhouse, or a line of stone pillars with crosses above them and inscriptions asking a prayer for the souls of the persons they commemorated, or a few hovels by the roadside.

I met few people, but here and there a band of tall girls passed me on their way to Kilronan, and called out to me in humorous wonder as they went by, speaking English with a slight foreign intonation that differed a good deal from the brogue of Galway. The rain and cold seemed to have no influence on their vitality, and as each band hurried past with eager talking and laughter they left the wet masses of rock more desolate than before.

A little after midday, when I was coming back to the village, an old, half-blind man spoke to me in Gaelic, but, in general, I was surprised at the abundance and fluency of the foreign tongue. In the afternoon the rain continued, and I sat here in the inn, looking out through the mist at a few men who were unloading hookers with turf from Connemara and at the long-legged pigs that were playing in the surf. As the fishermen came in and out from the public-house underneath I could hear through the broken panes of my window that a number of them still used the Gaelic, though it seems to be falling out of use among the younger people of this district. I had made the old woman of the house promise to get me a teacher of the language, and after a while I heard a great shuffling on the stairs, and the old dark man I had spoken to in the morning groped his way into my room.[36] I brought him over to the fire, and we

---

36. Martin Coneely (Máirtín Ó Conghaile, 1824?–1904) whom Synge calls 'Mourteen' in *The Aran Islands*, and whose local name was Máirtín Neile, had told stories to many visitors to the island. For those collected by Holger Pedersen (see n. 39 below), see Ole Munch-Pedersen (ed.), *Scéalta Mháirtín Neile* (Baile Átha Chliath: Comhairle Bhéaloideas Éireann

talked for many hours. He told me that he had known Petrie[37] and Sir William Wilde[38] and many living antiquaries and had taught Irish to Dr Finck and Dr Pedersen,[39] and given stories to Mr Curtin, of America.[40] A little after middle age he had fallen over a cliff, and since then he had had little eyesight and a trembling of his hands and head. As we talked he sat huddled together over the fire, shaking and blind, yet his face was indescribably pliant, lighting up with an ecstasy of humour when he told me anything that had a point of wit or malice, and growing sombre and desolate again when he spoke of religion or the fairies. He had great confidence in his own powers and talent, and thought his stories superior to all other stories in the world. When we were talking of Mr Curtin he told me a gentleman had brought out a volume of Aran stories in America and made £500 by the sale of them. 'And what do you think he did then?' he continued; 'he wrote a book of his own stories after making that lot of money with mine, and he brought them out and the devil a halfpenny did he get for them. Would you believe that?'

Afterwards he told me how one of his children had been taken by the fairies. One day a neighbour passed when it was playing on the road and said, 'That's a fine child, surely.' Then its mother tried to say 'God bless it,'

An Coláiste Ollscoile, 1994). I am grateful to Angela Bourke for making me aware of this collection.

37. George Petrie (1790–1866), Irish artist, antiquarian and archaeologist.

38. Sir William Wilde (1815–76), Irish eye-surgeon, medical statistician and antiquarian who visited Aran in 1857.

39. Holger Pedersen (1867–1953), Danish linguist who specialized in comparative Celtic grammar, came to the island in August 1895, just after the departure of f. N. Finck (1867–1910), the German philologist, who was to publish his study of the Aran dialect, *Die araner Mundart* in Marburg in 1899.

40. Jeremiah Curtin (1835–1906), the American translator and folklorist, visited Aran with his wife in 1892, and left this record of his meeting with Coneely: 'One aged man, afflicted with palsy, told me a number of "true stories of the old time". In relating them he got so enthusiastic that he rapped on my knees or nudged me continually.' *Memoirs of Jeremiah Curtin*, edited with notes and introduction by Joseph Schafer (Milwaukee: State Historical Society of Wisconsin, 1940), pp. 463–64. I am grateful to Angela Bourke for drawing my attention to this passage.

but something choked the words in her throat. A while later there was a wound on its neck, and for three nights the house was filled with noises. 'I never wear a shirt at night,' he went on, 'but I got up out of my bed, all naked as I was, and I lighted a light, and there was nothing in it.' Then a dummy came and made signs of hammering nails into a coffin. The next day the seed potatoes were filled with blood, and the child told its mother it was going to America. That night it died, and 'believe me,' said the old man, 'the fairies were in it'.

When he left me the rain cleared off, and I went out through the south end of the village to a long neck of sandhill that runs out into the sea towards the south-east. As I lay there on the grass the clouds lifted from the mountains of Connemara, and for a moment the green undulating foreground, backed in the distance by a mass of hills, reminded me of the country near Rome. Then the dun topsail of a hooker swept past the edge of the sandhill and revealed the presence of the sea.

When I moved on a boy and a man came down from the next village to talk to me, and I found that here at least English was imperfectly understood. When I asked them if there were any trees on the island they held a hurried consultation in Gaelic, and then the man asked if 'tree' meant the same thing as 'bush', for if so there were a few in sheltered hollows towards the west. They walked on with me to the channel that separates this island from Inishmaan – the middle island of the group – and showed me the roll from the Atlantic running up the sound between two walls of cliff. The boy pointed out a cottage on Inishmaan where several Gaelic students have lodged,[41] in a long village which runs like a belt of straw round the middle of the island. The place looked hardly fit for habitation. There was no green to be seen and no sign of humanity except the beehive-like roofs and the outline of a Dun that stood out above them against the edge of the sky.

On my way home I was joined by a man who had spent twenty years in America, and then returned as he was losing his health. His English was so imperfect that I understood him only at intervals. He seemed dirty,

---

41. Evidently the cottage of the McDonaghs: see n. 13 above.

hopeless, and asthmatic, and after going with me a few hundred yards he stopped and asked for coppers. I had none left so I gave him a fill of tobacco, and he went back to his hovel. When he was gone two little girls took their place at my heels, and I drew them in turn into conversation. They spoke with a delicate intonation that was full of charm, and told me in a sort of chant how they guide 'ladies and gintlemins' in the summer to all that is worth seeing in their neighbourhood, and sell them cowskin shoes and maiden-hair ferns, which are common among the rocks. We were now in Kilronan, and with some quaint words of blessing they turned away from me and went down to the pier.

All this walk back had been extraordinarily fine, for the intense insular clearness one sees only in Ireland after rain was throwing out every ripple in the sea and sky and every crevice in the hills beyond the bay.

Manchester Guardian (24 January 1905)

'The Oppression of the Hills' [42]

Among the cottages that are scattered through the hills of county Wicklow I have met with many people who show in a singular way the influence of a particular locality. These people live for the most part beside old roads and pathways where hardly one man passes in the day, and look out all the year on unbroken barriers of heath. At every season heavy rains fall for often a week at a time, till the thatch drips with water stained to a dull chestnut and the floor in the cottages seems to be going back to the condition of the bogs near it. Then the clouds break and there is a night of terrific storm from the south-west – all the larches that survive in these places are bowed and twisted towards the point where the sun rises in June – when the winds come down through the narrow glens with the congested whirl and roar of a torrent, breaking at times for sudden moments of silence that keep up the tension of the mind. At such times the people crouch all night over a few sods of turf and the dogs howl in the lanes.

When the sun rises there is a morning of almost supernatural radiance, and even the oldest men and women come out into the air with the joy of children who have recovered from a fever. In the evening it is raining again. This peculiar climate, acting on a population that is already lonely

---

42. Already written by 1902, when it was rejected for publication by *The Gael*: see diary entry for 26 March, MS 4421.

and dwindling, has caused or increased a tendency to nervous depression among the people, and every degree of sadness, from that of the man who is merely mournful to that of the man who has spent half his life in the madhouse, is common among these hills.

Not long ago in a desolate glen in the south of the county I met two policemen driving an ass-cart with a coffin on it, and a little further on I stopped an old man and asked him what had happened.

'This night three weeks,' he said, 'there was a poor fellow[43] below reaping in the glen, and in the evening he had two glasses of whiskey with some other lads. Then some excitement took him, and he threw off his clothes and ran away into the hills. There was great rain that night, and I suppose the poor creature lost his way and was the whole night perishing in the rain and darkness. In the morning they found his naked footmarks on some mud half-a-mile above the road, and again where you go up by a big stone. Then there was nothing known of him till last night, when they found his body on the mountain, and it near eaten by the crows.'

Then he went on to tell me how different the country had been when he was a young man.

'We had nothing to eat at that time,' he said, 'but milk and stirabout and potatoes, and there was a fine constitution you wouldn't meet this day at all. I remember when you'd see forty boys and girls below there on a Sunday evening, playing ball and diverting themselves; but now all this country is gone lonesome and bewildered, and there's no man knows what ails it.'

There are so few girls left in these neighbourhoods that one does not often meet with women that have grown up unmarried. I know one, however, who has lived by herself for fifteen years in a tiny hovel near a cross-roads much frequented by tinkers and ordinary tramps. As she has no one belonging to her, she spends a good deal of her time wandering through the country, and I have met her in every direction, often many miles from her own glen. 'I do be so afeard of the tramps,' she said to me one evening. 'I live all alone, and what would I do at all if one of them lads

---

43. John Winterbottom of Sheeanamore, Aughrim: for full details of his death by exposure in August 1901, see *Interpreting Synge*, pp. 34–5.

was to come near me? When my poor mother was dying, "Now, Nanny," says she, "don't be living on here when I'm dead," says she; "it'd be too lonesome." And now I wouldn't wish to go again my mother, and she dead – dead or alive I wouldn't go again my mother – but I'm after doing all I can, and I can't get away by any means.' As I was moving on she heard, or thought she heard, a sound of distant thunder.

'Ah, your honour,' she said, 'do you think it's thunder we'll be having? There's nothing I fear like the thunder. My heart isn't strong – I do feel it – and I have a lightness in my head, and often when I do be excited with the thunder I do be feared I might die there alone in the cottage and no one know it. But I do hope that the Lord, bless His holy name, has something in store for me. I've done all I can, and I don't like going again my mother, and she dead. And now good evening, your honour, and safe home.'

Intense nervousness is common also with much younger women. I remember one night hearing someone crying out and screaming in the house where I was staying.[44] I went downstairs and found it was a girl who had been taken in from a village a few miles away to help the servants. That afternoon her two younger sisters had come to see her, and now she had been taken with a panic that they had been drowned going home through the bogs, and she was crying and wailing and saying she must go to look for them. It was not thought fit for her to leave the house alone so late in the evening so I went with her. As we passed down a steep hill of heather, where the night-jars were clapping their wings in the moonlight, she told me a long story of the way she had been frightened. Then we reached a solitary cottage on the edge of the bog, and as a light was still shining in the window I knocked at the door, and asked if they had seen or heard anything. When they understood our errand three half-dressed generations came out to jeer at us on the door-step.

'Ah, Maggie,' said the old woman, 'you're a cute one. You're the girl likes a walk in the moonlight. Whisht your talk of them big lumps of childer, and look at Martin Edward there, who's not six itself, and he can go through the bog five times in an hour and not wet his feet.'

---

44. The house was Castle Kevin, near Annamoe, where Synge was staying with his family in June 1899: see Stephens, MS 6192, f. 1545 for the details of the incident.

My companion was still unconvinced, so we went on. The rushes were shining in the moonlight, and one flake of mist was lying on the river. We looked into one bog-hole, then into another, where a snipe rose and terrified us. We listened; a cow was chewing heavily in the shadow of a bush, two dogs were barking on the side of a hill, and there was a cart far away upon the road. Our teeth began to chatter with the cold of the bog air and the loneliness of the night. I could see that the actual presence of the bog had shown my companion the absurdity of her fears, and in a little while we went home.

The older people in county Wicklow, as in the rest of Ireland, still show a curious affection for the landed classes wherever they have lived for a generation or two upon their property. I remember an old woman who told me, with tears streaming on her face, how much more lonely the country had become since the 'quality' had gone away, and gave me a long story of how she had seen her landlord shutting up his house and leaving his property, and of the way he had died afterwards, when the 'grievance' of it broke his heart. The younger people feel differently, and when I was passing this landlord's house,[45] not long afterwards, I found these lines written in pencil on the doorpost:

> In the days of rack-renting
> And land-grabbing so vile
> A proud, heartless landlord
> Lived here a great while.
> When the League it was started,
> And the land-grabbing cry,
> To the cold North of Ireland
> He had for to fly.

A year later the doorpost had fallen to pieces, and the inscription with it.

Manchester Guardian (15 February 1905)

---

45. Again Castle Kevin, frequently rented by Synge's mother as a holiday home for the family, in spite of the fact that it had been boycotted by the Land League; the landlord was Charles W. Frizell, who lived in Belfast at this time.

'In the "Congested Districts": From Galway to Gorumna'

Some of the worst portions of the Irish congested districts – of which so much that is contradictory has been spoken and written – lie along the further north coast of Galway Bay and about the whole seaboard from Spiddal to Clifden. Some distance inland there is a line of railway,[46] and in the bay itself a steamer passes in and out to the Aran Islands; but this

---

46. The Midland and Great Western Railway ran from Galway to Clifden through Oughterard and Maam Cross.

particular district can only be visited thoroughly by driving or riding over some thirty or forty miles of desolate roadway. If one takes this route from Galway one has to go a little way only to reach places and people that are fully typical of Connemara. On each side of the road one sees small square fields of oats, or potatoes, or pasture, divided by loose stone walls that are built up without mortar. Wherever there are a few cottages near the road one sees bare-footed women hurrying backwards and forwards with hampers of turf or grass slung over their backs and generally a few children running after them, and if it is a market-day, as was the case on the day of which I am going to write, one overtakes long strings of country people driving home from Galway in low carts drawn by an ass or pony. As a rule one or two men sit in front of the cart driving and smoking, with a couple of women behind them stretched out at their ease among sacks of flour or young pigs, and nearly always talking continuously in Gaelic. These men are all dressed in homespuns of the grey natural wool, and the women in deep madder-dyed petticoats and bodices, with brown shawls over their heads. One's first feeling as one comes back among these people and takes a place, so to speak, in this noisy procession of fishermen, farmers, and women, where nearly everyone is interesting and attractive, is a dread of any reform that would tend to lessen their individuality rather than any very real hope of improving their well-being. One feels then, perhaps a little later, that it is a part of the misfortune of Ireland that nearly all the characteristics which give colour and attractiveness to Irish life are bound up with a social condition that is near to penury, while in countries like Brittany the best external features of the local life – the rich embroidered dresses, for instance, or the carved furniture – are connected with a decent and comfortable social condition.

About twelve miles from Galway one reaches Spiddal; a village which lies on the borderland between the fairly prosperous districts near Galway and the barren country further to the west. Like most places of its kind, it has a double row of houses – some of them with two storeys – several public-houses, and a large police barrack among them, and a little to one side a coastguard station, ending up at either side of the village with a chapel and a church. It was evening when we drove into Spiddal, and a little after sunset we walked on to a rather exposed quay where a few weather-beaten hookers were moored with many ropes. As we came down none of the crews were to be seen, but threads of turf smoke rising from the open manhole of the forecastle showed that the men were probably on board. While we were looking down on them from the pier – the tide was far out – an old grey-haired man with the inflamed eyes that are so common here from the continual itching of the turf smoke peered up through the manhole and watched us with vague curiosity. A few moments later a young man came down from a field of black earth, where he had been digging a drain, and asked the old man, in Gaelic, to throw him a spark for his pipe. The latter disappeared for a moment, then came up again with a smouldering end of a turf sod in his hand, and threw it up on the pier, where the young man caught it with a quick downward grab without burning himself, blew it into a blaze, lit his pipe with it, and went back to his work. These people are so poor that many of them do not spend any money on matches. The spark of lighting turf is kept alive day and night on the hearth, and when a man goes out fishing or to work in the fields he usually carries a lighted sod with him, and keeps it all day buried in ashes or any dry rubbish, so that he can use it when he needs it. On our way back to the village an old woman begged from us, speaking in English, as most of the people do to anyone who is not a native. We gave her a few halfpence, and as she was moving away with an ordinary 'God save you!' I said a blessing to her in Irish to show her I knew her own language if she chose to use it. Immediately she turned back towards me and began her thanks again, this time with extraordinary profusion. 'That the blessing of God may be on you', she said, 'on road and on ridge way, on sea and on land, on flood and on mountain in all the kingdoms of the world' – and so on, till I was too far off to hear what she was saying.

In a district like Spiddal one sees curious gradations of type, especially on Sundays and holidays, when everyone is dressed as their fancy leads them and as well as they can manage. As I watched the people coming from Mass the morning after we arrived this was curiously noticeable. The police and coastguards came first in their smartest uniforms; then the shopkeepers, dressed like the people of Dublin, but a little more grotesquely; then the more well-to-do country folk, dressed only in the local clothes I have spoken of, but the best and newest kind, while the wearers themselves looked well-fed and healthy, and a few of them, especially the girls, magnificently built; then, last of all one saw the destitute in still the same clothes, but this time patched and threadbare and ragged, the women mostly barefooted, and both sexes pinched with hunger and the fear of it. The class that one would be most interested to see increase is that of the typical well-to-do people, but except in a few districts it is not numerous, and it is always aspiring after the dress of the shop people or tending to sink down again among the paupers.

Later in the day we drove on another long stage to the west. As before, the country we passed through was not depressing, though stony and barren as a quarry. At every cross roads we passed groups of young, healthy-looking boys and men amusing themselves with hurley or pitching, and further back on little heights, a small field's breadth from the road, there were many groups of girls sitting out by the hour, near enough to the road to see everything that was passing, yet far enough away to keep their shyness undisturbed. Their red dresses looked peculiarly beautiful among the fresh green of the grass and opening bracken, with a strip of sea behind them, and, far away, the grey cliffs of Clare. A little further on some ten miles from Spiddal, inlets of the sea begin to run in towards the mountains, and the road turns north to avoid them across an expanse of desolate bog far more dreary than the rocks of the coast. Here one sees a few wretched sheep nibbling in places among the turf, and occasionally a few ragged people walking rapidly by the roadside. Before we stopped for the night we had reached another bay coast-line[47] and were among stones again. Later in the evening we walked out round another small quay with the usual little band of shabby hookers, and then along a road that rose in some places a few hundred feet above the sea, and as one looked down into the little fields that lay below it they looked so small and rocky that

---

47. Cashla or Costelloe Bay; the Jack Yeats drawing illustrating this article is entitled 'Near Castelloe', though the title was not included in the newspaper reproduction: see Hilary Pyle, *The Different Worlds of Jack B. Yeats* (Dublin: Irish Academic Press, 1994), pp. 129–33 for a catalogue of all the drawings.

the very thought of tillage in them seemed like the freak of an eccentric. Yet in this particular place tiny cottages, some of them without windows, swarmed by the roadside and in the 'boreens', or laneways, at either side, many of them built on a single sweep of stone with the naked living rock for their floor. A number of people were to be seen everywhere about them, the men loitering by the roadside and the women hurrying among the fields, feeding an odd calf or lamb or driving in a few ducks before the night. In one place a few boys were playing pitch with trousers buttons, and a little further on half-a-score of young men were making donkeys jump backwards and forwards over a low wall. As we came back we met two men, who came and talked to us, one of them, by his hat and dress, plainly a man who had been away from Connemara. In a little while he told us that he had been in Gloucester and Bristol working on public works, but had wearied of it and come back to his country.

'Bristol', he said, 'is the greatest town, I think, in all England, but the work in it is hard.'

I asked him about the fishing in the neighbourhood we were in. 'Ah,' he said, 'there's little fishing in it at all, for we have no good boats. There is no one asking for boats for this place, for the shopkeepers would rather have the people idle, so that they can get them for a shilling a day to go out in their old hookers and sell turf in Aran and on the coast of Clare.' Then we talked of Aran, and he told me of people I knew there who had died or got married since I had been on the islands, and then they went on their way.

Manchester Guardian (10 June 1905)

'In the "Congested Districts": Between the Bays of Carraroe'

In rural Ireland very few parishes only are increasing in population, and those that are doing so are usually in districts of the greatest poverty. One of the most curious instances of this tendency is to be found in the parish of Carraroe, which is said to be, on the whole, the poorest parish in the country, although many worse cases of individual destitution can be found elsewhere. The most characteristic part of this district lies on a long promontory between Cashla Bay and Greatman's Bay. On both coast-lines one sees a good many small quays, with, perhaps, two hookers moored to them, and on the roads one passes an occasional flat space covered with small green fields of oats – with whole families on their knees weeding among them – or patches of potatoes, but for the rest one sees little but an endless series of low stony hills with veins of grass. Here and there, however, one comes in sight of a fresh-water lake, with an island or two, covered with seagulls, and many cottages round the shore, some of them standing almost on the brink of the water, others a little higher up, fitted in among the rocks, and one or two standing out on the top of a ridge against the blue of the sky or of the Twelve Bens of Connaught.

At the edge of one of these lakes,[48] near a school of lace or knitting – one of those that have been established by the Congested Districts Board – we met a man driving a mare and foal that had scrambled out of their enclosure although the mare had her two off-legs chained together. As soon as he had got them back into one of the fields and built up the wall with loose stones he came over to a stone beside us and began to talk about horses and the dying out of the ponies of Connemara. 'You will hardly get any real Connemara ponies now at all,' he said, 'and the kind of horses they send down to us to improve the breed are no use,[49] for the horses we breed from them will not thrive or get their health on the little patches where we have to put them. This last while most of the people in this parish are giving up horses altogether. Those that have them sell their foals when they are about six months old for four pounds, or five maybe; but the better part of the people are working with an ass only, that can carry a few things on a straddle over her back.'

'If you've no horses,' I said, 'how do you get to Galway if you want to go to a fair or to market?'

'We go by the sea,' he said, 'in one of the hookers you've likely seen at the little quays while walking down by the road. You can sail to Galway

---

48. Loughaunwillan: the knitting-factory, which continued in operation well into the twentieth century, is still identifiable.

49. Most likely Yorkshire Hackneys, a preferred breed of Land Commissioner Frederick Wrench who was responsible for this part of the Congested District Boards scheme for horse improvement; 'none of the Board's schemes were so fiercely attacked', Micks, p. 28.

if the wind is fair in four hours or less, maybe; and the people here are all used to the sea, for no one can live in this place but by cutting turf in the mountains and sailing out to sell it in Clare or Aran, for you see yourselves there's no good in the land, that has little in it but bare rocks and stones. Two years ago there came a wet summer, and the people were worse off then than they are now, maybe, with their bad potatoes and all; for they couldn't cut or dry a load of turf to sell across the bay, and there was many a woman hadn't a dry sod itself to put under her pot, and she shivering with cold and hunger.'

A little later, when we had talked of one or two other things, I asked him if many of the people who were living round in the scattered cottages we could see were often in real want of food. 'There are a few, maybe, have enough all times', he said, 'but the most are in want one time or another, when the potatoes are bad or few, and their whole store is eaten; and there are some who are near starving all times, like a widow woman beyond who has seven children with hardly a shirt on their skins, and they with nothing to eat but the milk from one cow, and a handful of meal they will get from one neighbour or another.'

'You're getting an old man,' I said, 'and do you remember if the place was as bad as it is now when you were a young man growing up?'

'It wasn't as bad, or a half as bad,' he said, 'for there were fewer people in it and more land to each, and the land itself was better at that time, for now it is drying up or something, and not giving its fruits and increase as it did.'

I asked him if they used bought manures.

'We get a hundredweight for eight shillings now and again, but I think there's little good in it, for it's only a poor kind they send out to the like of us. Then there was another thing they had in the old times,' he continued, 'and that was the making of poteen (illicit whiskey), for it was a great trade at that time, and you'd see the police down on their knees blowing the fire with their own breath to make a drink for themselves, and then going off with the butt of an old barrel, and that was one seizure, and an old bag with a handful of malt, and that was another seizure, and would satisfy the law; but now they must have the worm and the still and a prisoner, and there is little of it made in the country. At that time a man would get ten shillings for a gallon, and it was a good trade for poor people.'

As we were talking a woman passed driving two young pigs, and we began to speak of them.

'We buy the young pigs and rear them up,' he said, 'but this year they are scarce and dear. And indeed what good are they in bad years, for how can we go feeding a pig when we haven't enough, maybe, for ourselves? In good years when you have potatoes and plenty you can rear up two or three pigs and make a good bit on them, but other times, maybe, a poor man will give a pound for a young pig that won't thrive after, and then his pound will be gone, and he'll have no money for his rent.'

The old man himself was cheerful and seemingly fairly well-to-do, but in the end he seemed to be getting dejected as he spoke of one difficulty after another, so I asked him, to change the subject, if there was much dancing in the country. 'No,' he said, 'this while back you'll never see a piper coming this way at all, though in the old times it's many a piper would be moving around through those houses for a whole quarter together, playing his pipes and drinking poteen and the people dancing round him; but now there is no dancing or singing in this place at all, and most of the young people is growing up and going to America.'

I pointed to the lace school near us,[50] and asked how the girls got on with the lace, and if they earned much money. 'I've heard tell', he said, 'that in the four schools round-about this place there is near six hundred pounds paid out in wages every year, and that is a good sum, but there isn't a young girl going to them that isn't saving up, and saving up till she'll have enough gathered to take her to America, and then away she will go, and why wouldn't she?'

Often the worst moments in the lives of these people are caused by the still frequent outbreaks of typhus fever, and before we parted I asked him if there was much fever in the particular district where we were.

'Just here,' he said, 'there isn't much of it at all, but there are places

---

50. The CDB employed German and French instructresses to teach girls specialist lace-making skills for curtain factories opened in Carraroe and Gorumna Island in 1902: see Breathnach, *Congested Districts Board*, p. 65.

round about where you'll sometimes hear of a score and more stretched out waiting for their death; but I suppose it is the will of God. Then there is a sickness they call consumption that some will die of, but I suppose there is no place where people aren't getting their death one way or other, and the most in this place are enjoying good health, glory be to God! for it is a healthy place and there is a clean air blowing.'

Then with a few of the usual blessings, he got up and left us, and we walked on through more of similar or still poorer country. It is remarkable that from Spiddal onward – that is, in the whole of the most poverty-stricken district of Ireland – no one begs, even in a roundabout way. It is the fashion with many of the officials who are connected with relief works and such things to compare the people of this district rather unfavourably with the people of the poor districts of Donegal, but in this respect at least Donegal is not the more admirable.

Manchester Guardian (14 June 1905)

'In the "Congested Districts": Among the Relief Works'

Beyond Carraroe, the last promontory on the north coast of Galway Bay, one reaches a group of islands which form the lower angle of Connemara. These islands are little more than a long peninsula broken through by a number of small straits, over which, some twelve years ago, causeways and swing bridges were constructed, so that one can now drive straight on through Annaghvaan, Lettermore, Gorumna, Lettermullan, and one or two smaller islands. When one approaches this district from the east a long detour is made to get round the inner point of Greatman's Bay, and then the road turns to the south-west till one reaches Annaghvaan, the first of the islands. This road is a remarkable one. Nearly every foot of it, as it now stands, has been built up in different years of famine by the people of the neighbourhood working on Government relief works, which are now once more in full swing, making improvements in some places, turning primitive tracts into roadways in others, and here and there building a new route to some desolate village.

We drove many miles, with Costello and Carraroe behind us, along a bog road of curious formation built up on a turf embankment, with broad grassy sods at either side – perhaps to make a possible way for the barefooted people – then two spaces of rough broken stones where the wheel-ruts are usually worn, and in the centre a track of gritty earth for the horses. Then at a turn of the road we came in sight of a dozen or more men and women working hurriedly and doggedly improving a further portion of this road, with a ganger swaggering among them and directing their work. Some of the people were cutting out sods from grassy patches near the road, others were carrying down bags of earth in a slow, inert procession, a few were breaking stones, and three or four women were scraping out a sort of sandpit at a little distance. As we drove quickly by we could see that every man and woman was working with a sort of hang-dog dejection that would be enough to make any casual passer mistake them for a band of convicts. The wages given on these works are usually a shilling a day, and as a rule one person only, generally the head of the family, is taken from each house. Sometimes the best worker in a family is thus forced away from his ordinary work of farming or fishing or kelp-making for this wretched remuneration at a time when his private industry is most needed. If this system of relief has some things in its favour, it is far from satisfactory in other ways and is not always economical. I have been told of a district not very far from here where there is a ganger, an overseer, an inspector, a paymaster, and an engineer superintending the work of two paupers only. This is possibly an exaggerated account of what is really taking place, yet it probably shows, not too inexactly, a state of things that is not rare in Ireland.

A mile or two further on we passed a similar band of workers, and then the road rose for a few feet and turned sharply on to a long causeway with a swing bridge in the centre that led to the island of Annaghvaan. Just as we reached the bridge our driver jumped down and took his mare by the head. A moment later she began to take fright at the hollow noise of her own hoofs on the boards of the bridge and the blue rush of the tide which she could see through them, but the man coaxed her forward, and got her over without much difficulty. For the next mile or two there was a continual series of small islands and causeways and bridges that the mare grew accustomed to, and trotted gaily over, till we reached Lettermore, and drove for some distance through the usual small hills of stone. Then we came to the largest causeway of all, between Lettermore and Gorumna, where the proportion of the opening of the bridge to the length of the embankment is so small that the tide runs through with extraordinary force. On the outer side the water was banked up nearly a yard high against the buttress of the bridge, and on the other side there was a rushing, eddying torrent that recalled some mountain salmon stream in flood, except that here, instead of the brown river water, one saw the white and blue foam of the sea.

The remainder of our road to the lower western end of Gorumna led through hilly districts that became more and more white with stone, though one saw here and there a few brown masses of bog or an oblong lake with many islands and rocks. In most places if one looked round the hills a little distance from the road one could see the yellow roofs and white gables of cottages scattered everywhere through this waste of rock, and on the ridge of every hill one could see the red dresses of women who were gathering turf or looking for their sheep or calves. Near the village where we stopped things are somewhat better, and a few fields of grass and potatoes were to be seen, and a certain number of small cattle grazing among the rocks. Here also one is close to the sea, and fishing and kelp-making are again possible. In the village there is a small private quay in connection with a shop where everything is sold, and not long after we arrived a hooker sailed in with a cargo of supplies from Galway. A number of women were standing about expecting her arrival, and soon afterwards several of them set off for different parts of the island with a bag of flour slung over an ass. One of these, a young girl of seventeen or eighteen, drove on with her load far into Lettermullan, the next island, on a road that we were walking also, and then sent the ass back to Gorumna in charge of a small boy and took up the sack of flour, which weighed at least 16 stone,[51] on her back, and carried it more than a mile, through a narrow track to her own home. This practice of allowing young girls to carry great weights frequently injures them severely, and is the cause of much danger and suffering in their after lives. They do not seem, however, to know anything of the risks they run, and their loads are borne gaily.

A little further on we came on another stretch of the relief works, where there were many elderly men and young girls working with the same curious aspect of shame and dejection. The work was just closing for the evening, and as we walked back to Gorumna an old man who had been working walked with us, and complained of his great poverty and the small wages he was given. 'A shilling a day', he said, 'would hardly keep a man in tea and sugar and tobacco and a bit of bread to eat, and what good is it at all when there is a family of five or six maybe, and often more?' Just as we reached the swing-bridge that led back to Gorumna another hooker sailed carefully in through the narrow rocky channel with a crowd of men and women sitting along the gunwale. They edged in close to a flat rock near the bridge and made her fast for a moment while the women jumped on shore, some of them carrying bottles, others with little children, and all dressed out in new red petticoats and shawls. They looked as they crowded up on the road as fine a body of peasant women as one could see anywhere, and were all talking and laughing eagerly among themselves. The old man told me in Irish that they had been at a pattern – a sort of semi-religious festival like the well-known festivals of Brittany – that had just been held some distance to the east on the Galway coast. It was reassuring to see that some, at least, of these island people are, in their own

---

51. 224 lbs, 102 kg.

way, prosperous and happy. When the women were all landed the swing-bridge was pushed open, and the hooker was poled through to the bay on the north side of the islands. Then the men moored her and came up to a little public-house, where they spent the rest of the evening talking and drinking and telling stories in Irish.

Manchester Guardian (17 June 1905)

'In the "Congested Districts": The Ferryman of Dinish Island'

When wandering among lonely islands on the West of Ireland like those of the Gorumna group one seldom fails to meet with some old sailor or pilot who has seen something of the world, and it is often from a man of this kind that one learns most about the island or hill that he has come back to, in middle age or towards the end of his life. An old seafaring man[52] who ferries chance comers to and from Dinish Island is a good example of this class. The island is separated from Furnace – the last of the group that is linked together by causeways and bridges – by a deep channel between two chains of rock. As we went to this channel across a strip of sandhill a wild-looking old man appeared at the other side and began making signs to us and pushing off a heavy boat from the shore. Before he was half-way across we could hear him calling out to us in a state of almost incoherent excitement, and directing us to a ledge of rock where he could take us off. A moment later we scrambled into his boat upon a mass of seaweed that he had been collecting for kelp, and he poled us across, talking at random about how he had seen His Royal Highness the Duke of Edinburgh[53] and gone to America as interpreter for the emigrants in a bad season twenty-one years ago. As soon as we landed we walked across a bay of sand to a tiny schoolhouse close to the sea, and the old man turned back across the channel with a travelling tea merchant and a young girl who had come down to the shore. All the time they were going across we could hear him talking and vociferating at the top of his voice, and then, after a moment's silence, he came in sight again, on our side, running towards us over the sand. After he had been a little while with us, and got over the excitement caused by the sudden arrival of two strangers – we could judge how great it was by a line of children's heads who were peeping over the rocks and watching us with amazement – he began to talk clearly and simply. After a few of the remarks one hears from everyone about the loneliness of the place, he spoke about the school behind us.

'Isn't it a poor thing', he said, 'to see a school lying closed up the like of that, and twenty or thirty scholars, maybe, running wild along the sea? I am very lonesome since that school was closed, for there was a school-mistress used to come for a long while from Lettermullan, and I used to

---

52. Probably identifiable as Robert Audley, a widower of 50 with two children at the time of the 1901 Census.

53. Alfred, Duke of Edinburgh (1844–1900), a son of Queen Victoria, had visited Galway and neighbouring districts in April 1880 to help in distributing relief to the people of the western islands.

ferry her over the water, and maybe ten little children along with her. And then there was a mistress living here for a long while, and I used to ferry the children only; but now she has found herself a better place, and this three months there's no school in it at all.'

One could see when he was quiet that he differed a good deal both in face and in his way of speaking from the people of the islands, and when he paused I asked him if he had spent all his life among them, excepting the one voyage to America.

'I have not,' he said, 'but I've been in many places, though I and my fathers have rented the sixth of this island for near two hundred years. My own father was a sailorman who came in here by chance and married a woman and lived, a snug decent man, with five cows or six, till he died at a hundred and three. And my mother's father, who had the place before him, died at a hundred and eight, and he wouldn't have died then, I'm thinking, only he fell down and broke his hip. They were strong, decent people at that time, and I was going to school – travelling out over the islands with my father ferrying me – till I was twenty years of age, and then I went to America and got to be a sailorman, and was in New York, and Baltimore, and New Orleans, and after that I was coasting till I knew every port and town of this country and Scotland and Wales.'

One of us asked him if he had stayed at sea till he came back to this island.

'I did not,' he said, 'for I went ashore once in South Wales, and I'm telling you Wales is a long country, for I travelled all a whole summer's day from that place till I reached Birkenhead at nine o'clock. And then I went to Manchester and to Newcastle-on-Tyne, and I worked there for two years. That's a rich country, dear gentlemen, and when the payman would come into the works on a Saturday you'd see the bit of board he had over his shoulder bending down with the weight of sovereigns he had for the men. And isn't it a queer thing to be sitting here now thinking on those times, and I after being near twenty years back on this bit of a rock that a dog wouldn't look at, where the pigs die and the spuds die, and even the judges and quality do come out and do lower our rents when they see the wild Atlantic driving in across the cursed stones.'[54]

'And what is it brought you back', I said, 'if you were doing well beyond in the world?'

'My two brothers went to America', he said, 'and I had to come back because I was the eldest son, and I got married then, and I after holding out till I was forty. I have a young family now growing up, for I was snug for a while; and then bad times came, and I lost my wife, and the potatoes went bad, and three cows I had were taken in the night with some disease of the brain and they swam out and were drowned in the sea. I got back their bodies in the morning and took them down to a gentleman beyond who understands the diseases of animals, but he gave me nothing for them at all. So there I am now with no pigs, and no cows, and a young family running round with no mother to mind them, and what can you do with children that know nothing at all, and will often put down as much in the pot one day as would do three days, and do be wasting the meal, though you can't say a word against them, for it's young and ignorant they are? If it wasn't for them I'd be off this evening, and I'd earn my living easy on the sea, for I'm only fifty-seven years of age, and I have good health; but how can I leave my young children? And I don't know what way I'm to go on living in this place that the Lord created last, I'm thinking, in the end of time, and it's often when I sit down and look around on it I do begin cursing and damning and asking myself how poor people can go on executing their religion at all.'

For a while he said nothing, and we could see tears in his eyes; then I asked him how he was living now from one day to another.

'They're letting me out advanced meal and flour from the shop,' he said, 'and I'm to pay it back when I burn a ton of kelp in the summer. For two months I was working on the relief works at a shilling a day, but what good is that for a family? So I've stopped now to rake up weed for a ton, or maybe two tons, of kelp. When I left the works I got my boy put on in my place, but the ganger put him back; and then I got him on again, and the ganger put him back. Then I bought a bottle of ink and a pen and a

---

54. The Land Commission, established by the Land Act of 1881, frequently reduced rents which it judged poor tenants unable to pay.

bit of paper to write a letter and make my complaint, but I never wrote it to this day, for what good is it harming him more than another? Then I've a daughter in America has only been there nine months, and she's sent me £3 already. I have another daughter, living above with her married sister, will be ready to go in the autumn, and another little one will go when she's big enough. There is a man above has four daughters in America and gets a pound a quarter from each one of them, and that is a great thing for a poor man. It's to America we'll all be going, and isn't it a fearful thing to think I'll be kept here another ten years maybe tending the children and striving to keep them alive, when I might be abroad in America living in decency and earning my bread?'

Afterwards he took us up to the highest point of the island and showed us a fine view of the whole group and of the Atlantic beyond them, with a few fishing-boats in the distance and many large boats nearer the rocks rowing heavily with loads of weed. When we got into the ferry again the channel had become too deep to pole, and the old man rowed with a couple of long sweeps from the bow.

'I go out alone in this boat,' he said as he was rowing, 'across the bay to the northern land. There is no other man in the place that would do it, but I'm a licensed pilot these twenty years, and a seafaring man.'

Then as we finally left him he called after us:

'It has been a great consolation to me, dear gentlemen, to be talking with your like, for one sees few people in this place, and so may God bless and reward you and see you safely to your homes.'

Manchester Guardian (21 June 1905)

'In the "Congested Districts": The Kelp Makers'

Some of those who have undertaken to reform the congested districts have shown an unfortunate tendency to give great attention to a few canonised industries, such as horse-breeding and fishing, or even bee-keeping, while they neglect local industries that have been practised with success for a great number of years. Thus, in the large volume issued a couple of years ago by the Department of Agriculture and Technical Instruction for Ireland, which claims to give a comprehensive account of the economic resources of the country, hardly a word has been said of the kelp industry, which is a matter of the greatest importance to the inhabitants of a very large district. The Congested Districts Board seems to have left it on one side also,[55] and in the Galway neighbourhood, at least, no steps appear to have been taken to ensure the people a fair market for the kelp they produce or to revise the present unsatisfactory system by which it is tested and paid for. In some places the whole buying trade falls into the hands of one man, who can then control the prices at his pleasure, while one hears on all sides of arbitrary decisions by which good kelp is rejected and what the people consider an inferior article is paid for at a high figure. When the buying is thus carried on no appeal can be made from the decision of one individual, and I have sometimes seen a party of old men sitting nearly in tears on a ton of rejected kelp that had cost them weeks of hard work, while, for all one knew, it had very possibly been refused on account of some grudge or caprice of the buyer.

The village of Trawbaun,[56] which lies on the coast opposite the Aran Islands, is a good instance of a kelp-making neighbourhood. We reached it through a narrow road, now in the hands of the relief workers, where we hurried past the usual melancholy line of old men breaking stones and younger men carrying bags of earth and sods. Soon afterwards the road fell away quickly towards the sea, through a village of many cottages huddled together with bare walls of stone that had never been whitewashed, as often happens in places that are peculiarly poor. Passing through these, we came out on three or four acres of sandhill that brought us to a line of rocks with a narrow sandy cove between them just filling with the tide. All along the coast a little above high-water mark we could see a number of tall reddish stacks of dried seaweed, some of which had probably been standing for weeks, while others were in various unfinished stages or had only just been begun. A number of men and women and boys were hard at work in every direction gathering fresh weed and spreading it out to dry

---

55. Consideration had, in fact, been given to kelp making by the CDB, but there was a declining market for the product, and it was an industry in which the Board had limited opportunities for investment: see Breathnach, *Congested Districts Board*, pp. 84–5.

56. In the south-east of Gorumna Island on Greatman's Bay.

on the rocks. In some places the weed is mostly gathered from the foreshore, but in this neighbourhood, at least in the early summer, it is pulled up from rocks under the sea at low water by men working from a boat or curragh with a long pole furnished with a short crossbar nailed to the top, which they entangle in the weeds.[57] Just as we came down a curragh lightly loaded by two boys was coming in over a low bar into the cove I have spoken of, and both of them were slipping over the side every moment or two to push their canoe from behind. Several bare-legged girls, crooning merry songs in Gaelic, were passing backwards and forwards over the sand, carrying heavy loads of weed on their backs. Further out many other curraghs, more heavily laden, were coming slowly in, waiting for the tide; and some old men on the shore were calling out directions to their crews in the high-pitched tone that is so remarkable in this Connaught Irish. The whole scene, with the fresh smell of the sea and the blueness of the shallow waves, made a curious contrast with the dismal spectacle of the relief workers we had just passed, for here the people seemed as light-hearted as a party of schoolboys.

Further on we came to a rocky headland where some men were burning down their weed into kelp, a process that, in this place, is given nearly twelve hours. As we came up dense volumes of rich creamy-coloured smoke were rising from a long pile of weed, in the centre of which we could see here and there a molten mass burning at an intense heat. Two men and a number of boys were attending to the fire, laying on fresh weed wherever the covering grew thin enough to receive it. A little to one side a baby, rolled up in a man's coat, was asleep beside a hamper, as on occasions like this the house is usually shut up and the whole family scatters for work of various kinds. The amount of weed needed to make a ton of kelp varies, I have been told, from three tons to five. The men of a family working busily on a favourable day can take a ton of the raw weed, and the kelp is sold at from £3 15s. or a little less to £5 a ton, so it is easy to see the importance of this trade. When all the weed intended for

---

57. For an account of this sort of seaweed-gathering with the *croisín* (= 'cross-stick', literally 'little cross'), see Tim Robinson, *Stones of Aran: Pilgrimage* (Harmondsworth: Penguin, 1990 [1986]), p. 147.

one furnace has been used the whole is covered up and left three or four days to cool; then it is broken up and taken off in boats or curraghs to a buyer. He takes a handful, tests it with certain chemicals, and fixes the price accordingly; but the people themselves have no means of knowing whether they are getting fair play, and although many buyers may be careful and conscientious there is a very general feeling of dissatisfaction among the people with the way they are forced to carry on the trade. When the kelp has been finally disposed of it is shipped in schooners and sent away – for the most part, I believe to Scotland – where is it used for the manufacture of iodine.

Complaints are often heard about the idleness of the natives of Connemara, yet at the present time one sees numbers of the people drying and arranging their weed until nightfall, and the bays where the weed is found are filled with boats at four or five o'clock in the morning when the tide is favourable. The chances of a good kelp season depend to some extent on suitable weather for drying and burning the weed, yet on the whole this trade is probably less precarious than the fishing industry or any other source of income now open to the people of a large portion of these congested districts. In the present year the weather has been excellent, and there is every hope that a good quantity of kelp may be obtained. The matter is of peculiar importance this year, as for the last few months the shopkeepers have been practically keeping the people alive by giving out meal and flour on the security of the kelp harvest – one house alone, I am told, distributed fourteen tons during the last ten days – so that if the kelp should not turn out well or the prices should be less than what is expected whole districts will be placed in the greatest difficulty.

It is a remarkable feature of the domestic finance of this district that although the people are so poor they are used to dealing with fairly large sums of money. Thus four or five tons of kelp well sold may bring a family between twenty and thirty pounds, and their bills for flour (which is bought in bags of two hundredweight at a good deal over a pound a bag) must also be considerable. It is the same with their pig-farming, fishing, and other industries, and probably this familiarity with considerable sums causes a part, at least, of the sense of shame that is shown by those who are reduced to working on the roadside for the miserable pittance of a shilling a day.

Manchester Guardian (24 June 1905)

'In the "Congested Districts": The Boat-Builders'

We left Gorumna in a hooker managed by two men, and sailed north to another district of the Galway coast.⁵⁸ Soon after we started the wind fell, and we lay almost becalmed in a curious bay so filled with islands that one could hardly distinguish the channel that led to the

---

58. Carna in Ard Bay, a well-established centre of boat building.

open sea. For some time we drifted slowly between Dinish Island and Illaunearach, a stony mound inhabited by three families only. Then our pace became so slow that the boatmen got out a couple of long sweeps and began rowing heavily, with sweat streaming from them. The air was heavy with thunder, and on every side one saw the same smoky blue sea and sky, with grey islands and mountains beyond them, and in one place a ridge of yellow rocks touched by a single ray of sunlight. Two or three pookawns[59] – lateen-rigged[60] boats, said to be of Spanish origin – could be seen about a mile ahead of us sailing easily across our bows where some opening in the islands made a draught from the east. In half an hour our own sails filled, and the boatmen stopped rowing and began to talk to us. One of them gave us many particulars about the prices of hookers and their nets, and the system adopted by the local boatbuilders who work for the poorer fishermen of the neighbourhood.

'When a man wants a boat,' he said, 'he buys the timber from a man in Galway and gets it brought up here in a hooker. Then he gets a carpenter to come to his house and build it in some place convenient to the sea. The whole time the carpenter will be working at it the other man must support him and give him whiskey every day. Then he must stand around while he is working, holding boards and handing nails, and if he doesn't do it smart enough you'll hear the carpenter scolding him and making a row. A carpenter like that will be six weeks or two months, maybe, building a boat, and he will get £2 for his work when he is done. The wood and everything you need for a 15ft boat will cost £4 or beyond it, so a boat like that is a dear thing for a poor man.'

We asked him about the boats that had been made by the local boatwrights for the Congested Districts Board.

'There were some made in Lettermullan,' he said, 'and beyond in an island west of where you're going to-day there is an old man has been building boats for thirty years, and he could tell you all about them.'

---

59. From Irish *púcán*, 'a fishing smack; an open boat with mainsail and jib', Ó Muirithe, p. 155.

60. A 'lateen' is a triangular sail.

Meanwhile we had been sailing quickly, and were near the north shore of the bay. The tide had gone so far out while we were becalmed that it was not possible to get in alongside the pier, so the men steered for a ledge of rock further out, where it was possible to land. As we were going in an anchor was dropped, and then when we were close to the rocks the men checked the boat by straining on the rope and brought us in to the shore, with a great deal of nicety.

Not long afterwards we made our way to see the old carpenter the boatman had told us of, and found him busy with two or three other men caulking the bottom of a boat that was propped up on one side. As we came towards them along the low island shore the scene reminded one curiously of some old picture of Noah building the Ark. The old man himself was rather remarkable in appearance, with strongly formed features, and an extraordinarily hairy chest showing through the open neck of his shirt. He told us that he had made several nobbies[61] for the Board, and showed us an arrangement that had been supplied for steaming the heavy timber needed for boats of this class.

'At the present time,' he said, 'I am making our own boats again, and the fifteen-foot boats the people do use here have light timber, and we don't need to trouble steaming them at all. I get eight pounds for a boat when I buy the timber myself and fit her all out ready for the sea. But I am working for poor men, and it is often three years before I will be paid the full price of a boat I'm after making.'

From where we stood we could see another island across a narrow sound, studded with the new cottages that are built in this neighbourhood by the Congested Districts Board.

'That island, like another you're after passing has been bought by the Board,' said the old man, who saw us looking at them, 'and it is a great thing for the poor people to have their holdings arranged for them in one strip instead of the little scattered plots the people have in all this neighbourhood, where a man will often have to pass through the ground of, maybe, three men to get to a plot of his own.'

---

61. 'A small single-masted sailing boat of a type used esp. for fishing in the Irish Sea', OED, n3.

This rearrangement of the holdings that is being carried out in most places where estates have been bought up by the Board and resold to the tenants is a matter of great importance that is fully appreciated by the people. Mere tenant purchase[62] in districts like this may do some good for the moment by lowering rents and interesting the people in their land, yet in the end it is likely to prove disastrous, as it tends to perpetuate holdings that are not large enough to support their owners and are too scattered to be worked effectively. In the relatively few estates bought by the Board – up to March, 1904, their area amounted to two or three hundred thousand acres out of the three and a half million that are included in the congested districts – this is being set right, yet some of the improvements made at the same time are perhaps a less certain gain, and give the neighbourhoods where they have been made an uncomfortable look that is, I think, felt by the people. For instance, there is no pressing need to substitute iron roofs – in many ways open to objection – for the thatch that has been used for centuries and is a part of the constructive tradition of the people. In many districts the thatching is done in some idle season by the men of a household themselves, with the help of their friends, who are proud of their skill, and it is looked on as a sort of festival where there is great talk and discussion, the loss of which is hardly made up for by the patch of ground which was needed to grow the straw and is now free for other use. In the same way, the improvements in the houses built by the Board are perhaps a little too sudden. It is far better, wherever possible, to improve the ordinary prosperity of the people till they begin to improve their houses themselves on their own lines than to do too much in the way of building houses that have no interest for the people and disfigure the country. I remember one evening, in another congested district – on the west coast of Kerry – listening to some peasants who discussed for hours the proportions of a new cottage that was to be built by one of them. They had never, of course, heard of proportion, but they had rules and opinions, in which they were deeply interested, as to how high a house should be if it was a certain length, with so many rafters, in order that it

---

62. Wyndham's Land Act (1903) had made it possible for landowners to sell and tenants to buy the land they rented on advantageous terms.

might look well. Traditions of this kind are destroyed for ever when too sweeping improvements are made in a district, and the loss is a great one. If any real improvement is to be made in many of these congested districts the rearrangement and sale of the holdings to the tenants, somewhat on the lines adopted by the Board, must be carried out on a large scale, but in doing so care should be taken to disorganise as little as possible the life and methods of the people. A little attention to the wells and, where necessary, greater assistance in putting up sheds for the cattle and pigs that now live in the houses would do a great deal to get rid of the epidemics of typhus and typhoid, and then the people should be left as free as possible to arrange their houses and way of life as it pleases them.

Manchester Guardian (28 June 1905)

'In the "Congested Districts": The Homes of the Harvestmen'

The general appearance of the North Mayo country round Belmullet – another district of the greatest poverty – differs curiously from that of Connemara. In Mayo a waste of turf and bog takes the place of the waste of stones that is the chief feature of the coast of Galway. Consequently sods of turf are used for all sorts of work – building walls and ditches and even the gables of cottages – instead of the loose pieces of granite or limestone that are ready to one's hand in the district we have left. Between every field one sees a thin bank of turf, worn away in some places by the weather, and covered in others with loose grass and royal flowering ferns. The rainfall of Belmullet is a heavy one, and in wet weather this absence of stone gives one an almost intolerable feeling of dampness and discomfort.

The last forty miles of our journey to Belmullet was made on the long car[63] which leaves Ballina at four o'clock in the morning. It was raining heavily as we set out, and the whole town was asleep, but during the first hour we met many harvestmen with scythe handles and little bundles tied in red handkerchiefs walking quickly into Ballina to embark for Liverpool or Glasgow. Then we passed Crossmolina, and were soon out on the bogs, where one drives for mile after mile, seeing an odd house only, scattered in a few places with long distances between them. We had been travelling all night from Connemara,[64] and again and again we dozed off into a sort of dream, only to wake up with a start when the car gave a dangerous lurch and see the same dreary waste with a few wet cattle straggling about the road, or the corner of a lake just seen beyond them through a break in the clouds. When we had driven about fifteen miles we changed horses at a village of three houses, where an old man without teeth brought out the new horses and harnessed them slowly as if he was half in his sleep. Then we drove on again, stopping from time to time at some sort of post-office, where a woman or boy usually came out to take the bag of letters. At Bangor Erris four more passengers got up, and as the roads were heavy with the rain we settled into a slow jog trot that made us almost despair of arriving at our destination. The people were now at work weeding potatoes in their few patches of tillage and cutting turf in the bogs, and their draggled, colourless clothes – so unlike the homespuns of Connemara – added indescribably to the feeling of wretchedness one gets from the sight of these miserable

---

63. A descendant of the 'Bianconi cars', a scheduled service of horse-drawn carriages carrying passengers seated on outside benches from canal stops and railheads to more remote destinations: see Introduction, p. xxvi.

64. A train journey from Recess via Galway back to Athlone, to connect with a train to Ballina: see Introduction, p. xxvi.

cottages, many of them with an old hamper or the end of a barrel stuck through the roof for a chimney, and the desolation of the bogs.

Belmullet itself is curiously placed on an isthmus – recently pierced by a canal[65] – that divides Broad Haven from Blacksod Bay. Beyond the isthmus there is a long peninsula some fourteen miles in length, running north and south, and separating these two bays from the Atlantic. As we were wandering through this headland in the late afternoon the rain began again, and we stopped to shelter under the gable of a cottage. After a moment or two a girl came out and brought us in out of the rain. At first we could hardly see anything with the darkness of the rain outside and the small window and door of the cottage, but after a moment or two we grew accustomed to it, and the light seemed adequate enough. The woman of the house was sitting opposite us at the corner of the fire, with two children near her, and just behind them a large wooden bed with a sort of red covering, and red curtains above it. Then there was the door, and a spinning wheel, and at the end opposite the fire a couple of stalls for cattle and a place for a pig with an old brood sow in it, and one young one a few weeks old. At the edge of the fireplace a small door opened into an inner room, but in many cottages of this kind there is one apartment only. We talked, as usual, of the hardships of the people, which are worst in places like this, at some distance from the sea, where no help can be got from fishing or making kelp.

'All this land about here', said the woman, who was sitting by the fire, 'is stripped bog' – that is, bog from which the turf has been cut – 'and it is no use at all without all kinds of stuff and manure mixed through it. If you went down a little behind the house you'd see that there is nothing but stones left at the bottom and you'd want great quantities of sand and seaweed and dung to make it soft and kind enough to grow a thing in it at all. The big farmers have all the good land snapped up, and there is nothing left but stones and bog for poor people like ourselves.'

The sow was snorting in the corner, and I said, after a moment, that it was probably with the pigs that they made most of their money.

---

65. Carter's Canal, in fact built 1845–51, hardly 'recently' in 1905.

'In bad years', she said, 'like the year we've had, when the potatoes are rotten and few, there is no use in our pigs, for we have nothing to give them. Last year we had a litter of pigs from that sow, and they were little good to us, for the people were afraid to buy at any price for fear they'd die upon their hands.'

One of us said something of the relief works we had seen in Connemara.

'We have the same thing here', she said, 'and I have a young lad who is out working on them now, and he has a little horse beast along with him, so that he gets a week's pay for three days or four, and has a little moment over for our own work on the farm'.

I asked her if she had many head of cattle.

'I have not, indeed,' she said, 'nor any place to feed. There is some small people do put a couple of yearlings out on the grass you see below you running out to the sands; but where would I get the money to buy one, or to pay the £1 8s, or near it, you do pay for every yearling you have upon the grass? A while since', she went on, 'we weren't so bad as we are at this time, for we had a young lad who used to go to Scotland for the harvest and be sending us back a pound or two pounds maybe in the month, and bringing five or six or beyond it when he'd come home at the end of autumn; but he got a hurt and never overed it, so we have no one at this time can go from us at all.'

One of the girls had been carding wool for the spinning wheel, so I asked about the spinning and weaving.

'Most women spin their wool in this place,' she said, 'and the weaver weaves it afterwards for 3d a yard if it is a single weaving, and for 6d a yard if it is double woven, as we do have it for the men. The women in this place have little time to be spinning, but the women back on the mountains do be mixing colours through their wool till you'd never ask to take your eyes from it. They do be throwing in a bit of stone colour, and a bit of red madder, and a bit of crimson, and a bit of stone colour again, and, believe me, it is nice stuffs they do make that you'd never ask to take your eyes from.'

The shower had now blown off, so we went out again and made our way down to a cove of the sea where a seal was diving at some distance from the shore, putting up its head every few moments to look at us with a curiously human expression. Afterwards we went on to a jetty north of the town, where the Sligo boat had just come in.[66] One of the men told us that they were taking over a hundred harvestmen to Sligo the next morning, where they would take a boat for Glasgow, and that many more would be going during the week. This migratory labour has many unsatisfactory features, yet in the present state of the country it may tend to check the longing for America that comes over those that spend the whole year on one miserable farm.

Manchester Guardian (1 July 1905)

---

66. A 'useful but not regular' steamer service between Sligo and Belmullet was subsidized by the CDB: see Micks, p. 89.

'In the "Congested Districts": The Smaller Peasant Proprietors'

The car drivers that take one round to isolated places in Ireland seem to be the cause of many of the misleading views that chance visitors take up about the country and the real temperament of the people. These men spend a great deal of their time driving a host of inspectors and officials connected with various Government Boards, who, although they often do excellent work, belong for the most part to classes that have a traditional misconception of the country people. It follows naturally enough that the carmen pick up the views of their patrons, and when they have done so they soon find apt instances from their own local knowledge that give a native popular air to opinions that are essentially foreign. That is not all. The car driver is usually the only countryman with whom the official is kept in close personal contact, so that while the stranger is bewildered, many distinguished authorities have been pleased and instructed by this version of their own convictions. It is fair to add that the carman is usually a small-town's man, so that he has a not unnatural grudge against the mountain squatter,[67] for whom so much has apparently been done while the towns are neglected, and also that the carman may be generally relied on when he is merely stating facts to anyone who is not a total stranger to the country.

We drove out recently with a man of this class, and as we left Belmullet he began to talk of an estate that has been sold to the tenants by the Congested Districts Board.

'Those people pay one or two pounds in the year,' he said, 'and for that they have a house, and a stripe of tilled land, and a stripe of rough land, and an outlet on the mountain for grazing cattle, and the rights of turbary,[68] and yet they aren't satisfied, while I do pay five pounds for a little house with hardly enough land to grow two score of cabbages.'

He was an elderly man, and as we drove on through many gangs of relief workers he told us about the building of the Belmullet workhouse in 1857, and I asked him what he remembered or had heard of the great famine ten years earlier.

'I have heard my father to say', he said, 'that he often seen the people dragging themselves along to the workhouse in Binghamstown[69] and some

---

67. Synge uses this term frequently to mean a tenant farmer, not necessarily someone occupying land without legal title, the normal meaning of the word, OED, n. 1a.

68. Short for 'common of turbary', 'the right to cut turf or peat for fuel on a common or on another person's land', OED, n. 2.

69. Former name for An Geata Mór, village on the Belmullet peninsula.

of them falling down and dying on the edge of the road. There were other places where he'd seen four or five corpses piled up on each other against a bit of a bank or the butt of a bridge, and when I began driving I was in great dread in the evenings when I'd be passing those places on the roads.'

It was a dark, windy day, and we went on through endless wastes of brown mountain and bog, meeting no one but an occasional woman driving an ass with meal or flour, or a few people drying turf and building it up into ricks on the roadside or near it. In the distance one could see white roads – often relief roads – twisting among the hills, with no one on them but a man here and there riding in with the mails from some forlorn village. In places we could see the white walls and gables of one of these villages against the face of a hill, and fairly frequently we passed a few tumbled-down cottages with plots of potatoes about them. After a while the carman stopped at a door to get a drink for his horse, and we went in for a moment or two to shelter from the wind. It was the poorest cottage we had seen. There was no chimney, and the smoke rose by the wall to a hole in the roof at the top of the gable. A boy of ten was sitting near the fire minding three babies, and at the other end of the room there was a cow with two calves and a few sickly looking hens. The air was so filled with turf smoke that we went out again in a moment into the open air. As we were standing about we heard the carman ask the boy why he was not at school.

'I'm spreading turf this day,' he said, 'and my brother is at school. To-morrow he'll stay at home, and it will be my turn to go.'

Then an old man came up and spoke of the harm the new potato crop is getting from the high wind, as indeed we had seen ourselves in several fields that we had passed, where whole lines of the tops were broken and withered.

'There was a storm like this three weeks ago,' he said, 'and I could hardly keep my old bonnet on me going round through the hills. This storm is as bad, or near it, and wherever there are loops and eddies in the wind you can see the tops all fluttered and destroyed, so that I'm thinking another windy day will leave us as badly off as we were last year.'

It seems that about here the damage of the sea winds, where there is no shelter, does as much or more harm than the blight itself. Still the blight is always a danger, and for several years past the people have been spraying their crops, with sufficiently good results to make them all anxious to try it.[70] Even an old woman who could not afford to get one of the machines used for this purpose was seen out in her field a season or two ago, with a bucketful of the solution, spraying her potatoes with an old broom – an instance which shows how eager the people are to adopt any improved methods that can be shown to be of real value. This took place in the neighbourhood of Aghoos – the place we were driving to – where an estate has been bought by the Congested Districts Board and resold to the tenants. The holdings are so small that the rents are usually about three pounds a year, though in some cases they are much less, and it is easily seen that the people must remain for a while, at least, as poor, or nearly as poor, as they have been in the past. In barren places of this kind the enlarging of the holdings is a matter of the greatest difficulty, as good land is not to be had in the neighbourhood, and it is hard to induce even a few families to migrate to another place where holdings could be provided for them, while their absence would liberate part of the land in a district that is overcrowded. At present most of the holdings have, besides their tilled land, a stripe of rough bog land, which is to be gradually reclaimed, but even when this is done the holdings will remain poor and small, and if a bad season comes the people may be again in need of relief. Still no one can deny the good that is done by making the tenants masters of their own ground and consolidating their holdings, and when the old fear of improvements, caused by the landlord system, is thoroughly forgotten, something may be done.[71]

A great deal has been said of the curse of the absentee landlord, but in reality the small landlord who lived on his property and knew how much

70. Spraying with a mixture of copper suphate and lime, an experimental treatment initially 'borrowed from the use of vine-dressing solution in France' had been introduced by the CDB in the 1890s and soon 'was universally recognized as most effective in warding off or mitigating the devastation of potato-blight', Micks, p. 33.

71. Tenants in Ireland, before the introduction of the Land Acts in the late nineteenth century, held their land on short term leases and could have their rents increased at will by the landlord if they improved their holdings.

money every tenant possessed was a far greater evil. The judicial rent system[72] was not a great deal better, as when the term came to an end the careless tenant had his rent lowered, while the man who had improved his holding remained as he was – a fact, which, of course, meant much more than the absolute value of the money lost. For one reason or another, the reduction of rents has come to be, in the tenants' view, the all-important matter, so that this system kept down the level of comfort, as every tenant was anxious to appear as poor as possible for fear of giving the landlord an advantage. These matters are well known; but at the present time the state of suspended land purchase[73] is tending to reproduce the same fear in a new form, and any tenants who have not bought out are naturally afraid to increase the price they may have to pay by improving their land. In this district, however, there is no fear of this kind, and a good many small grants have been given by the Board for rebuilding cottages and other improvements. A new cottage can be built by the occupier himself for a sum of about £30, of which the Board pays only a small part, while the cottages built by the Board, on their own plan, with slated roofs on them, cost double, or more than double, as much. We went into one of the reslated cottages with concrete floor, and it was curious to see that, however awkward the building looked from the outside, in the kitchen itself the stain of the turf smoke and the old pot-ovens and stools made the place seem natural and local. That at least was reassuring.

Manchester Guardian (5 July 1905)

---

72. That is the fixing of rents by the Land Commission: see n. 54 above.

73. 'The suspension of land purchase probably refers to difficulties in reimbursing landlords under Wyndham's Land Act, 1903, which were only resolved by further legislation in 1909'. Personal e-mail from David Fitzpatrick 17 September 2008.

'In the "Congested Districts": Erris'

In the poorest districts of Connemara the people live, as I have already pointed out, by various industries, such as fishing, turf-cutting, and kelp-making, which are independent of their farms, and are so precarious that many families are only kept from pauperism by the money that is sent home to them by daughters or sisters who are now servant girls in New York. Here in the congested districts of Mayo the land is still utterly insufficient – held at least in small plots, as it is now – as a means of life, and the people get the more considerable part of their funds by their work on the English or Scotch harvest, to which I have alluded before. A few days ago a special steamer went from Achill Island to Glasgow with five hundred of these labourers, most of them girls and young boys. From Glasgow they spread through the country in small bands and work together under a ganger, picking potatoes or weeding turnips, and sleeping for the most part in barns and outhouses. Their wages vary from a shilling a day to perhaps double as much in places where there is more demand for their work. The men go more often to the North of England, and usually work together, where it is possible, on small contracts for piecework arranged by one of themselves until the hay harvest begins, when they work by the day. In both cases they get fairly good wages, so that if they are careful and stay for some months they can bring back eight or nine pounds with them.

This morning people were passing through the town square of Belmullet – where our windows look out[74] – towards the steamer from two o'clock in small bands of boys and girls, many of them carrying their boots under their arms and walking in bare feet, a fashion to which they are more used. Last night also, on our way back from a village that is largely inhabited by harvest people, we saw many similar bands hurrying in towards the town as the steamer was to sail soon after dawn. This part of the coast is cut into by a great number of shallow tidal estuaries which are dry at low tide, while at full tide one sees many small roads that seem to run down aimlessly into the sea, till one notices, perhaps half a mile away, a similar road running down on the opposite headland On our way, as the tide was out, we passed one of these sandy fords where there were a number of girls gathering cockles, and drove into Geesala, where we left our car and walked on to the villages of Dooyork, which lies on a sort of headland, cut off on the south by another long estuary.[75] It is in places like this, where there is no thoroughfare in any direction to bring strangers to the country, that one meets with the most individual local life. There are two villages of Dooyork, an upper and lower, and as soon as we got into

---

74. Synge and Yeats were staying at Deehan's Royal Hotel, Belmullet.
75. Tullaghan Bay.

the first every doorway was filled with women and children looking after us with astonishment. All the houses were quite untouched by improvements, and a few of them were broken-down hovels of the worst kind. On the road there were several women bringing in turf or seaweed on horses with large panniers slung over a straw straddle, on which usually a baby of two or three years old was riding with delight. At the end of the village we talked to a man who had been in America, and before that had often gone to England as a harvestman.

'Some of the men get a nice bit of money,' he said, 'but it is hard work. They begin at three in the morning, and they work on till ten at night. A man will sometimes get twelve shillings an acre for hoeing turnips, and a skilful man will do an acre or the better part of it in one day; but I'm telling you it is hard work, and before the day is done a man will be hard set to know if it's the soil or the turnips he's striking down on.'

I asked him where and how they lodged.

'Ah,' he said, 'don't ask me to speak to you of that, for the lodging is poor, surely.'

We went on then to the next village, a still more primitive and curious one. The houses were built close together, with passages between them, and low square yards marked round with stones. At one corner we came on a group of dark brown asses with panniers, and women standing among them in red dresses with white or coloured handkerchiefs over their heads, and the whole scene had a strangely foreign, almost Eastern, look, though in its own way it was peculiarly characteristic of Ireland. Afterwards we went back to Geesala along the edge of the sea. This district has, unexpectedly enough, a strong branch of the Gaelic League, and small Irish plays are acted frequently in the winter, while there is also an Agricultural Co-operative Bank, which has done excellent work. These banks, on the Raiffeisen system,[76] have been promoted in Ireland for the last nine or

---

76. The Raiffeisen Banking Group was founded in Austria in 1886 by Friedrich Wilhelm Raiffeisen (1818–88), with the aim of providing basic banking services to the rural population based on co-operative principles. The Irish banks made small loans to farmers at low rates of interest.

ten years by the Irish Agricultural Society,[77] with aid from the Congested Districts Board, and in a small way they have done much good and shown – to those who wished to question it – the business intelligence of the smallest farmers. The interest made by these local associations tends to check emigration, but in this district the distress of last year has a bad effect. In the last few months a certain number of men have sold out the tenant-right of their holdings – usually to the local shopkeeper, to whom they are always in debt – and shipped themselves and their whole families to America with what remained of the money. This is probably the worst kind of emigration, and one fears the sufferings of these families who are suddenly moved to such different surroundings must be great.

This district of the Erris Union, which we have now been through, is the poorest in the whole of Ireland, and during the last few months six or seven hundred people have been engaged on the relief works. Still, putting aside exceptionally bad years, there is certainly a tendency towards improvement. The steamer from Sligo, which has only been running for a few years, has done much good by bringing in flour and meal much more cheaply than could be done formerly. Typhus is less frequent than it used to be, probably because the houses and holdings are improving gradually, and we have heard it said that the work done in Aghoos by the fund raised by the 'Manchester Guardian' some years ago was the beginning of this better state of things. The relief system as it is now carried on is an utterly degrading one, and many things will have to be done before the district is in anything like a satisfactory state. Yet the impression one gets of the whole life is not a gloomy one. Last night was St John's Eve,[78] and bonfires – a relic of Druidical rites – were lighted all over the country, the largest of all being placed in the town square of Belmullet, where a number of small boys shrieked and cheered and threw up firebrands for hours together. To-day, again, there was a large market in the square, where a number of country people with their horses and donkeys stood about bargaining for

---

77. Irish Agricultural Organization Society, set up in Dublin in 1894, largely at the instigation of Sir Horace Plunkett (1854–1932), to promote co-operative organization among Irish farmers; Plunkett was also a member of the CDB from its establishment.

78. 23 June, eve of the Feast of St John the Baptist.

young pigs, heather brooms, homespun flannels, second-hand clothing, blacking brushes, tinkers' goods, and many other articles. Once when I looked out the blacking-brush man and the card-trick man were getting up a fight in the corner of the square. A little later there was another stir, and I saw a Chinaman wandering about followed by a wondering crowd. The sea in Erris, as in Connemara, and the continual arrival of islanders and boatmen from various directions tend to keep up an interest and movement that is felt even far away in the villages among the hills.

Manchester Guardian (8 July 1905)

'In the "Congested Districts": The Inner Lands of Mayo – The Village Shop'

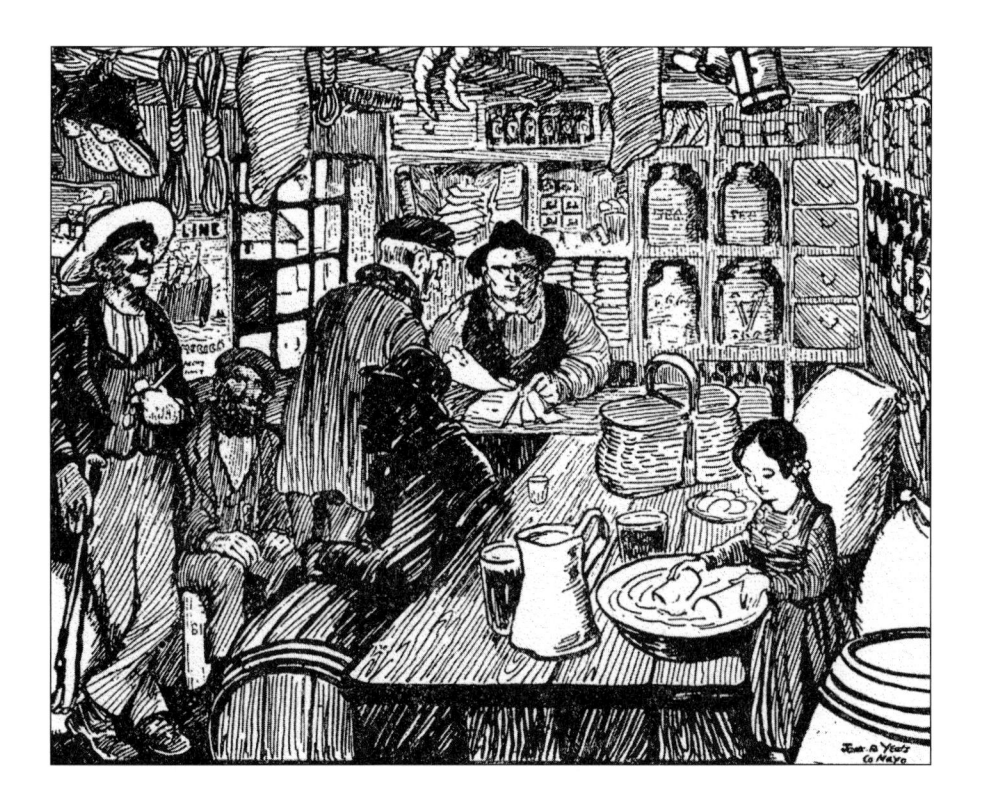

There is a curious change in the appearance of the country when one moves inland from the coast districts of Mayo to the congested portion of the inner edge of the county. In this place there are no longer the Erris tracts of bog or the tracts of stone of Connemara, but one sees everywhere low hills and small farms of poor land that is half turf bog, already much cut away, and half narrow plots of grass or tillage. Here and there one meets with little villages, built on the old system, with cottages closely grouped together and filled with primitive people, and the women mostly in bare feet with white handkerchiefs over their heads. On the whole, however, one soon feels that this neighbourhood is far less destitute than those we have been in hitherto. Turning out of Swinford, soon after our arrival, we were met almost at once by a country funeral coming towards the town with a large crowd, mostly of women, walking after it. The coffin was tied on one side of an outside car, and two old women, probably the chief mourners, were sitting on the other side. In the crowd itself we could see a few men leading horses or bicycles, and several young women who seemed by their dress to be returned Americans. When the funeral was out of sight we walked on for a few miles and then turned into one of the wayside public-houses, at the same time general shop and bar, which are a peculiar feature of most of the country parts of Ireland. An old one-eyed man with a sky-blue handkerchief round his neck was standing at the counter making up his bill with the publican, and disputing loudly over it. Here, as in most of the congested districts, the shops are run on a vague system of credit that is not satisfactory, though one does not see at once what other method could be found to take its place. After the sale of whatever the summer season has produced – pigs, cattle, kelp, &c – the bills are paid off, more or less fully, and all the ready money of a family is thus run away with. Then about Christmas time a new bill is begun, which runs on till the following autumn – or later in the harvesting districts – and quite small shopkeepers often put out relatively large sums in this way. The people keep no pass-books, so they have no check on the traders, and although direct fraud is probably rare, it is likely that the prices charged are often exorbitant. What is worse, the shopkeeper in out-of-the-way places is usually the only buyer to be had for a number of home products, such as eggs, chickens, carrageen moss,[79] and sometimes

---

79. Carrageen (from Irish *carraigín*, 'little rock') moss, edible seaweed used in jellies.

even kelp, so that he can control the prices both of what he buys and what he sells, while as a creditor he has an authority that makes bargaining impossible. Another of the many complicated causes that keep the people near to pauperism! Meanwhile the old man's bill was made out, and the publican came to serve us. While he did so the old man spoke to us about the funeral, and I asked him about the returned Americans we had seen going after it.

'All the girls in this place,' he said, 'are going out to America when they are about seventeen years old. Then they work there for six years or more, till they do grow weary of that fixed kind of life, with the early rising and the working late, and then they do come home with a little stocking of fortune with them, and they do be tempting the boys with their chains and their rings, till they get a husband and settle down in this place. Such a lot of them is coming now there is hardly a marriage made in the place that the woman hasn't been in America.'

I asked a woman who had come in for a moment if she thought the girls kept their health in America.

'Many of them don't,' she said – 'working in factories with dirty air; and then you have likely seen that the girls in this place is big, stout people, and when they get over beyond they think they should be in the fashions, and they begin squeezing themselves in till you hear them gasping for breath, and that's no healthy way to be living.'

When we offered the old man a drink, a moment later, he asked for two-penny ale.

'This is the only place in Ireland', he said, 'where you'll see people drinking ale, for it is from this place that the greatest multitudes go harvesting to England – it's the only way they can live – and they bring the taste for ale back along with them. You'll see a power of them that come home at Michaelmas or Martinmas[80] itself that will never do a hand's turn the rest of the year, but they will be sitting around in each other's houses playing cards through the night, and a barrel of ale set up among them.'

---

80. Michaelmas is 29 September, the Feast of Michael and all Angels, Martinmas is 11 November, the Feast of St Martin of Tours.

I asked him if he could tell about how many went from Swinford and the country round in each year.

'Well,' he said, 'you'd never reckon them, but I've heard people to say that there are six thousand or near it. Trains full of them do be running every week to the city of Dublin for the Liverpool boat, and I'm telling you it's many are hard set to get a seat in them at all. Then if the weather is too good beyond and the hay is near saved of itself, there is some that get little to do, but if the Lord God sends showers and rain there is work and plenty, and a power of money to be made.'

While he was talking some men who were driving cattle from a fair came in and sat about in the shop drinking neat glasses of whiskey. They called for their drinks so rapidly that the publican called in a little bare-footed girl in a green dress who stood on a box beside a porter barrel rinsing glasses while he served the men. They all appeared to know the old man with one eye, and they talked to him about some job he had been doing on the relief works in this district. Then they made him tell a story for us of a morning when he had killed three wild ducks 'with one skelp of a little gun he had', and the man who was sitting on a barrel at my side told me that the old man had been the best shot in the place till he got too fond of porter, and had had his gun and his licence taken from him because he was shooting wild over the roads. Afterwards they began to make fun of him because his wife had run away from him and gone over the water, and he began to lose his temper. On our way back an old man who was driving an ass with heavy panniers of turf told us that all the turf of this district will be cut away in the next twenty years, and the people will be left without fuel. This is taking place in many parts of Ireland, and unless the Department of Agriculture or the Congested Districts Board can take steps to provide plantations for these districts there may be considerable suffering, as it is not likely that the people even then will be able to buy coal. Something has been done and a great deal has been said on the subject of growing timber in Ireland, but so far there has been little result. An attempt was made to establish an extensive plantation near Carna, in Connemara, first by the Irish Government in 1890 and then by the Congested Board since 1902, but the work has been a complete failure.[81] Efforts have been made on a smaller scale to encourage planting among the people, but I have not seen much good come of them. Some turf tracts in Ireland are still of great extent, but they are not inexhaustible, and even if turf has to be brought from them, in a few years, to cottages great distances away, the cost of it will be a serious and additional hardship for the people of many poor localities.

Manchester Guardian (19 July 1905)

---

81. W.L. Micks is defensive on the subject of this plantation at Knockboy, which he claims was an unsuitable site, donated not chosen by the CDB; the Board's policy was to encourage the planting of trees as shelter belts for farms: see Micks, pp. 26–7.

'In the "Congested Districts": The Small Town'

Many of the smaller towns of the west and south of Ireland – the towns chiefly that are in or near the congested districts – have a peculiar character. If one goes into Swinford or Charlestown, for instance, one sees a large dirty street strewn in every direction with loose stones, paper, and straw, and edged on both sides by a long line of deserted-looking shops, with a few asses with panniers of turf standing about in front of them. These buildings are mostly two or three storeys high, with smooth slate roofs, and they show little trace of the older sort of construction that was common in Ireland, although there are often a few tiny and miserable cottages at the ends of the town that have been left standing from an older period. Nearly all towns of this class are merely trading centres kept up by the country people that live round them, and they usually stand where several main roads come together from large out-of-the-way districts. In Swinford, which may be taken as a good example of these market towns, there are seven roads leading into the country, and it is likely that a fair was started here at first, and that the town as it is now grew up afterwards. Although there is at present a population of something over 1,300 people and a considerable trade, the place is still too small to have much genuine life, and the streets look empty and miserable till a market-day arrives. Then early in the morning old men and women, with a few younger women of about thirty who have been in America, crowd into the town and range themselves with their asses and carts at both sides of the road, among the piles of goods which the shopkeepers spread out before their doors.

The life and peculiarities of the neighbourhood – the harvesting and the potato blight, for instance – are made curiously apparent by the selection of these articles. Over nearly every shop door we could see, as we wandered through the town, two scythe blades fixed at right angles over the doorways with the points and edges uppermost, and in the street below them there were numbers of hayrakes standing in barrels, scythe handles, scythe blades bound in straw rope, reaping hooks, scythe stones, and other things of the kind. In a smith's forge at the end of the town we found a smith fixing blades and hand-grips to scythe handles for a crowd of men who stood round him with the blades and handles, which they had bought elsewhere, ready in their hands. In front of many shops, also, one could see old farmers bargaining eagerly for second-hand spraying machines or buying supplies of the blue sulphate of copper that was displayed in open sacks all down the street. In other places large packing cases were set up, with small trunks on top of them, and pasted over with advertisements of the various Atlantic lines that are used by emigrants, and large pictures of the Oceanic[82] and other vessels. Inside many of the shops and in the windows one could see an extraordinary collection of objects – saddles, fiddles, rosaries, rat-traps, the Shorter Catechism,[83] castor oil, rings, razors, rhyme-books, fashion plates, nit-killer, and fine-tooth combs. Other houses had the more usual articles of farm and household use, but nearly all of them, even drapers' establishments with stays and ribbons in the windows, had a licensed bar at the end, where one could see a few old men or women drinking whiskey or beer. In the streets themselves there was a pig market going on at the upper end of the town near the Courthouse, and in another place a sale of barrels and churns, made apparently by a local cooper, and also of many sized wooden bowls, pig-troughs, and the wooden bars and pegs that are used on donkeys' saddles to carry the panniers. Further down there were a number of new panniers set out, with long bundles of willow boughs set up beside them, and offered for sale by old women and children. As the day went on six or seven old-clothes brokers did a noisy trade from three large booths set up in the street. A few of the things sold were new, but most of them were more or less worn out, and the sale was carried on as a sort of auction, an old man holding up each article in turn and asking first, perhaps two shillings for a greasy blouse, then cutting away the price to sixpence or even fourpence-halfpenny. Near the booths a number of strolling singers and acrobats were lounging about, and starting off now and then to sing or do contortions in some part of the town. A couple of these men began to give a performance near a booth where we were listening to the bargaining and the fantastic talk of the brokers. First one of them, in a yellow and green jersey, stood on his hands and did a few feats; then he went round with his hat and sold ballads, while the other man sang a song, to a banjo, about a girl –

---

82. The SS *Oceanic* of the White Star Line, in service since 1899, was at this time the largest transatlantic passenger liner.

83. The much reprinted and adapted Westminster Shorter Catechism of 1647, a fundamental document of Protestant doctrine.

> ... whose name it was I don't know,
> And she passed her life in a barber's shop
> making wigs out of sawdust and snow.

Not far away another man set up a stall, with tremendous shouting, to sell some little packets, and we could hear him calling out, 'There's envelopes, notepaper, a pair of boot-laces, and corn cure for one penny. Take notice, gentlemen.'

All the time the braying of the asses that were standing about the town was incessant and extraordinarily noisy, as sometimes four or five of them took it up at the same time. Many of these asses were of a long-legged, gawky type, quite unusual to this country, and due, we were told, to a Spanish ass sent here by the Congested Districts to improve the breed. It is unfortunate that most attempts to improve the live stock of Ireland have been made by some offhand introduction of a foreign type which often turns out little suited to the new conditions it is brought to, instead of by the slower and less exciting method of improving the different types by selection from the local breeds. We have heard a great deal in passing through Connemara of the harm that has been done by injudicious 'improving' of the ponies and horses,[84] and while it is probable that some of the objections made to the new types may be due to local prejudice, it should not be forgotten that the small farmer is not a fool, and that he knows perfectly well when he has an animal that is suited to his needs.

Towards evening, when the market was beginning to break up, an outside car drove through the town laden on one side with an immense American trunk belonging to a woman who had just come home after the usual period of six years that she had spent making her fortune. A man at a shop door who saw it passing began to talk about his own time in New York, and told us how often he had had to go down to Coney Island at night to 'recoup' himself after the heat of the day. It is not too much to say that one can hardly spend an hour in one of these Mayo crowds without being reminded in some way of the drain of the people that has been and is still running from Ireland. It is, however, satisfactory to note that in

---

84. See n. 49 above.

this neighbourhood and west of it on the Dillon estate,[85] which has been bought out and sold to the tenants by the Congested Districts Board, there is a current of returning people that may do much good. A day or two ago we happened to ask for tea in a cottage which was occupied by a woman in a new American blouse, who had unmistakably come home recently from the States. Her cottage was perfectly clean and yet had lost none of the peculiar local character of these cottages. Almost the only difference that one could point to was a large photograph of the head of the Sistine Madonna hanging over the fire in the little room where we sat, instead of the hideous German oleographs[86] on religious subjects that are brought round by pedlars and bought by most of the simpler Irish women for the sake of the subjects they represent.

Manchester Guardian (22 July 1905)

---

85. The estate of Viscount Dillon, partly in Roscommon, amounted to 93,000 acres: see Micks, p. 227.

86. 'A type of coloured lithograph which has been impressed with a canvas grain and varnished, in order to make it look like an oil painting,' OED.

'In the "Congested Districts": Possible Remedies – Concluding Article'

It is not easy to improve the state of the people in the congested districts by any particular remedy or set of remedies. As we have seen, these people are dependent for their livelihood on various industries, such as fishing, kelpmaking, turf-cutting, or harvesting in England, and yet the failure of a few small plots of potatoes brings them literally to a state of famine. Near Belmullet during a day of storm we saw the crop for next year in danger of utter ruin, and if the weather had not changed, by good luck, before much harm was done, the whole demoralising and wretched business of the relief works would have had to be taken up again in a few months. It is obvious that the earnings of the people should be large enough to make them more or less independent of one particular crop, and yet, in reality, it is not easy to bring about such a state of things, for the moment a man earns a few extra pounds in the year he finds many good and bad ways of spending them, so that when a quarter of his income is cut away unexpectedly once in seven or eight years he is as badly off as before. To make the matter worse, the pig trade – which is often relied on to bring in the rent-money – is, as I have shown, dependent on the potatoes, so that a bad potato season means a dearth of food, as well as a business difficulty which may have many consequences. It is possible that by giving more attention to the supply of new seed potatoes and good manure – something in this direction is being done by the co-operative societies – the failure of the crop may be made less frequent. Yet there is little prospect of getting rid of the danger altogether, and as long as it continues the people will have many hardships.

The most one can do for the moment is to improve their condition and solvency in other ways, and for this purpose extended purchase on the lines adopted by the Congested Districts Board seems absolutely necessary. This will need more funds than the Board has now at its disposal, and probably some quicker mode of work. Perhaps in places where relief has to be given some force may have to be brought to bear on landlords who refuse to sell at fair terms. No amount of purchase in the poorer places will make the people prosperous – even if the holdings are considerably enlarged – yet there is no sort of doubt that in all the estates which the Board has arranged and sold to the tenants there has been a steady tendency towards improvement. A good deal may be done also by improved communications, either by railroad or by sea, to make life easier for the people. For instance, before the steamer was put on a few years ago between Sligo and Belmullet the cost of bringing a ton of meal or flour by road from Ballina to Belmullet was £1, and one can easily estimate the consequent dearness of food. That is perhaps an extreme case, yet there are still a good many places where things are almost as bad, and in these places the people suffer doubly, as they are usually in the hands of one or two small shopkeepers, who can dictate the price of eggs and other small articles which they bring in to sell. At present a steamer running between Westport and Belmullet, in addition to the Sligo boat, is badly needed, and would probably do a great deal of good more cheaply than the same service could be done by a line of railway. If the communications to the poorest districts could be once made fairly satisfactory it would be much easier for the Congested Districts Board or some similar body to encourage the local industries of the people and to enable them to get the full market value for what they produce.

The cottage industries that have been introduced or encouraged by the Board – lacemaking, knitting, and the like – have done something, yet at best they are a small affair. In a few places the fishing industry has been most successfully developed, but in others it has practically failed and led to a good deal of disappointment and wasted energy. In all these works it needs care and tact to induce the people to undertake new methods of work, but the talk sometimes heard of their sloth and ignorance has not much foundations. The people have traditional views and instincts about agriculture and live stock, and they have a perfectly natural slowness to adopt the advice of an official expert who knows nothing of the peculiar conditions of their native place. The advice given is often excellent, but there have been a sufficient number of failures in the work done by the Congested Board, such as the attempt at forestry in Carna and the bad results got on certain of their example plots laid out to demonstrate the best methods of farming,[87] to make the conservatism of the people a sign of, perhaps, valuable prudence. The Board and the Department of Agriculture and Technical Education have done much excellent work, and it is not to be expected that improvements of this kind, which must be largely experimental, can be carried on without failures; yet one does not always pardon

---

87. The 'example plots' were farms, half of which were farmed according to the advice of CDB agricultural instructors in return for free fertiliser: see Micks, p. 25.

a sort of contempt for the local views of the people which seems rooted in nearly all the official workers one meets with through the country.

One of the chief problems that one has to deal with in Ireland is, of course, the emigration that I have mentioned so often. It is probably the most complicated of all Irish affairs, and in dealing with it it is important to remember that the whole moral and economic condition of Ireland has been brought into a diseased state by prolonged misgovernment and many misfortunes, so that at the present time normal remedies produce abnormal results. For instance, if it is observed in some neighbourhood that the girls are going to America because they have no work at home, and a lace school is started to help them, it too often happens that the girls merely use it as a means of earning money enough to pay for their passage and outfit, and the evil is apparently increased. Further, it should not be forgotten that emigrants are going out at the present time for quite opposite reasons. In the poorest districts of all they go reluctantly, because they are unable to keep themselves at home; but in places where there has been much improvement the younger and brighter men and girls get ambitions which they cannot satisfy in this country, and so they go also. Again, where there is no local life or amusements they go because they are dull, and when amusements and races are introduced, they get the taste for amusements, and go because they cannot get enough of them. They go as much from districts where the political life has been allowed to stagnate as from districts where there has been an excess of agitation that has ended only in disappointment. For the present the Gaelic League is probably doing more than any other movement to check this terrible evil, and yet one fears that when the people realise in five, or perhaps in ten, years that this hope of restoring a lost language is a vain one the last result will be a new kind of hopelessness and many crowded ships leaving Queenstown and Galway. Happily in some places there is a counter-current of people returning from America. Yet they are not very numerous, and one feels that the only real remedy for emigration is the restoration of some national life to the people. It is this conviction that makes most Irish politicians scorn all merely economic or agricultural reforms, for if Home Rule would not of itself make a national life it would do more to make such a life possible than half a million creameries.[88] With renewed life in the country many changes of the methods of government and the holding of property would inevitably take place, which would all tend to make life less difficult even in bad years and in the worst districts of Mayo and Connemara.

Manchester Guardian (26 July 1905)

---

88. The *Manchester Guardian*, under the editorship of C.P. Scott, was a strong supporter of Irish Home Rule: see Introduction, p. xl.

'The Vagrants of Wicklow'

Some features of County Wicklow, such as the position of the principal workhouses[89] and holiday places, on either side of the coach road from Arklow to Bray, have made this district a favourite with the vagrants of Ireland. A few of these people have been on the roads for generations; but fairly often they seem to have merely drifted out from the ordinary people of the villages, and do not differ greatly from the class they come from. Their abundance has often been regretted; yet in one sense it is an interesting sign, for wherever the labourer of a country has preserved his vitality, and begets an occasional temperament of distinction, a certain number of vagrants are to be looked for. In the middle classes the gifted son of a family is always the poorest – usually a writer or artist with no sense for speculation – and in a family of peasants, where the average comfort is just over penury, the gifted son sinks also, and is soon a tramp on the roadside.

In this life, however, there are many privileges. The tramp in Ireland is little troubled by the laws, and lives in out-of-door conditions that keep him in good-humour and fine bodily health. This is so apparent, in Wicklow at least, that these men rarely seek for charity on any plea of ill-health, but ask simply when they beg – 'Would you help a poor fellow

---

89. Synge would have been thinking of the workhouse in Rathdrum; the other two workhouses, at Baltinglass and Shillelagh, were not close to the Arklow-Bray road.

along the road?' or – 'Would you give me the price of a night's lodging, for I'm after walking a great way since the sun rose?'

The healthiness of this life, again, often causes these people to live to a great age, though it is not always easy to test the stories that are told of their longevity. One man, however, who died not long ago, claimed to have reached 102 with a show of likelihood; for several old people remember his first appearance in a certain district as a man of middle age, about the year of the famine, in 1847 or 1848. This man could hardly be classed with ordinary tramps; for he was married several times in different parts of the world, and reared children of whom he seemed to have forgotten in his old age even the names and sex. In his early life he spent thirty years at sea, where he sailed with someone he spoke of afterwards as 'il mio capitane', visiting India and Japan, and gaining odd words and intonations that gave colour to his language. When he was too old to wander in the world, he learned all the paths of Wicklow, and till the end of his life he could go the thirty miles from Dublin to the Seven Churches,[90] without, as he said, 'putting out his foot on a white road, or seeing any Christian but the hares and moon'. When he was over ninety, he married an old woman of eighty-five. Before many days, however, they quarrelled so fiercely that he beat her with his stick, and came out again on the roads. In a few hours he was arrested at her complaint and sentenced to a month in Kilmainham. He cared nothing for the plank bed and uncomfortable diet; but he always gathered himself together and cursed with extraordinary rage as he told how they had cut off the white hair which had grown down upon his shoulders. All his pride and his half-conscious feeling for the dignity of his age seemed to have set themselves on this long hair, which marked him out from the other people of his district; and I have often heard him saying to himself, as he sat beside me under a ditch – 'What use is an old man without his hair? A man has only his bloom like the trees; and what use is an old man without his white hair?'

Among the country people of the East of Ireland the tramps and tinkers who wander round from the West have a curious reputation for witchery and unnatural powers.

---

90. Local name for Glendalough, the medieval monastic settlement.

'There's great witchery in that country,' a man said to me once, on the side of a mountain to the east of Aughavanna,[91] in Wicklow, 'there's great witchery in that country, and great knowledge of the fairies. I've had men lodging with me out of the West – men who would be walking the world looking for a bit of money – and every one of them would be talking of the wonders below in Connemara. I remember one time, a while after I was married, there was a tinker down there in the glen, and two women along with him. I brought him into my cottage to do a bit of a job, and my first child was there lying in the bed, and he covered up to his chin with the bed-clothes. When the tallest of the women came in, she looked around at him, and then she says –

"That's a fine boy, God bless him."

"How do you know it's a boy", says my woman, "when it's only the head of him you see?"

"I know rightly," says the tinker, "and it's the first too."

'Then my wife was going to slate[92] me for bringing in people to bewitch her child, and I had to turn the lot of them out to finish the job in the lane.'

I asked him where most of the tinkers came from that are met with in Wicklow.

'They come from every part,' he said. 'They're gallous[93] lads for walking round through the world. One time I seen fifty of them above on the road to Rathdangan,[94] and they all match-making and marrying themselves for the year that was to come. One man would take such a woman, and say he was going such roads and places, stopping at this fair and another fair, till he'd meet them again at such a place, when the spring was coming on. Another, maybe, would swap the woman he had with one from another man, with as much talk as if you'd be selling a cow. It's two hours I was there watching them from the bog underneath where I was

---

91. Small village on the road into the Glen of Imaal, site of one of the military barracks built by the British in the wake of the 1798 rebellion.

92. 'To beat or thrash severely,' OED v.² 2, a specifically Irish usage.

93. Corruption of 'gallows', used as an intensive adjective to mean 'fine' or 'excellent'.

94. Next village on the road from Aughavanna to Baltinglass in West Wicklow.

cutting turf, and the like of the crying, and the kissing, and the singing, and the shouting began when they went off this way and that way, you never heard in your life. Sometimes, when a party would be gone a bit down over the hill, a girl would begin crying out and wanting to go back to her ma. Then the man would say, "Black hell to your soul, you've come with me now, and you'll go the whole way." I often seen tinkers before and since, but I never seen such a power of them as were in it that day.'

It need hardly be said that in all tramp life plaintive and tragic elements are common, even on the surface. Some are peculiar to Wicklow. In these hills the summer passes in a few weeks from a late spring full of odour and colour to an autumn that is premature and filled with the desolate splendour of decay; and it often happens that, in moments when one is most aware of this ceaseless fading of beauty, some incident of tramp life gives a local human intensity to the shadow of one's own mood.

One evening, on the high ground near the Avonbeg,[95] I met a young tramp just as an extraordinary sunset had begun to fade, and a low white mist was rising from the bogs. He had a sort of table in his hands that he seemed to have made himself out of twisted rushes and a few branches of osier. His clothes were more than usually ragged, and I could see by his face that he was suffering from some terrible disease. When he was quite close, he held out the table.

'Would you give me a few pence for that thing?' he said. 'I'm after working at it all day by the river, and for the love of God give me something now, the way I can get a drink and lodging for the night.'

I felt in my pockets, and could find nothing but a shilling piece.

'I wouldn't wish to give you so much,' I said, holding it out to him; 'but it is all I have, and I don't like to give you nothing at all, and the darkness coming on. Keep the table; it's no use to me, and you'll maybe sell it for something in the morning.'

The shilling was more than he expected, and his eyes flamed with joy.

'May the Almighty God preserve you and watch over you, and reward

---

95. River running down the valley from Glenmalure to the Meeting of the Waters, supposed site of a famous song of Thomas Moore, where it joins the Avonmore. All three of Synge's Wicklow plays are set in this valley.

you for this night,' he said; 'but you'll take the table. I wouldn't keep it at all, and you after stretching out your hand with a shilling to me, and the darkness coming on.'

He forced it into my hands so eagerly that I was not able to refuse it, and set off down the road with tottering steps. When he had gone a few yards, I called after him – 'There's your table; take it, and God speed you.'

Then I put down his table on the ground, and set off as quickly as I was able. In a moment he came up with me again, holding the table in his hands, and slipped round in front of me, so that I could not get away.

'You wouldn't refuse it,' he said, 'and I after working at it all day below by the river!'

He was shaking with excitement and the exertion of overtaking me; so I took his table and let him go on his way. A quarter of a mile further on I threw it over the ditch in a desolate place where no one was likely to find it.

In addition to the more genuine vagrants a number of wandering men and women are to be met with in the northern parts of the country, who walk out for ferns and flowers in bands of from four or five to a dozen. They usually set out in the evening, and sleep in some ditch or shed, coming home the next night with what they have gathered. If their sales are successful, both men and women drink heavily; so that they are always on the edge of starvation, and are miserably dressed, the women sometimes wearing nothing but an old petticoat and shawl – a scantiness of clothing that is sometimes met with also among the road women of Kerry.

These people are nearly always at war with the police, and are often harshly treated. Once after a holiday, as I was walking home through a village on the border of Wicklow, I came upon several policemen, with a crowd round them, trying to force a drunken flower-woman out of the village. She did not wish to go, and threw herself down raging and kicking on the ground. They let her lie there for a few moments, and then she propped herself up against the wall, scolding and storming at everyone till she became so outrageous the police renewed their attack. One of them walked up to her and hit her a sharp blow on the jaw with the back of his hand. Then two more of them seized her by the shoulders and forced her along the road for a few yards, till her clothes began to tear off with the violence of the struggle, and they let her go once more.

She sprang up at once when they did so.

'Let this be the barracks yard, if you wish it,' she cried out, tearing off the rags that still clung about her. 'Let this be the barracks yard, and come on now the lot of you.'

Then she rushed at them with extraordinary fury; but the police, to avoid scandal, withdrew into the town, and left her to be quieted by her friends.

Sometimes, it is fair to add, the police are generous and good-humoured. One evening many years ago, when Whit Monday in Enniskerry[96] was a very different thing from what it is now, I was looking out of a window in that village, watching the police, who had been brought in for the occasion, getting ready to start for Bray. As they were standing about a young ballad-singer came along from the Dargle, and one of the policemen who seemed to know him, asked him why a fine stout lad the like of him wasn't earning his bread instead of straying on the roads.

Immediately the young man drew up on the spot where he was, and began shouting a loud ballad at the top of his voice. The police tried to stop him; but he went on, getting faster and faster, till he ended, swinging his head from side to side, in a furious patter, of which I seem to remember:

> Botheration
>   Take the nation,
> Calculation,
>   In the stable,
> Cain and Abel,
>   Tower of Babel,
> And the Battle of Waterloo.

Then he pulled off his hat, dashed in among the police, and did not leave them till they had given him the share of money he felt he had earned for his bread.

---

96. Village on the river Dargle, 20 km south of Dublin.

In all the circumstances of this tramp life there is a certain wildness that gives it romance and a peculiar value for those who look at life in Ireland with an eye that is aware of the arts also. In all the healthy movements of art variations from the ordinary types of manhood are made interesting for the ordinary man, and in this way only the higher arts are universal. Beside this art, however, founded on the variations which are a condition and effect of all vigorous life, there is another art – sometimes confounded with it – founded on the freak of nature, in itself a mere sign of atavism or disease. This latter art, which is occupied with the antics of the freak, is of interest only to the variation from ordinary minds, and, for this reason, is never universal. To be quite plain, the tramp in real life, Hamlet and Faust in the arts, are variations; but the maniac in real life, and Des Esseintes[97] and all his ugly crew in the arts, are freaks only.

The Shanachie (Autumn 1906)

97. Central figure of J-K Huysman's 'decadent' novel *À Rebours* (1884). In the 1890s Synge read much of Huysmans' work but had turned against him at this stage.

'The People of the Glens'

Here and there in County Wicklow there are still a number of little known places – places with curiously melodious names such as Aughavanna, Glenmalure, Annamoe, or Lough Nahanagan – where the people have retained a peculiar simplicity, and speak a language in some ways more Elizabethan than the English of Connaught, where Irish was generally used till a much later date. In these glens many women still wear old-fashioned bonnets, with a white frill round the face, and the old men, when they are going to the fair, or to Mass, are often seen in curiously-cut frock-coats, tall hats, and breeches buckled at the knee. When they meet a wanderer on foot, these old people are always glad to stop and talk to him for hours, telling him stories of the Rebellion, or the fallen angels that ride across the hills, or alluding to the three shadowy countries that are never forgotten in Wicklow – America (their El Dorado), the union,[98] and the madhouse.

'I had a power of children,' an old man, who was born in Glenmalure, said to me once; 'I had a power of children, and they all went to California with what I could give them, and bought a bit of a field. Then, when they put in the plough, it stuck fast on them. They looked in beneath it, and there was fine gold stretched within the earth. They're rich now, and their

---

98. The workhouse, from Poor Law Union, the administrative district made up of a group of parishes, responsible for the support of the poor under the Poor Relief Act of 1838.

daughters are riding on fine horses with new saddles on them, and elegant bits in their mouths, yet not a ha'porth did they ever send me, and may the devil ride with them to hell.'

Not long afterwards I met an old man wandering about a hill-side, where there was a fine view of Lough Dan, in extraordinary excitement and good spirits.

'I landed in Liverpool two days ago,' he said, when I had wished him the time of day; 'then I came to the city of Dublin this morning, and took the train to Bray, where you have the blue salt water on your left, and the beautiful valleys, with trees in them, on your right. From that I drove to this place on a jaunting-car to see some brothers and cousins I have living below. They're poor people, Mister honey,[99] with bits of cabins, and mud floors under them, but they're as happy as if they were in heaven, and what more would a man want than that? In America and Australia, and on the Atlantic Ocean, you have all sorts, good people and bad people, and murderers, and thieves, and pick-pockets; but in this place there isn't a being isn't as good and decent as yourself or me.'

I saw he was one of the old people one sometimes meets with who emigrated when the people were simpler than they are at present, and who often come back, after a lifetime in the States, as Irish as any old man who has never been twenty miles from the town of Wicklow. I asked him about his life abroad, when we had talked a little longer.

'I've been through perils enough to slay nations,' he said, 'and the people here think I should be rotten with gold, but they're better off the way they are. For five years I was a ship's smith, and never saw dry land, and I in all the danger and peril of the Atlantic Ocean. Then I was a veterinary surgeon, curing side-slip, splay-foot, spavin, splints, glanders, and the various ailments of the horse and ass. The lads in this place think you've nothing to do but to go across the sea and fill a bag with gold; but I tell you it is hard work, and in those countries the workhouses is full, and

---

99. 'Honey' as a term of endearment, though common in the speech of older women in Ireland, could be used by men to men: see Michael Traynor, *The English Dialect of Donegal* (Dublin: Royal Irish Academy, 1953), p. 145. This form, prefaced by the honorific 'Mister', reappears in *The Playboy* (CW IV 75).

the prisons is full, and the crazy-houses is full, the same as in the city of Dublin. Over beyond you have fine dwellings, and you have only to put out your hand from the window among roses and vines, and the red wine grape; but there is all sorts in it, and the people is better in this country, among the trees and valleys, and they resting on their floors of mud.'

In Wicklow, as in the rest of Ireland, the union, though it is a home of refuge for the tramps and tinkers, is looked on with supreme horror by the peasants. The madhouse, which they know better, is less dreaded.

One night I had to go down, late in the evening, from Annamoe to the town of Wicklow, and come back again into the hills. As soon as I came near Rathnew[100] I passed many bands of girls and men making rather ruffianly flirtation on the pathway, and women who surged up to stare at me, as I passed in the middle of the road. The thick line of trees from Ashford to Rathnew makes the way intensely dark even on clear nights, and when one is riding quickly, the contrast, when one reaches the lights of Wicklow, is singularly abrupt. The town itself after nightfall is gloomy and squalid. Half-drunken men and women stand about, wrangling and disputing in the dull light from the windows, which is only strong enough to show the wretchedness of the figures which pass and repass across them. I did my business quickly and turned back to the hills, passing for the first few miles the same noisy groups and couples on the roadway. After a while I stopped at a lonely public-house to get a drink and rest for a moment before I came to the hills. Six or seven men were talking drearily at one end of the room, and a woman I knew, who had been marketing in Wicklow, was resting nearer the door. When I had been given a glass of beer, I sat down on a barrel near her, and we began to talk.

'Ah, your honour,' she said, 'I hear you're going off in a short time to Dublin, or to France, and maybe we won't be in the place at all when you come back. There's no fences to the bit of farm I have, the way I'm destroyed running. The calves do be straying, and the geese do be straying, and the hens do be straying, and I'm destroyed running after them. We've no man in the place since himself died in the winter, and he ailing these

---

100. Village 3 km west of Wicklow on the way from the market town of Ashford.

five years, and there's no one to give us a hand, drawing the hay, or cutting the bit of oats we have above on the hill. My brother Michael has come back to his own place after being seven years in the Richmond Asylum; but what can you ask of him, and he with a long family of his own? And, indeed, it's a wonder he ever came back when it was a fine time he had in the asylum.'

She saw my movement of surprise, and went on.

'There was a son of my own, as fine a lad as you'd see in the county – though I'm his mother that says it, and you'd never think it to look at me. Well, he was a keeper in a kind of a private asylum, I think they call it; and when Michael was taken bad, he went to see him, and didn't he know the keepers that were in charge of him, and they promised to take the best of care of him, and indeed he was always a quiet man that would give no trouble. After the first three years he was free in the place, and he walking about like a gentleman, doing any light work he'd find agreeable. Then my son went to see him a second time, and "You'll never see Michael again," says he when he came back, "for he's too well off where he is". And indeed it was well for him, but now he's come home'. Then she got up to carry out some groceries she was buying to the ass-cart that was waiting outside.

'It's real sorry I do be when I see yous going off,' she said, as she was turning away, 'I don't often speak to you, but it's company to see yous passing up and down over the hill, and now may the Almighty God bless and preserve you, and see you safe home.'

A little later I was walking up the long hill which leads from Ashford to the high ground from Laragh to Sugar Loaf.[101] The solitude was intense. Towards the top of the hill I passed through a narrow gap, with high rocks on one side of it, and fir trees above them, and a handful of jagged sky filled with extraordinarily brilliant stars. In a few moments I passed out on the brow of the hill that runs behind the Devil's Glen,[102] and smelt the fragrance of the bogs. I mounted again. There was not light enough to

---

101. The Sugar Loaf is the distinctive conical-shaped volcanic peak at the northern end of the Wicklow Mountains.

102. The deep valley culminating in a waterfall, which was part of the Synge estate of Glanmore.

show the mountains round me, and the earth seemed to have dwindled away into a mere platform where an astrologer might watch. Among these intense emotions of the night one cannot wonder that the madhouse is so often named in Wicklow.

Many of the old people of the county, however, when they have no definite sorrow, are not mournful, and are full of curious whims and observations. One old woman, who lived near Glen Macanass,[103] told me that she had seen her sons had no hope of making a livelihood in the place where they were born, so, in addition to their schooling, she engaged a master to come over the bogs every evening and teach them sums and spelling. One evening she came in behind them, when they were at work, and stopped to listen.

'And what do you think my son was after doing?' she said. 'He'd made a sum of how many times a wheel on a cart would turn round between the bridge below and the Post Office in Dublin. Would you believe that? I went out without saying a word, and I got the old stocking where I keep a bit of money, and I made out what I owed the master. Then I went in again, and "Master," says I, "Mick's learning enough for the likes of him. You can go now and safe home to you." And, God bless you, Avourneen, Mick got a fine job after on the railroad.'

Another day when she was trying to flatter me, she said: 'Ah, God bless you, Avourneen, you've no pride. Didn't I hear you yesterday, and you talking to my pig below in the field as if it was your brother? And a nice clean pig it is, too, the crathur.' A year or two afterwards I met this old woman again. Her husband had died a few months before of the 'Influence',[104] and she was in pitiable distress, weeping and wailing while she talked to me. 'The poor old man is after dying on me,' she said, 'and he was great company. There's only one son left me now, and we do be killed

---

103. Valley of the Glenmacnass river, north of Laragh, well known for the waterfall at its head. The woman, identifiable by her favourite tag 'Avourneen', was in fact a close neighbour of the Synges when they stayed at Castle Kevin, Annamoe; according to the 1901 Census, she was Catherine Rochford, a widow of 74, living with her unmarried son Michael, aged 32. It is likely that Synge here deliberately misplaces her to disguise her identity.

104. Influenza.

working. Ah, Avourneen, the poor do have great stratagems to keep in their little cabins at all. And did ever you see the like of the place we live in? Isn't it the poorest, lonesomest, wildest, dreariest bit of a hill a person ever passed a life on?' When she stopped a moment, with the tears streaming on her face, I told her a little about the poverty I had seen in Paris.

'God Almighty forgive us, Avourneen,' she went on when I had finished, 'we don't know anything about it. We have our bit of turf, and our bit of sticks, and our bit to eat, and we have our health. Glory be to His holy Name, not a one of the childer was ever a day ill, except one boy was hurted off a cart and he never overed it. It's small right we have to complain at all.'

She died the following winter, and her son went to New York.

The old people who have direct tradition of the Rebellion, and a real interest in it, are growing less numerous daily, but one still meets with them here and there in the more remote districts.

One evening at the beginning of harvest, as I was walking into a straggling village, far away in the mountains, in the southern half of the county, I overtook an old man[105] walking in the same direction with an empty gallon can. I joined him; and when he had talked for a moment, he turned round and looked at me curiously.

'Begging your pardon, sir,' he said, 'I think you aren't Irish'. I told him he was mistaken.

'Well,' he went on, 'you don't speak the same as we do; so I was thinking maybe you were from another country.'

'I came back from France,' I said, 'two months ago, and maybe there's a trace of the language still upon my tongue.' He stopped and beamed with satisfaction.

'Ah,' he said, 'see that now. I knew there was something about you. I do be talking to all who do pass through this glen, telling them stories of the Rebellion, and the old histories of Ireland, and there's few can puzzle me, though I'm only a poor ignorant man.' He told me some of his adventures, and then he stopped again.

---

105. Patrick Kehoe of Aughavanna (1819–1906), whom Synge calls Cavanagh here; for the identification see Hannigan & Nolan, p. 720.

'Look at me now,' he said, 'and tell me what age you think I'd be.'

'You might be seventy,' I said.

'Ah,' he said, with a piteous whine in his voice, 'you wouldn't take me to be as old as that? No man ever thought me that age to this day.'

'When I look at you better,' I said, fearing I had blundered, 'I see you can't be far over sixty. Maybe you're sixty-four'. He beamed once more with delight and hurried along the road. 'Go on, now', he said, 'I'm eighty-two years, three months and five days. Would you believe that? I was baptized on the fourth of June, eighty-two years ago, and it's the truth I'm telling you.'

'Well, it's a great wonder,' I said, 'to think you're that age, when you're as strong as I am to this day.'

'I'm not strong at all,' he went on, more despondingly, 'not strong the way I was. If I had two glasses of whiskey, I'd dance a hornpipe would dazzle your eyes; but the way I am at this minute you could knock me down with a rush. I have a noise in my head, so that you wouldn't hear the river at the side of it, and I can't sleep at nights. It's that weakens me. I do be lying in the darkness thinking of all has happened in threescore years to the families of Wicklow, what this son did, and what that son did, and of all that went across the sea, and wishing black hell would seize them that never wrote three words to say were they alive or in good health. That's the profession I have now to be thinking of all the people, and of the times that's gone. And begging your pardon, might I ask your name?'

I told him.

'There are two branches of the Synges in the County Wicklow,' he said; and then he went on to tell me fragments of folklore connected with my forefathers: how a lady used to ride through Roundwood 'on a curious beast' to visit an uncle of hers in Roundwood Park, and how she married one of the Synges and got her weight in gold – eight stone of gold – as her dowry. Stories that referred to events which took place more than a hundred years ago.[106] When he had finished, I told him how much I wondered at his knowledge of the county.

---

106. For the details of Synge family history which Kehoe may here be retailing, see Mc Cormack, pp. 124-5.

'There's not a family I don't know,' he said, 'from Baltinglass to the sea, and what they've done, and who they've married. You don't know me yet, but if you were a while in this place talking to myself, it's more pleasure and gratitude you'd have from my company than you'd have maybe from many a gentleman you'd meet riding or driving a car. Did you ever hear tell of Mr. ——, the Member of Parliament?'[107]

I told him I had heard his name.

'Well, one day I was near striking him on this stretch of the road. I was after telling him about two men were piked beyond by that corner, at the time of the Rebellion, and when I came to an end, "It's all lies you're telling," says he, "there's not a word of it true." "How's that?" says I, "what in the name of God do you know of the histories of the world?" "It's all in my history book", says he, "and another way altogether." "Go home, then," says I, "and burn your history book for it's all lies is in it, and you're the first man ever thought he knew the history of these places better than old Cavanagh" – that's myself. "Well," says he, "I'm going home to-morrow, and I'll find out in the city of Dublin whether it's you is right or the book. Then when I come back in a twelve-month – if we both have our health, by the grace of God – I'll tell you about it." A year after he came back late in the evening, and down he comes to my little dwelling with the rage he had to see me. I wasn't in at that time, so he came down again to me at the dawn of day. "Ah, Cavanagh," says he, "you're the finest man for histories ever I seen. It's you were right, and the book was wrong." Would you believe that?'

By this time we had reached a wayside public-house, where he was evidently going with his can, so, as I did not wish to part with him so soon, I asked him to come in and take something with me. When we went into the little bar-room, which was beautifully clean, I asked him what he would have. He turned to the publican – 'Have you any good whiskey at the present time?' he said. 'Not now, nor at any time', said the publican, 'we only keep bad; but isn't it all the same for the likes of you that wouldn't know the difference?'

---

107. W.J. Corbet, Parnellite M.P. in the period 1880–1900; for details see Hannigan & Nolan, p. 720.

After prolonged barging[108] he got a glass of whiskey, took off his hat before he tasted it to say a prayer for my future, and then sat down with it on a bench in the corner.

I was served in turn, and we began to talk about horses and racing, as there had been races in Arklow a day or two before.[109] I alluded to some races I had seen in France, and immediately the publican's wife, a young woman who had just come in, spoke of a visit she had made to the Grand Prix a few years before.

'Then you have been in France?' I asked her.

'For eleven years,' she replied.

'Alors vous parlez Français, Madame?'

'Mais oui, Monsieur,' she answered with pure intonation.

We had a little talk in French, and then the old man got his can filled with porter – the mid-day drink for a party of reapers who were working on the hill – bought a pennyworth of sweets, and went back down the road.

'That's the greatest old rogue in the village,' said the publican, as soon as he was out of hearing, 'he's always making up to all who pass through the place, and trying what he can get out of them. The other day a party told me to give him a bottle of XXX porter[110] he was after asking for. I just gave him the dregs of an old barrel we had finished, and there he was, sucking in his lips, and saying it was the finest drink ever he tasted, and that it was rising to his head already, though he'd hardly a drop of it swallowed. Faith in the end I had to laugh to hear the talk that he was making.' A little later I wished them good evening and started again on my walk, as I had two mountains to cross.

The younger people of these glens are not so interesting as the old men and women; and though there are still many fine young men to be met with among them who are extraordinarily gifted and agile, it too often happens, especially in the more lonely places, that the men under thirty

---

108. Abuse.

109. Synge wrote up a description of the Arklow races in August 1901 but did not use it in his published essays: see CW II 197–8.

110. Extra strength stout.

are badly built, shy, and despondent. Even among the older people, whose singular charm I have tried to interpret, it should perhaps be added that it is possible to find many individuals who are far from admirable in temper or in morals. One would hardly stop to assert a fact so obvious if it had not become the fashion in Dublin, quite recently, to reject a fundamental doctrine of theology, and to exalt the Irish peasant into a type of almost absolute virtue, frugal, self-sacrificing, valiant, and I know not what. There is some truth in this estimate, yet it is safer to hold with the theologians that, even west of the Shannon, the heart of man is not spotless, for though the Irish peasant has many beautiful virtues, it is idle to assert that he is totally unacquainted with the deadly sins, or with any minor rogueries. He has, however, it should never be forgotten, a fine sense of humour, and the greatest courtesy. When a benevolent visitor comes to his cottage, seeking a sort of holy family, the man of the house, his wife, and all their infants, too courteous to disappoint him, play their parts with delight. When the amiable visitor, however, is once more in the boreen, a storm of good-tempered irony breaks out behind him that would surprise him could he hear it. This irony I have heard many times in places where I have been intimate with the people, and I have always been overjoyed to hear it. It shows that, in spite of relief-works, commissions, and patronizing philanthropy – that sickly thing – the Irish peasant, in his own mind, is neither abject nor servile.[III]

The Shanachie (March 1907)

III. The final paragraph of this essay, written in the wake of the controversy over the *Playboy*, when Synge's critics accused him of misrepresenting the Irish peasants, was cut from the text used in *In Wicklow, West Kerry and Connemara*. See Introduction, p. xliv.

'At a Wicklow Fair: The Place and the People'[112]

A year or two ago I wished to visit a fair in county Wicklow, and as the buying and selling in these fairs are got through very early in the morning I started soon after dawn to walk the ten or twelve miles that led to Augrim,[113] a village in the southern half of the county, where the fair was to be held. When I came out into the air the cold was intense, though it was a morning of August, and the dew was so heavy that bushes and meadows of mountain grass seemed to have lost their greenness in a shroud of wet silvery grey. In the glens on either side on my road white mists were twisting and feathering themselves into extraordinary shapes, and showing blue hills here and there behind them, that looked singularly desolate and far away. At every turn I came on multitudes of rabbits feeding on the roadside, and at times I saw even shyer creatures – corncrakes, squirrels, and snipe – close to villages where no one was awake.

Then the sun rose, and I could see lines of smoke beginning to rise from farmhouses under the hills, and sometimes a sleepy, half-dressed girl looked out of the door of a cottage when my feet echoed on the road. About

---

112. Based on two visits by Synge to Aughrim fair in the summer of 1902, on 30 July and 27 August: see Stephens, MS 6193, ff. 1969, 2012.

113. Normally spelled Aughrim.

six miles from Augrim I began to fall in with droves of bullocks and sheep, in charge of two or three dogs and a herd, or with whole families of mountain people, sometimes driving nothing but a single donkey or kid. These people seemed to feel already the animation of the fair, and were talking eagerly and gaily among themselves. I did not hurry, and it was about nine o'clock when I made my way into the village, which was now thronged with cattle and sheep. On every side the usual halfhumorous bargaining could be heard above the noise of the pigs and donkeys and lambs. One man would say, 'Are you going to not divide a shilling with me? Are you going to not do it? You're the biggest schemer ever walked down into Augrim.'

A little further on a man said to a seller: 'You're asking too much for them lambs.' The seller answered: 'If I didn't ask it how would I ever get it? The lambs is good lambs, and if you buy them now you'll get home nice and easy in time to have your dinner in comfort, and if you don't buy them you'll be here the whole day sweating in the heat and dust, and maybe not please yourself in the end of all.' Then they began looking at the lambs again, talking of the cleanness of their skin and the quality of the wool, and making many extravagant remarks in their praise or against them. As I turned away I heard the loud clap of one hand into another which always marks the conclusion of a bargain.

A little further on I found a farmer I knew standing before a publichouse, looking radiant with delight. 'It's a fine fair, Mister,' he said, 'and I'm after selling the lambs I had here a month ago and no one would look at them. Then I took them to Rathdrum and Wicklow, getting up at three in the morning and driving them in the creel, and it all for nothing. But I'm shut of them now, and it's not too bad a price I've got either. I'm after driving the lambs outside the customs (the boundary where the fair-tolls are paid) and I'm waiting now for my money.' While we were talking a cry of warning was raised: 'Mind yourselves below, there's a drift of sheep coming down the road.' Then a couple of men and dogs appeared, trying to drive a score of sheep that someone had purchased out of the village between the countless flocks that were standing already on either side of the way. This task is peculiarly difficult. Boys and men collect round the flock that is to be driven out and try to force the animals down the narrow passage that is left in the middle of the road. It hardly ever happens, however, that they get through without carrying off a few of some one else's sheep, or losing some of their own, which have to be restored, or looked for afterwards as the case may be.

The flock was driven by as well as could be managed, and a moment later an old man came up to us and asked if we had seen a ewe passing from the west. 'A sheep is after passing,' said the farmer I was talking to, 'but it was not one of yours, for it was too wilful; it was a mountain sheep.' Sometimes animals are astray in this way for a considerable time – it is not unusual to meet a man the day after a fair wandering through the country, asking after a lost heifer or ewe – but they are always well marked and are found in the end.

When I reached the fair-green above the village I found the curious throng one always meets in these fairs, made up of wild mountain squatters,[114] sometimes dressed in knee-breeches and frock-coats, gentlemen farmers in sporting checks and knickerbockers, jobbers and herds. At one corner of the green there was the usual camp of tinkers, where a swarm of children had been left to play among the carts while the men and women wandered through the fair selling cans or donkeys. Many odd types of tramps and beggars had come together also, and were loitering about the green in the hope of getting some chance job, or of finding someone who would stand them a drink. Once or twice a stir was made by some unruly ram or bull, but in these smaller fairs there seldom is much real excitement till the evening, when the bad whiskey that is too freely drunk begins to make itself felt.

When I had spoken to one or two men that I wished to see I sat down near a bridge at the end of the green between a tinker who was mending a can and a herd who was minding some sheep that had not been sold. The herd spoke to me with some pride of his skill in dipping sheep to keep them from the fly[115] and other matters connected with his work. 'Let

---

114. See note 67 above.

115. In summer sheep are 'dipped', soaked in a bath of chemicals to stop flies hatching their eggs into maggots in the sheep's flesh.

you not be talking,' said the tinker when he paused for a moment. 'You've been after sheep since you were that height (holding his hand a little over the ground), and yet you're nowhere in the world beside the herds that do be reared beyond on the mountains. Those men are a wonder, for I'm told they can tell a lamb from their own ewes before it is marked, and that when they have five hundred sheep on the hills – five hundred is a big number – they don't need to count them or reckon them at all, but they just walk here and there where they are, and if one is gone away they'll miss it from the others.'[116]

Then a woman came up and spoke to the tinker, and they went down the road together into the village. 'That man is a great villain,' said the herd when he was out of hearing. 'One time he and his woman went up to a priest in the hills and asked him would he wed them for half a sovereign, I think it was. The priest said it was a poor price, but he'd wed them surely if they'd make him a tin can along with it." I will, faith," said the tinker, "and I'll come back when it's done." They went off then, and in three weeks they came back, and they asked the priest would he wed them a second time. "Have you the tin can?" said the priest. "We have not," said the tinker; "we had it made at the fall of night, but the ass gave it a kick this morning the way it isn't fit for you at all." "Go on, now," says the priest. "It's a pair of rogues and schemers you are, and I won't wed you at all." They went off then, and they were never married to this day.'

As I went up again through the village a great sale of old clothing was going on from booths at each side of the road, and further on boots were set out for sale on boards laid across the tops of barrels, a very usual counter. In another place old women were selling quantities of damaged fruit, kippered herrings, and an extraordinary collection of old ropes and iron. In front of a public-house a ballad-singer was singing a song in the middle of a crowd of people. As far as I could hear it, the words ran like this:

---

116. This praise of mountain shepherds Synge in fact heard from Willie Coleman, owner of Tomrilands House, Annamoe, which Mrs Synge rented as a holiday home in 1902, and where Synge wrote *The Shadow of the Glen* and *Riders to the Sea*. See Hannigan & Nolan, 712.

> As we came down from Wicklow
> With our bundle of switches;
> As we came down from Wicklow,
> Oh! what did we see?
> As we came to the city
> We saw maidens pretty,
> And we called out to ask them to buy our heath-broom.
> Heath-broom, freestone, black turf, gather them up.
> Oh! Gradh, Macree, Mavourneen,
> Won't you buy our heath-broom?
>
> When the season is over
> Won't we be in clover,
> With the gold in our pockets
> We got from heath-broom.
> It's home we will toddle,
> And we'll get a naggin,
> And we'll drink to the maidens that bought our heath-broom.
> Heath-broom, freestone, black turf, gather them up.
> Oh! Gradh, Macree, Mavourneen,
> Won't you buy my heath-broom?

Before he had finished a tinker arrived, too drunk to stand or walk, but leading a tall horse with his left hand, and inviting anyone who would deny that he was the best horseman in Wicklow to fight with him on the spot. Soon afterwards I started on my way home, driving most of the way with a farmer from the same neighbourhood. Still, our progress was slow, and it was nearly midnight when I reached the cottage I had left at dawn.

Manchester Guardian (9 May 1907)

'A Landlord's Garden In County Wicklow'

A stone's throw from an old house where I spent several summers in county Wicklow,[117] there was a garden that had been left to itself for fifteen or twenty years. Just inside the gate, as one entered, two paths led up through a couple of strawberry beds, half choked with leaves, where a few white and narrow strawberries, not bigger than a lady's thimble, were still hidden away. Further on there was nearly half an acre of tall raspberry canes and thistles five feet high, which had grown together in a dense mass, where, with perseverance, one could still pick raspberries enough to last a household for the season. Then, in a waste of hemlock, there were some half-dozen apple trees covered with lichen and moss, and against the northern walls a few dying plum trees hanging from their nails. Beyond them there was a dead pear tree, and just inside the gate, as one came back to it, a large fuchsia filled with empty nests. A few lines of box here and there showed where the flower beds had been laid out, and when anyone who had the knowledge looked carefully among them many remnants could be found of beautiful and rare plants.

All round this garden there was a wall seven or eight feet high, in which one could see three or four tracks, with well-worn holes, like the

---

117. Castle Kevin: see note 44 above.

paths down a cliff in Kerry, where boys and tramps came over to steal and take away any apples or other fruits that were in season. Above the wall on the three windy sides there were rows of finely-grown lime trees, the place of meeting in the summer for ten thousand bees. Under the east wall there was the roof of a greenhouse where one could sit, when it was wet or dry, and watch the birds and butterflies, many of which were not common. The seasons were always late in this place – it was high above the sea – and redpoles often used to nest not far off late in the summer; siskins did the same once or twice, and greenfinches till the beginning of August used to cackle endlessly in the lime trees.

Everyone is used in Ireland to the tragedy that is bound up with the lives of farmers and fishing people, but in this garden one seemed to feel the tragedy of the landlord class also, and of the innumerable old families that are quickly dwindling away. These owners of the land are not much pitied at the present day, or much deserving of pity, and yet one cannot quite forget that they are the descendants of what was at one time, in the eighteenth century, a high-spirited and highly cultivated aristocracy. The broken greenhouses and mouse-eaten libraries that were designed and collected by men who voted with Grattan are perhaps as mournful in the end as the four mud walls that are so often left in Wicklow as the only remnants of a farmhouse. The desolation of this life is often of a peculiarly local kind, and if a playwright chose to go through the Irish countryhouses he would find material, it is likely, for many gloomy plays that would turn on the dying away of these old families, and on the lives of the one or two delicate girls that are left so often to represent a dozen hearty men who were alive a generation or two ago. Many of the descendants of these people have of course drifted into professional life in Dublin, or have gone abroad, yet wherever they are they do not equal their forefathers, and where men used to collect fine editions of 'Don Quixote' and Molière, in Spanish and French, and luxuriantly bound copies of Juvenal and Persius and Cicero, nothing is read now but Longfellow and Hal Caine[118] and

---

118. Thomas Henry Hall Caine (1853–1931), one of the most popular British novelists of his time, many of whose works were successfully dramatized and later filmed.

Miss Corelli.[119] Where good and roomy houses were built a hundred years ago, poor and tawdry houses are built now, and bad bookbinding, bad pictures, and bad decoration are thought well of, where rich bindings, beautiful miniatures and finely carved chimney-pieces were once prized by the old Irish landlords.

To return to our garden. One year the apple crop was unusually plentiful, and every Sunday inroads were made upon it by some unknown persons.[120] At last I decided to lie in wait at the dangerous hour – about twelve o'clock, when the boys of the neighbourhood were on their way home from Mass, and we were supposed to be busy with our devotions three miles away. A little before eleven I slipped out, accordingly, with a book, locked the door behind me, put the key in my pocket, and lay down under a bush. When I had been reading for some time, and had quite forgotten the thieves, I looked up at some little stir and saw a young man, in his Sunday clothes, walking up the path towards me. He stopped when he saw me, and for a moment we gazed at each other with astonishment. At last, to make a move, I said it was a fine day. 'It is indeed, sir', he answered with a smile, and then he turned round and ran for his life. I realized that he was a thief, and jumped up and ran after him, seeing, as I did so, a flock of small boys swarming up the walls of the garden. Meanwhile the young man ran round and round through the raspberry canes, over the strawberry beds, and in and out among the apple trees. He knew that if he tried to get over the wall I should catch him, and that there was no other way out, as I had locked the gate. It was heavy running, and we both began to get weary. Then I caught my foot in a briar and fell. Immediately the young man rushed to the wall and began scrambling up it, but just as he was drawing his leg over the top I caught him by the heel. For a moment he struggled and kicked, then by sheer weight I brought him down at my feet, and an armful of masonry along with him. I caught him by the neck and tried to ask his name, but found we were too breathless to speak.

---

119. Marie Corelli (1855–1924), hugely successful British novelist of romantic fiction.

120. The incident on which this is based took place in the summer of 1901; the fruit were in fact cherries not apples: see *Interpreting Synge*, pp. 25–6.

For I do not know how long we sat glaring at each other, and gasping painfully. Then by degrees I began to upbraid him in a whisper for coming over a person's wall to steal his apples, when he was such a fine well-dressed, grown-up young man. I could see that he was in mortal dread that I might have him up in the police courts, which I had no intention of doing; and when I finally asked him his name and address he invented a long story of how he lived six miles away and had come over to this neighbourhood for Mass and to see a friend, and then how he had got a drought upon him[121] and thought an apple would put him in spirits for his walk home. Then he swore he would never come over the wall again if I would let him off, and that he would pray God to have mercy on me when my last hour was come. I felt sure his whole story was a tissue of lies, and I did not want him to have the crow of having taken me in. 'There is a woman belonging to the place', I said, 'inside in the house helping the girl to cook the dinner.[122] Walk in now with me, and we'll see if you're such a stranger as you'd have me think'. He looked infinitely troubled, but I took him sternly by the neck and wrist and we set off for the gate. When we had gone a pace or two he stopped. 'I beg your pardon,' he said. 'My cap's after falling down on the over side of the wall. May I cross over and get it?' That was too much for me. 'Well, go on,' I said, 'and if ever I catch you again, woe betide you.' I let him go then, and he rushed madly over the wall and disappeared. A few days later I discovered, not at all to my surprise, that he lived half a mile away and was intimately related to a small boy who came to the house every morning to run messages and clean the boots. Yet it must not be thought that this young man was dishonest; I would have been quite ready the next day to trust him with a ten pound note.

Manchester Guardian (1 July 1907)

---

121. Felt thirsty.

122. Evidently a local woman hired to assist the Synges' own cook whom they brought with them from Dublin on their summer holidays.

'In West Kerry'[123]

At Tralee station – I was on my way to Ballyferriter, a village near the end of the Dingle peninsula – I found a boy who carried my bag a couple of hundred yards along the road, to an open yard where the light railway starts for the west.[124] There was a confused mass of peasants struggling on the platform with all sorts of baggage, which the people lifted into the train for themselves as well as they were able. The seats ran up either side of the cars, and the space between them was soon filled with sacks of flour, cases of porter, pots, chairs rolled in straw, and other household goods. A drunken young man got in, just before we started, and sang songs for a few coppers, telling us that he had spent all his money, and had nothing left to pay for his ticket to Dingle. Then, when the carriage was closely packed, we moved slowly out of Tralee. At my side there was an old man who explained the Irish names of the stations, and pointed out

---

123. This was the first of the three essays published in *The Shanachie* as a planned series in 1907. These were quite heavily revised by Synge in manuscript on the printed *Shanachie* texts in preparation for what he planned as his 'Wicklow and Kerry book'. This provided the basis for the version published in the 1910 *Works* and subsequent editions as a single undivided 'In West Kerry' essay from which the separate sub-titles were removed. This essay, like the following one on the Blaskets, was based on Synge's visit to the Dingle peninsula in August 1905.

124. The Tralee-Dingle light railway: see Introduction p. xxvii.

the Seven Pigs, a group of islands in Tralee bay, Kerry Head further off, and other mountains we came to. Beyond him there was a crowd of big women in shawls, who seemed to be coming from market, and just opposite me a young woman wearing a wedding-ring, who was a perfect type of the refined women of Kerry, with supreme charm in every movement and expression. The big woman talked to her about some elderly man who had been sick, her husband it was likely, and some young man who had gone away to England, and was breaking his heart with loneliness. 'Ah, poor fellow,' she said, 'I suppose he will get used to it like another; and wouldn't he be worse off if he was beyond the seas in Saint Louis, or the towns of America?'

This woman seemed to unite in a curious way the healthy look of the peasant with the greatest sensitiveness and delicacy; and whenever there was any little stir or joke in the carriage, her face and neck flushed with pleasure and amusement.

As we went on there were superb views, first on our north, towards Loop Head, and then, when we reached the top of the ridge we had to cross,[125] to the south also, past Dingle Bay to Drung Hill, Macgillicuddy's Reeks, and other mountains of South Kerry. A little further on nearly all the people got out at Anascaul, a small station; and the young woman I had admired gathered up most of the household goods, and got down also, lifting heavy boxes with the power of a man. Then two returned American girls got in, fine stout-looking women, with distress in their expressions, and we started again. Dingle Bay could now be seen at times through narrow valleys on our left, and had always extraordinary beauty in the evening light. In the carriage next ours a number of herds and jobbers were travelling, and for the last hour they kept up a furious altercation that seemed always on the verge of breaking out into a dangerous quarrel, but no blows were given.

At Dingle I got my bags out of the train as quickly as I could and found an old blue side-car waiting to drive me to Ballyferriter.[126] I was some time

---

125. Slieve Mish mountains.

126. In the revised text, Synge suppressed the name calling it only 'the village where I was

tying on my goods with the raggedy boy who was to drive me, and then we set off, passing through the usual streets of a Kerry town, with public-houses at the corners, and then past a narrow quay with a few sailing-boats and a small steamer with coal. Then we went over a bridge near a large water-mill, where we met a number of girls with the black shawls that are so typical of Kerry, and turned sharp to the right, into the heart of the mountains. At first we went up hill for several miles, and our progress was slow, though the boy got down once or twice and gathered a handful of switches to beat the tall mare we were driving. Just as the twilight was beginning to deepen we reached the top of the ridge, and came out through a gap that brought us into sight of Smerwick Harbour, a wild bay with magnificent headlands visible beyond it, and a long stretch of the Atlantic. We drove on again for a long time, sometimes very quickly, where the slope was gradual, and then slowly for a moment where the road seemed to fall away under us like the wall of a house. As the night fell the sea became like a piece of white silver on our right, and the mountains got black on our left, and heavy night smells began to come up out of the bogs. Once or twice I noticed a blue cloud over the edge of the road, and then I saw suddenly that we were almost against the gables of a little village, where the houses were so closely packed together there was no light to be seen from any of them. It was now quite dark, and the boy got cautious in his driving, pulling the car almost into the ditch once or twice to avoid an enormous cavity where the centre of the road had subsided into the bogs. At last we passed another river and a public-house, and went up a hill, from which we could see the outline of a chapel. Then the boy turned to me: 'Is it ten o'clock yet?' he said, 'for we're mostly now in Ballyferriter.'[127] A moment later he drew up at a shop where I was to lodge, and I was shown upstairs to a sort of inn-parlour.

 When I had had some tea, the landlord came up,[128] and we had a long,

---

going'; this seems to have been a deliberate policy of anonomyzing places, adopted elsewhere in the text as well.

127. The name of the village here, and the whole following passage down to 'left me for the night' was cut from the revised text.

128. William Long, with whom Synge stayed 7–13 August: see CL I pp. 119–20. Long was the National School teacher as well as keeping a pub and letting rooms.

interesting talk. He was an excellent Gaelic scholar, with much knowledge of the country. First he told me a good deal about the extraordinary antiquities of this neighbourhood, that I knew of already; then we talked of the language.

'The boys and young men of this place', he said, 'are keeping steadily to Irish; but the girls are all for taking up with newdies and nodies, and it is hard to make anything of them.' Then he lent me some Gaelic books, and left me for the night.

The next morning, a Sunday, rain was threatening; but I went out west after my breakfast under Croagh Martin, in the direction of the Atlantic. At one of the first villages I came to I had a long talk with a man who was sitting on the ditch waiting till it was time for Mass. Before long we began talking about the Irish language.

'A few years ago,' he said, 'they were all for stopping it off; and when I was a boy, they tied a gobban[129] into my mouth for the whole afternoon, because I was heard speaking Irish. Wasn't that great cruelty? And now when I hear the same busybodies coming around and telling us for the love of God to speak nothing but Irish, I've a good mind to tell them to go to hell. There was a priest out here a while since who was telling us to stay always where we are, and to speak nothing but Irish; but I suppose, although the priests are learned men and great scholars, they don't understand the life of the people the same as another man would. In this place the land is poor – you can see that for yourself – and the people have little else to live on; so that when there is a long family, one son will stay at home and keep on the farm, and the others will go away because they must go. Then when they once pass out of the Dingle Station in Tralee they won't hear a word of Irish, or meet anyone who'd understand it, so what good, I ask you, is a man who hasn't got the English and plenty of it?'

After I left him I went on towards Dunquin, and lay for a long time on the side of a magnificently wild road, where one could see the Blasket

---

129. From Irish *gobán*, 'a tin or porringer with breathing holes in the bottom, tied on a calf's snout to prevent it from sucking the cow,' Ó Muirithe, p. 113.

Islands and the end of Dunmore Head – the most westerly point of Europe. It was a grey day, with a curious silence on the sea and sky, and no sign of life anywhere, except the sail of one curragh – or niavogue,[130] as they are called here – that was sailing in from the islands. Now and then a cart passed me filled with old people and children, on their way to Mass, who saluted me in Irish. Then I turned back myself. I got on a long road running through a bog, with a smooth, green mountain on one side, and the sea on the other, and Brandon[131] in front of me, partly covered with the clouds. As far as I could see there were little groups of people – mostly women and children – on their way to the chapel in Ballyferriter. A few of the women wore round blue cloaks; but the larger number had simply black or blue shawls over their heads. This procession along the olive bog between the mountains and the sea, on this grey day of autumn, seemed to wring me with the pang of emotion one feels everywhere in Ireland – an emotion that is partly local and patriotic, and partly a share of the desolation that is mixed everywhere with the supreme beauty of the world.

In the evening, when I was walking about the village, I fell in with a man who could read Gaelic, and was full of enthusiasm for the old language, and of contempt for English. I mentioned the conversation I had had in the morning.

'Well,' he said, 'I can tell you that the English I have was never any more good to me than the cover of that pipe. Buyers come here from Dingle, and Cork, and Clare, and they have good Irish, and so has everyone we meet with, for there is no one can do business in this place who hasn't the language on his tongue.'

Then I asked him about the emigration.

'Many go away', he said, 'who could stay if they wished to, for it is a fine place for fishing, and a man will get more money, and better health for himself, and rear a better family, in this place than in many another. And now, with the help of God, the little children will all learn to read and write Irish in the schools, and that is a great thing; for how can people do any

---

130. Irish *naomhóg*: see Mac Conghail, *The Blaskets*, p. 50 for the traditions associated with this specifically Kerry form of the curragh.

131. The highest mountain on the Dingle peninsula.

good, or make a song even, if they cannot write? You will often be three weeks making a song,' he went on after a moment, 'and there will be times when you will think of good things to put into it, that could never be beaten in the whole world; but if you cannot write them down you will forget them maybe by the next day, and then what good will be your song?'

After a while we went upstairs to a large room in the inn, where a number of young men and girls were dancing jigs and reels. These young people of Ballyferriter, although they are as thoroughly Irish-speaking as the people of Connemara, are pushing forward in their habits of living and dress, so that this group of dancers could hardly have been distinguished by their appearance from any Sunday party in Limerick or Cork. After a long four-hand reel my friend, who was dressed in the homespuns of a fisherman, danced a jig to the whistling of a young man with the greatest energy and spirit. Then he sat down with me in the corner, and we talked about spring trawling and the price of nets. I told him about the ways of Aran and Connemara; and then he told me about the French trawlers who come to this neighbourhood in April and May.

'The Frenchmen from Fechamp',[132] he said, 'are Catholics and decent people; but those who come from Boulogne have no religion, and are little better than a wild beast would lep on you out of a wood. One night there was a drift of them below in the public-house, where there is a counter, as you've maybe seen, with a zinc top on it. Well, they were talking together, and they had some little difference among themselves, and from that they went on raising their voices, till one of them out with his knife and drove it down through the zinc into the wood. Wasn't that a dangerous fellow?'

Then he told me about their tobacco:

'The French do have two kinds of tobacco: one of them is called hay-tobacco, and if you give them a few eggs, or maybe nine little cabbage plants, they'll give you as much of it as would fill your hat. Then we get a pound of our own tobacco, and mix the two of them together, and put them away in a pig's bladder – it's that way we keep our tobacco – and then we have enough with that lot for the whole winter.'

---

132. For Fécamp, the fishing port on the coast of Normandy; Synge corrected his misspelling here in the revised text.

This evening a circus was advertised in Dingle, for one night only, so I made my way there towards the end of the afternoon, although the weather was windy and threatening. I reached the town an hour too soon, so I spent some time watching the wild types of fishermen and fishwomen who stand about the quays. Then I wandered up and saw the evening train coming in from Tralee,[133] with the usual number of gaily-dressed young women, and half-drunken jobbers and merchants; and, at last, about eight o'clock, I went to the circus-field, just above the town, in a heavy splash of thunder-rain. The tent was set up in the middle of the field, and a little to the side of it a large crowd was struggling for tickets at one of the wheeled-houses in which the acrobats live. I went round the tent in the hope of getting in by some easier means, and found a door in the canvas where a man was calling out: 'Tickets, or money, this way, tickets or money.' I passed in through a long passage of canvas, paying sixpence for admission. It was already some time after the hour announced for the show; but although the tent was almost full there was no sign of the performers, so I found a corner where I could stand and watch the crowd coming in, wet and dripping from the rain, which had now turned to a downpour. The tent was lighted by a few flaring gas-jets round the central pole, and there was an opening above them through which the rain shot down in straight, whistling lines. The top of the tent was dripping and saturated, and the gas shining sideways across it, made it glitter in many places with the brilliancy of golden silk. When a sudden squall came, with a rush, from the narrow valleys behind the town, the whole structure billowed, and flapped, and strained, till one waited every moment to see the canvas fall upon our heads. The people, who looked strangely black and swarthy in the flickering light, were seated all round, on three or four rows of raised wooden seats, and many who came late had crushed in between them, and were standing in dense masses wherever there was room. At the entrance a rather riotous crowd began to surge in so quickly that there was some danger of the place being rushed. Word was sent across the ring, and in a moment three or four of the women performers, with long,

---

133. There were three trains a day from Tralee to Dingle.

steaming ulsters[134] buttoned over their tights, ran out from behind the scenes and threw themselves into the crowd, forcing back the wild hillside people, fishwomen, and drunken sailors, in an extraordinary tumult of swearing, wrestling, and laughter. These women seemed to enjoy this part of their work, and shrieked with amusement when two or three of them fell on some enormous farmer or publican and nearly dragged him to the ground. Here and there among the people I could see a little party of frightened squireens[135] and their daughters, in the highest fashions of five years ago, trying, not very successfully, to reach the shilling seats. The crowd was now so thick I could see little more than the heads of the performers, who had at last come into the ring, and many of the shorter women who were near me must have seen nothing the whole evening, yet they showed no sign of impatience. The performance was begun by the usual dirty white horse that was brought out and set to gallop in a circle, with a gaudy horse-woman on his back who jumped through a hoop and did the ordinary feats, the horse's hoofs splashing and possing[136] all the time in the green slush of the ring. An old door-mat was laid down near the entrance for the performers, and, as they came out in turn, they wiped the mud from their feet before they got up on their horses. A little later the clown came out, to the great delight of the people. He was followed by some gymnasts, and then the horse-people came out again, in different dress and make-up, and went through their old turns once more. Then there was prolonged fooling between the clown and the chief horseman, who made many medieval jokes, that reminded me of little circuses on the outer Boulevards of Paris, and at last the horseman sang a song which won great applause:

> Here's to the man who kisses his wife,
> And kisses his wife alone;

---

134. 'A long, loose overcoat of frieze or other rough cloth, frequently with a waist-belt', *OED*, 3; originally an 'Ulster Overcoat,' introduced by J. G. M'Gee & Co. of Belfast in 1867.

135. Somewhat derogatory Irish term for 'a petty squire; a small landowner or country gentleman,' *OED*.

136. *OED*, v. 3, gives this as an obsolete meaning 'to splash or tramp in mud or water'.

> For there's many a man kissed another man's wife,
> When he thought he kissed his own.
>
> Here's to the man who rocks his child,
> And rocks his child alone;
> For there's many a man rocked another man's child,
> When he thought he rocked his own.

About ten o'clock there seemed to be a lull in the storm, so I made my way into the open air with a Gaelic Leaguer[137] and a young man who were going to Ballyferriter also. The rain had stopped for the moment, but a high wind was blowing, and the darkness was intense. We went to a public-house where we had left our cycles,[138] and got a few biscuits and a glass of beer before we started. A sleepy barmaid, who was lolling behind the counter with a novel, pricked up her ears when she heard us talking of our ride.

'Surely you are not going to Ballydavid,'[139] she said, 'at such an hour of a night like this?' We told her we were going to Ballyferriter, which was further away.

'Well,' she said, 'I wouldn't go to Ballyferriter to-night if you had a coach and four to drive me, and gave me twenty pounds into the bargain. How at all will you get on in the darkness when the roads will be running with water, and you'll be likely to slip down every place into some drain or ditch?'

When we went out the night seemed darker than ever after the brightly lighted bar, and we began to walk carefully down the steep hill through the town. Before we had gone many yards a woman's voice called out sharply from under the wall, 'Mind the horse.' I looked up, and saw the black outline of a horse's head with its ears pricked up, right over my

---

137. The details about the 'Gaelic Leaguer' and Synge's other companion are cut from the revised text here and later; they become 'two young men who were going the road I had to travel'.

138. In the revised text the phrase 'where we had left our cycles' is omitted; in the following sentence 'ride' is changed to 'journey'.

139. Small village on the east side of Smerwick Harbour.

head. If we had been riding, we should certainly have crashed into it.[140] It was evident that in such darkness we should never get to the end of our ten-mile journey. The young man after a moment suggested that he should try to borrow a lamp from some people of his acquaintance at the bottom of the town. We went to the house, and after waiting for some time he was admitted, and we saw him disappearing at the end of a long passage. Another squall of rain broke through the street while the Gaelic Leaguer and I stood in the darkness, for what seemed nearly a quarter of an hour, waiting for his return. Then a light flickered in the passage, and he came back to us with a lamp. We mounted at last, and made our way over the bridge in the teeth of a gale, and then up the hill, riding slowly and painfully with just light enough, when we kept close together, to avoid sloughs of water and piles of stones on the roadway. By the time we reached the top of the ridge, and began to work down carefully towards Smerwick, the rain had stopped, and we reached Ballyferriter before midnight.

All round this village the country is of the greatest interest. I go out very often to the site of Sybil Ferriter's Castle, on a little headland[141] reached by a narrow strip of rocks. As I lie there I can watch whole flights of cormorants, and choughs, and seagulls, that fly about under the cliffs, and beyond them a number of niavogues that are nearly always fishing in Ferriter's Cove. Further on there is Sybil Head and three other rocky points – the Three Sisters – then Smerwick Harbour, and Brandon far away, usually half covered with white airy clouds. Between these headlands and Ballyferriter there is a strip of sandhill, covered with sea-holly, and a low beach, where scores of bullocks lie close to the sea. To the west one

---

140. This sentence is cut from the revised text, and the following passage edited so that it would appear that Synge and his companions were walking rather than cycling.

141. Dun Point, which shelters the small Ferriter's Cove, just west of Ballyferriter. For the folklore associated with Sybil Ferriter and the ruined castle, see Steve McDonough, *The Dingle Peninsula: History, Folklore, Archaeology* (Dingle: Brandon Books, 1993) cited at http://www.dingle-peninsula.ie/ballyferriter/bf-history.html, accessed 22 September 2008.

can see the Blasket Islands, and the Tearaught,[142] a pointed rock, standing up like a pyramid in the grey light from the Atlantic. The rocks in this place are Old Red Sandstone and Silurian, and are curiously different in their effect from the granite of Wicklow, or the limestone of Aran and Clare. As one goes further on towards the headlands, one passes peculiar horse-shoe coves, with the contorted lines of sandstone on one side, and slaty, blue rocks on the other, and a neck of transparent sea, of wonderful blueness, between them.

I walked up this morning along the long slope from the east to the top of Sybil Head, where one comes out suddenly on the brow of a cliff, with a straight fall at one's feet of many hundred feet into the sea. It is a place of indescribable grandeur. East one sees Carrantuohill, in the south the Skellig Rocks many miles away, on the north Loop Head, in the west the full sweep of the Atlantic, and over all the wonderfully tender and searching colour that is peculiar to Kerry. Looking down the drop of five or six hundred feet, the height is so great that the gannets flying close over the sea look like white butterflies, and the choughs like flies fluttering behind them. One wonders in these places why anyone is left in Dublin or London or Paris, when it would be better, one would think, to live in a tent or hut with this magnificent sea and sky, and to breathe this wonderful air which is like wine in one's teeth.

Here and there on this headland, as indeed in all this neighbourhood, there are little villages of ten or twenty houses, closely packed together without any order or roadway. Usually there are one or two curious bee-hive-like structures in these villages, used here, I believe, as pig-sties or storehouses. On my way down from Sybil Head I was joined by a tall young man, who told me he had been in the navy, but had bought himself out before his time was over.

'Twelve of us joined from this place,' he said, 'and I was the last of them that stayed in it, for it is a life that no one could put up with. It's not the work that would trouble you, but it's that they can't leave you alone, and that you must be ever and always fooling over something.'

---

142. An Tiaracht, the most western of the six main Blasket Islands, site of a lighthouse.

He had been in South Africa during the war,[143] and in Japan, and all over the world; but he was now dressed in homespuns, and had settled down here, he told me, for the rest of his life. Before we reached the village we met Maurice, the fisherman I have spoken of,[144] and we sat down under a hedge to shelter from a shower. We began to talk of fevers and sicknesses and doctors – these little villages are often infested with typhus – and Maurice spoke about the traditional cures.

'There is a plant', he said, 'which is the richest that is growing out of the ground, and in the old times the women used to be giving it to their children till they'd be growing up, seven feet maybe in height. Then the priests and doctors began taking everything to themselves, and destroyed the old knowledge, and that is a poor thing, for you know well it was the Holy Mother of God who cured her own Son with plants the like of that, and said after, that no mother should be without a plant for ever to cure her child. Then she threw out the seeds of it over the whole world, so that it's growing every place from that day to this.'

The Shanachie (Summer 1907)

---

143. The Boer War (1899–1901) in which many Irishmen fought in the British army, as well as a number in the Irish Brigade on the Boer side. Synge's own sympathies were with the Boers: see Mc Cormack, pp. 241–2.

144. Presumably the enthusiast for Irish with whom Synge discussed fishing and French tobacco earlier in the essay. A reference in one of Synge's notebooks to 'Shaneen Manning', MS 4404, f. 27v, suggests that 'Maurice' may have been John Manning, listed as a 'farmer's son' of 21 in the 1901 Census, but it was a common name in the area.

'In West Kerry: the Blasket Islands'

When I had spent some time in Ballyferriter, I went out one Sunday[145] to the Great Blasket Island with a local schoolmaster,[146] and two young men from the village, who were going for the afternoon only. The day was admirably clear, with a blue sea and sky, and the voyage in the long canoe – I had not been in one for two or three years – gave me indescribable enjoyment. We passed Dunmore Head, and then stood out nearly due west towards the Great Blasket itself; the height of the mountains round the bay, and the sharpness of the rocks, making the place singularly different from the sounds about Aran, where I had last travelled in a curragh. As usual three men were rowing, my host,[147] his son,[148] and a tall man not unlike the types of Iar-Connaught,[149] all dressed in blue jerseys, homespun trousers, and shirts, and talking in Irish only, though my host could speak good English when he chose. As we came nearer the island,

---

145. 13 August 1905.

146. Possibly William Long, with whom Synge had been lodging in Ballyferriter: see n. 128 above.

147. Pádraig Ó Catháin (Patrick Keane), the so-called 'King' of the Blaskets; he was 40 in 1901. Here, and throughout, I am grateful to Muiris Mac Conghail for his help with identifying the people of the Blaskets.

148. Sean Ó Catháin (John Keane), 11 in 1901.

149. West Connacht, another name for Connemara.

'IN WEST KERRY: THE BLASKET ISLANDS'

which seemed to rise like a mountain straight out of the sea, we could distinguish a crowd of people in their holiday clothes, standing or sitting along the brow of the cliff watching our approach; and in one place only a patch of cottages with tarred roofs of felt, on the face of the hill several hundred feet about the line of surf. A little later we doubled into a cove among the rocks, and I landed at a boatslip,[150] with the sharp qualm of excitement I always feel when setting foot on one of these little islands where I am to stay for weeks. At the head of a steep zig-zag path we came out among the people, who crowded round us, and shook hands with the men who had come with me.

The cottage where I was to stay was one of the highest of the group; and, as we passed up to it through little paths among the cottages many white, wolfish-looking dogs came out and barked at us furiously. My host had gone in front with my bag, and when I reached his threshold, he came forward and shook hands with me again, with a finished speech of welcome. His eldest daughter, a young married woman of about twenty,[151] who manages the house, shook hands with me also, and then, without asking if we were hungry, began making us tea in a metal tea-pot, and frying us rashers of bacon. She was a small, beautifully-formed woman, with brown hair and eyes – instead of the black hair and blue eyes that are usually found with this type in Ireland – and delicate feet and ankles, that are not common in these places where the woman's work is so hard. Her sister,[152] who lives in the house also, was a bonny[153] girl of about eighteen, full of humour and spirits.

The schoolmaster made many jokes in English and Irish while the little hostess served our tea; and then the kitchen filled up with young men and women – the men dressed like ordinary fishermen, and the women wearing print bodices and coloured skirts that had none of the distinction

---

150. The rest of this sentence was cut from the revised text.

151. Máire Ní Cheatháin (Mary Keane), 16 in 1901, was married to Maidhc Léan Ó Guithín; her father, Pádraig, was a widower.

152. Cáit Ní Cheatháin (Kate Keane), 14 in 1901; she appears in two of Synge's Blasket photographs, see Mac Conghail, *The Blaskets*, pp. 121–2.

153. 'Bony' in the *Shanachie* text, a mistake Synge corrected in revision.

of the dress of Aran – and a polka was danced, with curious solemnity, in a whirl of dust.[154] When it was over, it was time for my companions to go back to the mainland, and as soon as we began to go down to the sea a large crowd, made up of nearly all the men and women and children of the island, came down also, closely packed round us. At the edge of the cliff the young men and the schoolmaster bid me good-bye, and disappeared down the zig-zag path, leaving me alone with the islanders on the ledge of rock, where I had seen the people as we came in. I sat for a long time watching the sail of the canoe moving away to Dunquin, and talking to a young man who had spent some years in Ballyferriter, and had good English. The evening was peculiarly fine, and after a while, when the crowd had scattered, I passed up through the cottages, and walked along a boreen towards the north-west, between a few plots of potatoes, and little fields of weeds, that seemed to have gone out of cultivation not long ago. Beyond these I turned up a sharp, green hill, and came out suddenly on the broken edge of a cliff. The effect was wonderful. The Atlantic was right underneath; then I could see the sharp rocks of several uninhabited islands a mile or two off, the Tearaught far away in the west, and, on my left, the whole northern edge of the island I was on, curving round towards the west, with a steep, heathery face a thousand feet high. The whole sight of wild islands and sea was as clear and cold and brilliant as what one sees in a dream, and alive with the singularly severe glory that is in the character of this place. As I was wandering about I saw many of the younger islanders, not far off, jumping, and putting the weight – a heavy stone – or running races on the grass. Then four girls, walking arm-in-arm, came up and talked to me in Irish. Before long they began to laugh loudly at some signs I made to eke out my meaning; and by degrees the men wandered up also, till there was a crowd round us. The cold of the night was growing stronger, however, so we turned back to the village, and sat round the fire in the kitchen the rest of the evening.

At eleven o'clock the people got up as one man, and went away, leaving me with the little hostess – the man of the house had gone to the main-

---

154. Tomás O'Crohan gives an account of the visit of a dancing-master to the island in *The Islandman*, trans. Robin Flower (Oxford: Oxford University Press, 1951 [1937]) pp. 82–3.

land with the young men – her husband and sister. I told them I was sleepy, and ready to go to bed, so the little hostess lighted a candle, carried it into the room beyond the kitchen, and stuck it up on the end of the bedpost of one of the beds with a few drops of grease. Then she took off her apron, and fastened it up in the window as a blind, laid another apron, her sister's, on the wet earthen floor for me to stand on, and told me I might go to bed. The room had two beds, running from wall to wall, with a small space between them, a chair that the little hostess had brought in, and an old hairbrush that was propping the window open, my bag, and no other article of any kind. When I had been in bed for some time, I heard the host's voice in the kitchen, and a moment or two later he came in with a candle in his hand, and made a long apology for having been away the whole of my first evening on the island, holding the candle while he talked very close to my face. I told that him I had been well entertained by his family and neighbours, and had hardly missed him. He went away, and half an hour later opened the door again with the iron spoon which serves to lift the latch, and came in, in a suit of white homespuns, and said he must ask me to let him stretch out in the other bed, as there was no place else for him to lie. I told him that he was welcome, and he got into the other bed, and lit his pipe. Then we had a long talk about this place, and America, and the younger generations.

'There has been no one drowned on this island,' he said, 'for forty years, and that is a great wonder, for it is a dangerous life. There was a man – the brother of the man you were talking to when the girls were dancing – was married to a widow had a public-house away to the west of Ballydavid, and he was out fishing for mackerel, and he got a great haul of them. Then he filled his canoe too full, so that she was down to the edge in the water, and a wave broke into her, when they were near the shore, and she went down under them. Two men got ashore, but the man from this island was drowned, for his oilskins went down about his feet, and he sank where he was.'

Then we talked about the chances of the mackerel season. 'If the season is good,' he said, 'we get on well; but it is not certain at all. We do pay £4 for a net, and sometimes the dogfish will get into it the first day and tear it into pieces as if you'd cut it with a knife. Sometimes the mackerel will die in the net, and then ten men would be hard set to pull them up into the canoe, so that if the wind rises on us we must cut loose, and let down the net to the bottom of the sea. When we get fish here in the night, we go to Dunquin and sell them to buyers in the morning; and believe me it is a dangerous thing to cross that sound when you have too great a load taken into your canoe. When it is too bad to cross over, we do salt the fish ourselves – we must salt them cleanly and put them in clean barrels – and then, the first day it is calm, buyers will be out after them from the town of Dingle.'

Afterwards he spoke of the people who go away to America and the younger generations that are growing up now in Ireland.

'The young people is no use,' he said. 'I am not as good a man as my father was, and my son is growing up worse than I am'. Then he put up his pipe on the end of the bedpost. 'You'll be tired now,' he went on, 'so it's time we were sleeping, and I humbly beg your pardon, might I ask your name?'

I told him. 'Well, good night so,' he said, 'and may you have a good sleep your first night in this island.'

Then he put out the candle and we settled to sleep. In a few minutes I could hear that he was in his dreams, and just as my own ideas were beginning to wander the house door opened and the son of the place, a young man of about twenty, came in and walked into our room with another candle, and came over to my bed. I lay with my eyes closed, and the young man did not seem pleased with my presence, though he looked at me with curiosity. When he was satisfied, he went back to the kitchen, and took a drink of whiskey and said his prayers. Then, after loitering about for some time and playing with a little mongrel greyhound that seemed to adore him, he took off his clothes, and clambering very artfully over his father, stretched out on the inner side of the bed.

I awoke the next morning about six o'clock, and not long afterwards the host awoke also, and asked how I did. Then he wanted to know if I ever drank whiskey; and, when he heard that I did so, he began calling for one of his daughters at the top of his voice. In a few moments the younger girl came in, looking very sleepy, and, at the host's bidding, got the whiskey-bottle, some water, and a green wine-glass out of the kitchen. She came first to my bedside and gave me a dram, then she did the same for her father and brother, handed us our pipes and tobacco, and went back to her bed.

There were to be sports at noon in Ballyferriter,[155] and when we had talked for a while I asked the host if he would think well of my going over to see them. 'I would not,' he said; 'you'd do better to stay quiet in this place where you are. The men will be all drunk coming back, fighting and kicking in the canoes, and a man the like of you who aren't used to us would be frightened out of his life. Then if you went the people would be taking you into one public-house, and then into another, till you'd maybe get drunk yourself, and that wouldn't be a nice thing for a gentleman. Stay where you are in this island, and you'll be safest so.'

When the son got up a little later and began going in and out of the kitchen, some of the neighbours, who had already come in, stared at me with curiosity as I lay in my bed. Then I got up myself and went into the kitchen. The little hostess set about getting my breakfast, but before it was ready, she partly rinsed the dough out of a pan, where she had been kneading bread, poured some water into it, and put it on a chair near the door. Then she hunted about the edges of the rafters till she found a piece of soap, which she put on the back of a chair with a towel, and told me I might wash my face. I did so as well as I was able, in the middle of the people, and dried myself with the towel, which was the one used by the whole family.

The morning looked as if it would turn to rain and wind, so I took the advice I had been given, and let the canoes go off without me to the sports. After a turn on the cliffs I came back to the house to write letters.[156] The little hostess was washing up the breakfast things when I arrived with my papers and pens; but she made room for me at the table, and spread out an

---

155. Races were traditionally held in August at Béal Bán by Smerwick Harbour just north of Ballyferriter: information from Muiris Mac Conghail.

156. A number of letters written by Synge from the Blaskets survive, to Yeats, Lady Gregory and his German translator Max Meyerfeld (1875–1940): see CL I pp. 122–6.

old newspaper for me to write on. A little later, when she had finished her washing, she came over to her usual place in the chimney-corner, not far from where I was sitting, sat down on the floor, and took out her hair-pins and began combing her hair. As I finished each letter I had to tell her who it was to, and where the people lived; and then I had to tell her if they were married or single, how many children they had, and make a guess at how many pounds they spent in the year, and at the number of their servants. Just before I finished, the younger girl came back with three or four other young women, who were followed in a little while by a party of men.

I showed them some photographs of the Aran Islands and Wicklow, which they looked at with eagerness. The little hostess was especially taken with two or three that had nicely dressed babies or children in their foreground; and as she put her hands on my shoulders and leaned over to look at them, with the confidence that is so usual in these places, I could see that she had her full share of the passion for children which is powerful in all women who are permanently and profoundly attractive. While I was telling her what I could about the children, I saw one of the men looking with peculiar amazement at an old photograph of myself, that had been taken by a friend many years ago in an alley of the Luxembourg gardens,[157] where there were many statues in the background. 'Look at that,' he whispered in Irish to one of the girls, pointing to the statues, 'in those countries they do have naked people standing about in their skins.'

I explained that the figures were of marble only, and then the little hostess and all the girls examined them also. 'Oh, dear me,' said the little hostess, 'Is deas an rud do bheith ag siubhal ins an domhain mor'[158] (it's a fine thing to be travelling in the big world).'

In the afternoon I went up and walked along the narrow central ridge of the island, till I came to the highest point,[159] which is nearly three miles west of the village. The weather was gloomy and wild, and there was some-

---

157. This photograph survives among the Synge papers in Trinity College Dublin Library: MS 6189/9.
158. Here and below, Synge's spelling in Irish has been left uncorrected.
159. Croaghmore.

thing nearly appalling in the loneliness of the place. I could look down on either side into a foggy edge of grey moving sea, and then further off I could see many distant mountains, or look out across the shadowy outline of Inishtooskert[160] to the Tearaught rock. While I was sitting on the little mound which marks the summit of the island – a mound stripped and riddled by rabbits – a heavy bank of fog began to work up from the south, behind Valentia, on the other jaw of Dingle Bay. As soon as I saw it I hurried down from the pinnacle where I was, so that I might get away from the more dangerous locality before the cloud overtook me. In spite of my haste, I had not gone half a mile when an edge of fog whisked and circled round me, and in a moment I could see nothing but a grey shroud of mist, and a few yards of steep, slippery grass. Everything was distorted and magnified to an extraordinary degree; but I could hear the moan of the sea under me, and I knew my direction, so I worked along towards the village without particular trouble. In some places the island on this southern side is bitten into by sharp, narrow coves, and when the fog opened a little I could see across them where gulls and choughs were picking about on the grass, looking as big as black Kerry cattle, or as mountain sheep. Before I reached the house the cloud had turned to a sharp shower of rain, and as I went in the water was dripping from my hat. 'Oh, dear me', said the little hostess, when she saw me, 'Ta tu an fhliuch anois (you are very wet now)'. She was alone in the house, breathing audibly, with a sort of simple self-importance, as she washed her jugs and tea-cups. While I was drinking my tea a little later, some women came in with three or four little girls – the most beautiful children I have ever seen – who live in one of the nearest cottages. They tried to get the little girls to dance a reel together, but the smallest of them was shy, and went and hid her head in the skirts of the little hostess. In the end, however, two of the little girls danced with two of those who were grown up, to the lilting of one of them. The little hostess sat at the fire while they danced, plucking and drawing a cormorant for the men's dinner, and calling out to the little girls when they lost the step of the dance.

---

160. Inis Tuaisceart, which lies to the north of the Great Blasket.

In the evenings of Sundays and holidays the young men and girls go out to a rocky headland on the north-west, where there is a long, grassy slope, to dance and amuse themselves; and this evening I wandered out there with two men, telling them ghost-stories in Irish as we went. When we turned over the edge of the hill, we came on a number of young men lying on the short grass playing cards. We sat down near them, and before long a party of girls and young women came up also and sat down, twenty paces off, on the brink of the cliff, some of them wearing the fawn-coloured shawls that are so attractive and so much thought of in the south. It was just after sunset, and Inishtooskert was standing out with a smoky blue outline against the redness of the sky. At the foot of the cliff a wonderful silvery light was shining on the sea, which already, before the beginning of September, was looking eager and wintry and cold. The little group of blue-coated men lying on the grass, and the group of girls further off, had a singular effect in this solitude of rocks and sea, and, in spite of their high spirits, it gave me a pang of grief to feel the utter loneliness and desolation of the place that has given these people their finest qualities.

One of the young men had been thrown from a car a few days before on his way home from Dingle, and his face was still raw and bleeding and horrible to look at, but the young girls seemed to find romance in his condition, and several of them went over and sat in a group round him, stroking his arms and face. When the card-playing was over, I showed the young men a few tricks and feats, which they worked at themselves, to the great amusement of the girls, till they had accomplished them all. On our way back to the village, the young girls ran wild in the twilight, flying and shrieking over the grass, or rushing up behind the young men and throwing them over, if they were able, by a sudden jerk or trip. The men in return caught them by one hand, and spun them round and round four or five times and then let them go, when they whirled down the grassy slope for many yards, spinning like peg-tops, and only keeping their feet by the greatest efforts or good luck.

When we got to the village, the people scattered for supper, and in our cottage the little hostess swept the floor, and sprinkled it with some sand she had brought home in her apron. Then she filled a crock with drinking-

'IN WEST KERRY: THE BLASKET ISLANDS'

water, lit the lamp, and sat down by the fire to comb her hair. Some time afterwards, when a number of young men had come in, as was usual, to spend the evening, someone said a niavogue was on its way home from the sports. We went out to the door, but it was too dark to see anything except the lights of a little steamer that was passing up the sound, almost beneath us, on its way to Limerick or Tralee. When it had gone by, we could hear a furious drunken uproar coming up from a canoe that was somewhere out in the bay. It sounded as if the men were strangling or murdering each other, and it seemed almost miraculous that they should be able to manage their canoe. The people seemed to think they were in no special danger, and we went in again to the fire and talked about porter and whiskey – I have never heard the men here talk for half an hour of anything without some allusion to drink – discussing how much a man could drink with comfort in a day, whether it is better to drink when a man is thirsty or at ordinary times, and what food gives the best liking for porter. Then they asked me how much porter I could drink myself, and I told them I could drink whiskey, but that I had no taste for porter, and would only take a pint or two at odd times when I was thirsty.

'The girls are laughing to hear you say that,' said an old man, 'but whiskey is a lighter drink, and I'd sooner have it myself, and any old man would say the same.' A little later some young men came in in their Sunday clothes, and told us the news of the sports.

This morning it was raining heavily, and the host got out some nets and set to work, with his son and son-in-law, mending many holes that had been cut by dogfish, as the mackerel season is soon to begin. While they were at work the kitchen emptied and filled continually with islanders passing in and out, and discussing the weather and the season. Then they started cutting each other's hair, the man who was being cut sitting with an oilskin round him on a little stool by the door, and some other men sharpened their razors on the host's razor-strop, which seems to be the only one on the island. I had not shaved since I arrived, so the little hostess asked me after a while if I would like to shave myself before dinner. I told her I would, so she got me some water in the potato-dish and put it on a chair. Then her sister got me a little piece of broken looking-glass and put it on a nail near the door where there was some light. I set to work, and as I stood with my back to the people I could catch a score of eyes here and there in the glass, watching me intently. 'That is a great improvement to you now,' said the host, when I had done, 'and whenever you want a beard, God bless you, you'll have a thick one surely.'

When I was coming down in the evening from the ridge of the island where I spend much of my time, looking at the richness of the Atlantic on one side, and the sad or brilliant greys of Dingle Bay on the other, I was joined by two young women, and we walked back together. Just outside the village we met an old woman who stopped and laughed at us. 'Well, aren't you in good fortune this night, stranger,' she said, 'to be walking up and down in the company of women?'

'I am surely,' I answered; 'isn't that the best thing to be doing in the whole world?'

At our own door I saw the little hostess sweeping the floor, so I went down for a moment to the gable of the cottage, and looked out over the roofs of the little village to the sound, where the tide was running with extraordinary force that makes the waves break and foam in the calmest weather. In a few minutes the little hostess came down and stood beside me – she thought I should not be left by myself when I had been driven away by the dust – and I asked her many questions about the names and relationships of the people that I am beginning to know.

Afterwards, when many of the people had come together in the kitchen, the men told me about their lobsterpots that are brought from Southampton, and cost half-a-crown each. 'In good weather,' said the man who was talking to me, 'they will often last for a quarter, but if storms come up on them, they will sometimes break up in a week or two. Still, it is a good trade;'[161] and we do sell lobsters and crayfish every week in the season to a boat from England or a boat from France that do come in here, as you'll maybe see before you go.'

---

161. In his notebook, Synge noted that ten men from the island who had spent the summer on Inishvickillaun had 'made about £50 each catching lobster and crayfish', MS 4404, f 18r.

'IN WEST KERRY: THE BLASKET ISLANDS'

I told them I had been often in France, and one of the boys began counting up the numerals in French to show what he had learnt from their buyers. A little later, when the talk was beginning to flag, I turned to a young man near me, the best fiddler, I was told, on the islands, and asked him to play us a dance. He made excuses, and would not get his fiddle; but two of the girls slipped off and brought it. The young man tuned it and offered it to me, but I insisted that he should open the evening. Then he played one or two tunes, without tone, but with good intonation and rhythm. When it was my turn I played a few tunes also; but the pitch was so low I could not do what I wanted, and I had not much success with the people, though the fiddler himself watched me with interest. 'That is great playing,' he said, when I had finished, 'and I never seen anyone the like of you for moving your hand and getting the sound out of it with the full drag of the bow.' Then he played a polka and four couples danced. The women as usual were in their naked feet, and whenever there was a figure for women only, there was a curious hush and patter of bare feet till the heavy pounding and shuffling of the men's boots broke in again. The whirl of music and dancing in this little kitchen stirred me with an extraordinary effect. The kindliness and merrymaking of these islanders, who, one knows, are full of riot and severity and daring, have a quality and attractiveness that are absent altogether from the life of towns, and makes one think of the life that is shown in the old ballads of Scotland.

After the dance the host, who had come in, sang a long English doggerel about a poor scholar who went to Maynooth and had great success in his studies, so that he was praised by the bishop. Then he went home for his holiday, and a young woman, who had great riches, asked him into her parlour, and told him it was no fit life for a fine young man to be a priest, always saying Mass for poor people, and that he would have a right to give up his Latin, and get married to herself. He refused her offers and went back to his college. When he was gone, she went to the justice, in great anger, and swore an oath against him, that he had seduced her and left her with child. He was brought back for his trial, and he was in risk to be degraded and hanged, when a man rode up on a horse and said it was himself was the lover of the lady, and the father of her child.

Then they told me about an old man of eighty years, who is going to spend the winter alone on Inishvickillaun,[162] an island six miles from this village. His son is making canoes and doing other carpenter's jobs on this island, and the other children have scattered also; but the old man refuses to leave the island he has spent his life on, so they have left him with a goat, and a bag of flour and stack of turf.

I have just been to the weaver's,[163] looking at his loom and appliances. The host took me down to his cottage over the brow of the village, where some young men were finishing the skeleton of a canoe, and we found his family crowded round a low table on green stools with rope-seats, finishing their dinner of potatoes. A little later the old weaver, who looks pale and sickly compared with the other islanders, took me into a sort of outhouse with a damp feeling in the air, where his loom was set up. He showed me how it was worked, and then brought out some pieces of stuff that he had woven. At first I was puzzled by the fine brown colour of some of the material, but they explained it was from selected wools of the black or mottled sheep that are common here, and are so variegated that many tints of grey or brown can be had from their fleeces. The wool for the flannel is sometimes spun on this island; sometimes it is given to women in Dunquin, who spin it cheaply for so much a pound. Then it is woven, and finally the stuff is sent to a mill in Dingle to be cleaned and dressed before it is given to a tailor in Dingle to be made up for their own use. Such cloth is not cheap, but is of wonderful quality and strength. When I came out of the weaver's, a little sailing-smack was anchored in the sound, and some one on board her was blowing a horn. They told me she was the French boat, and as I went back to my cottage I could see many canoes hurrying out to her with their cargoes of lobsters and crabs.

---

162. Inis Icíleáin, the most southerly of the Blasket group. The old man was almost certainly Muris Mór Ó Dálaigh: information from Muiris Mac Conghail.

163. Eoghan Bán Conchúir; he and his wife were the last of the Protestant community on the island where a Protestant mission school had been established in 1839: information from Muiris Mac Conghail.

I have left the island again. I walked round the cliffs in the morning, and then packed my bag in my room, several girls putting their heads into the little window while I did so, to say it was a great pity I was not staying on for another week or a fortnight. Then the men went off with my bag in a heavy shower, and I waited a minute or two while the little hostess buttered some bread for my lunch and tied it up in a clean handkerchief of her own. Then I bid them good-bye, and set off down to the slip with three girls, who came with me to see that I did not go astray among the innumerable paths. It was still raining heavily, so I told them to put my cape, which they were carrying, over their heads. They did so with delight, and ran down the path before me, to the great amusement of the islanders. At the head of the cliff, many people were standing about to bid me good-bye and wish me a good voyage.

The wind was in our favour, so the men took in their oars after rowing for about a quarter of a mile, and lay down in the bottom of the canoe, while one man ran up the sail, and the host steered with an oar. At Dunquin the host hired me a dray without springs, kissed my hand in farewell, and I was driven off to Ballyferriter.

The Shanachie (Autumn 1907)

'In West Kerry: To Puck Fair'

After a long day's wandering I reached, towards the twilight, a little cottage on the south side of Dingle Bay, where I have often lived.[164] There is no village near it; yet many other cottages are scattered on the little hills not far off; and as the people I lodge with are, in some ways, a leading family, many men and women look in during the day, or in the evening, to talk or tell stories, or to buy a few pennyworth of sugar or starch.[165] Although this cottage is not on the road anywhere – the main road passes a few hundred yards to the west – it is well known also to the peculiar race of local respectable tramps who move from one family to another in some special neighbourhood or barony. This evening when I came in I found a little old man, in a tall hat, and long brown coat, sitting up on the settle beside the fire, who was spending, one could see, a night or more in the place.

I had a great deal to tell the people at first of my travels in different parts of the county, to the Blasket Islands – which they can see from here

---

164. The cottage was that of Philly and Margaret Harris in Mountain Stage, near Glenbeigh, which Synge visited every summer from 1903 to 1906: see Introduction, p. xix. This essay is based on material from several of his visits there from 1904 to 1906.

165. Margaret Harris kept 'a cross-roads shop': RTÉ interview with Mrs Margaret (Pegeen) Feehan, daughter of Margaret and Philly Harris, broadcast on 16 April 1971. I am grateful to Eamon O Fiachán for making a recording of this interview available to me.

'IN WEST KERRY: TO PUCK FAIR'

– Corkaguiny,[166] and Tralee; and they had news to tell me also of people who have married or died since I was here before, or gone away, or come back from America. Then I was told that the old man, Dermot, or Darby, as he is called in English, was the finest story-teller in Iveragh;[167] and after a while he told us a long story in Irish, but spoke so rapidly and indistinctly – he had no teeth – that I could understand but few passages, and most of the younger people, fairly good native Irish-speakers, had difficulty also. When he finished, I asked him where he had heard the story.

'I heard it in the city of Portsmouth', he said. 'I worked there for fifteen years, and four years in Plymouth, and a long while in the hills of Wales; twenty-five years in all I was working at the other side; and there were many Irish in it, who would be telling stories in the evening, the same as we are doing here. I heard many good stories, but what can I do with them now, and I an old lisping fellow, the way I can't give them out like a ballad?'

When he had talked a little more about his travels, and a bridge over the Severn, that he thought the greatest wonder of the world, I asked him if he remembered the famine.

'I do well,' he said. 'I was living near Kenmare, and many's the day I saw them burying the corpses in the ditch by the road. It was after that I went to England; for this country was ruined and destroyed. I heard there was work at that time in Plymouth; so I went to Dublin, and took a boat that was going to England; but it was at a place called Liverpool they put me on shore, and then I had to walk to Plymouth, asking my way on the road. In that place I saw the soldiers after coming back from the Crimea,[168] and they all broken and maimed'.[169] Then he turned to one of the men: 'Do you know the story of the man who fished up the box of smoke, Thady?' he said.

'I do not,' said the man.

---

166. The barony of Corkaguiny included virtually all the Dingle peninsula.

167. Iveragh is the large Kerry peninsula south of Dingle Bay.

168. The Crimean War (1853–6), in which the British and French were allied with the Ottoman Empire against the Russians.

169. The passage that follows from 'Then he turned to one of the men' down to 'I let it slip' was omitted from the revised text of the essay.

Then he told another long, Irish story, with fine energy and expression, giving the 'runs' especially with extraordinary volubility. Whenever there was a purely rhetorical question, such as, 'Wasn't that a great wonder?' the people answered, 'It was indeed, Darby,' or whatever was expected. Just as he finished, a little old squatter, known as Danny-boy, came in, and shook me by the hand. 'Well,' he said to me, as he sat down in the corner, 'and where is your Missis?'

'Ah,' said the woman of the house, 'that's what I was going to ask the minute I seen him, but I let it slip.'[170]

A little later, when Darby went out for a moment, the people told me he beats up and down between Killorglin and Ballinskelligs and the Inny river,[171] and that he is a particular, crabby kind of man; and will not take anything from the people but coppers and eggs.

'And he's a wasteful old fellow with all,' said the woman of the house, 'though he's eighty years old or beyond it, for whatever money he'll get one day selling his eggs to the coastguards, he'll spend it the next getting a drink when he's thirsty, or keeping good boots on his feet.'

From that they began talking of misers, and telling stories about them.

'There was an old woman', said one of the men,[172] 'living beyond to the east, and she was thought to have a great store of money. She had one daughter only; and in the course of a year a young lad got married to her, thinking he'd have her fortune. The woman died after – God be merciful to her – and left the both of them as poor as they were before. Well, one night a man that knew them was passing to the Fair of Puck, and he came in, and asked would they give him a lodging for that night. They gave him what they had and welcome; and, after his tea, when they were sitting over

---

170. In 1906 Synge was engaged to Molly Allgood (Maire O'Neill), and had announced to the family that on his next visit he would be bringing his wife: Margaret Fehan, RTÉ interview, April 1971.

171. Killorglin is close to Glenbeigh at the north of the Iveragh peninsula, Ballinskelligs on its south coast, the Inny river inland in the mountains.

172. Denis Harris, younger brother of Philly, lived in the house next door. The tales of misers were recorded among the 'Stories of Denis Harris' which Synge collected in a notebook in 1905, MS 4401, ff. 1–6.

the fire – the way we are this night – the man asked them how they were so poor-looking, and if the old woman had left nothing behind her.

"Not a farthing did she leave," said the daughter.

"And did she give no word or warning, or message, in her last moments?" said the man.

"She did not," said the daughter, "except only that I shouldn't comb out the hair of her poll and she dead."

"And you heeded her," said the man.

"I did surely," said the daughter.

"Well," said the man, "to-morrow night, when I'm gone, let the two of you go down the Reilic (the graveyard) and dig up her coffin, and look in her hair, and see what it is you'll find in it."

"We'll do that," said the daughter, and with that they all stretched out for the night.

'The next evening they went down quietly with a shovel, and they dug up the coffin, and combed through her hair, and there behind her poll they found her fortune, five hundred pounds, in good notes and gold.'

'There was an old fellow living on the little hill beyond the graveyard,' said Danny-boy, when the man had finished, 'and he had his fortune some place hid in his bed; and he was an old, weak fellow, so that they were all watching him to see he wouldn't hide it away. One time there was no one in it but himself and a young girl; and the old fellow slipped out of his bed, and went out of the door, as far as a little bush and some stones. The young girl kept her eye on him, and she made sure he'd hidden something in the bush; so, when he was back in his bed, she called the people, and they all came and looked in the bushes, but not a thing could they find. The old man died after, and no one ever found his fortune to this day.'

'There were some young lads, a while since,' said the old woman, 'and they went up of a Sunday and began searching through those bushes to see if they could find anything; but a kind of a turkey-cock came up out of the stones and drove them away.'

'There was another old woman,' said the man of the house, 'who tried to take down her fortune into her stomach. She was near death, and she was all day stretched in her bed at the corner of the fire. One day when the girl was tinkering about, the old woman rose up and got ready a little skillet that was near the hob, and put something into it, and put it down by the fire; and the girl watching her all the time under her oxter, not letting on she seen her at all. When the old woman lay down again, the girl went over to put on more sods on the fire, and she got a look into the skillet; and what did she see but sixty sovereigns? She knew well what the old woman was striving to do, so she went out to the dairy, and she got a lump of fresh butter, and put it down into the skillet, when the woman didn't see her do it at all. After a bit the old woman rose up and looked into the skillet; and when she saw the froth of the butter, she thought it was the gold that was melted. She got back into her bed – a dark place maybe – and she began sipping and sipping at the butter till she had the whole of it swallowed. Then the girl made some trick to entice the skillet away from her, and she found the sixty sovereigns in the bottom, and she kept them for herself.'

By this time it was late; and the old woman brought over a mug of milk and a piece of bread to Darby at the settle; and the people gathered at the table for their supper; so I went into the little room at the end of the cottage where I am given a bed.

When I came into the kitchen in the morning, old Darby was still asleep on the settle, with his coat and trousers over him, a little red nightcap on his head, and his half-bred terrier, Jess, chained, with a little chain he carries with him, to the leg of the settle.

'That's a poor way to lie on the bare board,' said the woman of the house when she saw me looking at him; 'but when I filled a sack with straw for him last night, he wouldn't have it at all.'

While she was boiling some eggs for my breakfast, Darby roused up from his sleep, pulled on his trousers and coat, slipped his feet into his boots, and started off, when he had eaten a few mouthfuls of bread, for another house, where he is known, some five miles away.

'IN WEST KERRY: TO PUCK FAIR'

Afterwards I went out on the cnuceen,[173] a little hill between this cottage and the sea, to watch the people gathering carrageen moss, a trade which is much followed in this district during the springtides of summer. I lay down on the edge of the cliff where the heathery hill comes to an end and the steep rocks begin. About a mile to the west there was a long headland Feakle Callaigh[174] (the Witch's Tooth), covered with mists, that blew over me from time to time with a swish of rain, followed by sunshine again. The mountains on the other side of the bay were covered; so I could see nothing but the strip of brilliant sea below me, thronged with girls and men up to their waists in the water, with a hamper in one hand and a stick in the other, gathering the moss, and talking and laughing loudly as they worked. The long frill of dark, golden rocks covered with weed, with the asses and children slipping about on it, and the bars of silvery light breaking through on the further inlets of the bay, had the singularly brilliant liveliness one meets everywhere in Kerry.

When the tide began to come in, I went down one of the passes to the sea, and met many parties of girls and old men and women coming up with what they had gathered, most of them still wearing the clothes that had been in the sea, and were heavy and black with salt water. A little further on I met Danny-boy, and we sat down to talk.

'Do you see that sandy head?' he said, pointing out to the east; 'That is called the Stooks of the Dead Women; for one time a boat came ashore there with twelve dead women on board her, big ladies with green dresses and gold rings, and fine jewelries, and a dead harper or fiddler along with them. Then there are graves again in the little hollow by the cnuceen, and what we call them is the Graves of the Sailors; for some sailors, Greeks or great strangers were washed in there, a hundred years ago, and it is there that they were buried.' Then we began talking of the carrageen he had gathered, and the spring-tides that will come again this summer. I took out my diary to tell him the times of the moon but he would hardly listen

---

173. From Irish *cnocán*, 'little hill'. The hill here is Knockboy, on which Harris family tradition locates 'Synge's stone' as his favourite vantage point on the neighbourhood: I am grateful to Pat O'Shea for this information.

174. Feaklecally, on the south coast of Dingle Bay.

to me. When I stopped, he gave his ass a cut with his stick. 'Go on now,' he said; 'I wouldn't believe those almanacks at all; they do not tell the truth about the moon.'

The greatest event in West Kerry is the horse-fair, known as Puck Fair, which is held yearly in August.[175] If one asks anyone, many miles east or west of Killorglin, when he reaped his oats or sold his pigs or heifers, he will tell you it was four or five weeks, or whatever it may be, before or after Puck. On the main roads for many days past I have been falling in with tramps and trick characters of all kinds, sometimes single and sometimes in parties of four or five; and as I am on the roads a great deal, I have often met the same persons several days in succession – one day perhaps at Ballinskelligs, the next day at Feakle Callaigh, and the third in the outskirts of Killorglin.

Yesterday cavalcades of every sort were passing from the west with droves of horses, mares, jennets, foals, and asses, with their owners going after them in flat or railed carts, or riding on ponies.

The men of this house – they were going to buy a horse – went to the fair last night; and I followed at an early hour in the morning. As I came near Killorglin, the road was much blocked by the latest sellers pushing eagerly forward, and early purchasers who were anxiously leading off their young horses, before the roads became dangerous from the crush of drunken drivers and riders.

Just outside the town, near the first public-house, blind beggars were kneeling on the pathway, praying with almost oriental volubility for the souls of anyone who would throw them a coin.

'May the Holy Immaculate Mother of Jesus Christ', said one of them, 'intercede for you in the hour of need. Relieve a poor blind creature, and may Jesus Christ relieve yourselves in the hour of death. May He have mercy, I'm saying, on your brothers, and fathers, sisters, for evermore.'

Further on, stalls were set out with cheap cakes and refreshments, and one could see that many houses had been arranged as lodging and dining

---

175. Held in Killorglin over three days 10–12 August; Synge visited the Fair on 11 August 1904.

houses to supply the crowds who had come in. Then I came to the principal road that goes round the fair-green, where there was a great concourse of horses, trotting, and walking, and galloping in every direction. Most of them were of the lighter, cheaper class of animal, and were selling, apparently to the people's satisfaction, at prices that reminded one of the time when fresh meat was sold for three pence a pound. At the further end of the green there were one or two rough shooting galleries; and a number of women – not very rigid one could see – selling, or appearing to sell, all kinds of trifles, a set that come in, I am told, from towns not far away. At the end of the green I turned past the chapel, where a little crowd had just carried in a man who had been killed or badly wounded by a fall from a horse, and went down to the bridge of the river, and then back again into the main road of the town. Here there were a number of people who had come in for amusement only, and were walking up and down, looking at each other – a crowd is as exciting as champagne to these lonely people who live in long glens among the mountains – and meeting with cousins and friends. Then, in the three-cornered space in the middle of the town, I came on Puck himself, a magnificent he-goat (Irish *puc*), raised on a platform twenty feet high, and held by a chain from each horn, with his face down the road. He is kept in this position, with a few cabbages to feed on, for three days, so that he may preside over the pig-fair, and the horse-fair, and the day of winding-up.

At the foot of this platform, where the crowd was thickest, a young ballad-singer was howling a ballad in honour of Puck, making one think of the early Greek festivals, since the time of which, it is possible the goat has been exalted yearly in Killorglin.

The song was printed on a green slip by itself. It ran:

A New Song on the Great Puck Fair.
BY JOHN PURCELL.
All young lovers that are fond of sporting, pay attention for
    a while,
I will sing you the praises of Puck Fair, and I'm sure it will make
    you smile;

Where the lads and lassies coming gaily to Killorglin can be seen,
To view the puck upon the stage, as our hero dressed in green.

Chorus.
And hurra for the gallant puck so gay,
For he is a splendid one;
Wind and rain don't touch his tail,
For his hair is thirty inches long.

Now it is on the square he's erected with all colours grand and gay;
There's not a fair throughout Ireland but Puck Fair it takes the sway.
Where you see the gamblers in rotation, trick-o'-the-loops and other games,
The ballad-singers and the wheel-of-fortune, and the shooting-gallery for to take aim.

Chorus.
Where is the tyrant dare oppose it
Our old customs we will hold up still,
And I think we will have another –
That is Home Rule and Purchase Bill.[176]

Now all young men that are not married, next Shrove can take a wife,
For before next Puck Fair we will have Home Rule, and then you will be settled down in life.
Now the same advice I give young girls for to get married and have pluck:
Let the landlords see that you defy them when coming to Fair of Puck.
Céad míle Fáilte to The Fair of Puck.

---

176. Home Rule, limited legislative autonomy for Ireland, and land purchase by tenants from landlords, facilitated under a number of Land Acts from 1881 to 1903, had been the two great political objectives of Irish nationalism for a generation.

When one makes the obvious elisions, the lines are not so irregular as they look, and are always sung to a measure; yet the whole, in spite of the assonance rhymes, and the 'colours grand and gay' seems pitifully remote from any good spirit of ballad-making.

Across the square, a man and a woman who had a baby tied on her back, were singing another ballad on the Russian and Japanese War,[177] in the curious method of antiphony that is still sometimes heard in the back streets of Dublin. These are some of the verses:

> *Man.* Now provisions are rising, 'tis sad for to state,
> The flour, tea and sugar, tobacco, and meat;
> But God help us poor Irish, how must we stand the test
> *Both.* If they only now stop the trade of commerce.
> *Woman.* Now the Russians are powerful on sea and on land
> But the Japs they are active, they will them command.
> Before this war it is finished I have one word to say
> *Both.* There will be more shot and drowned than in the Crimea.
> *Man.* Now the Japs are victorious up to this time,
>   And thousands of Russians I hear they are dying.
>   Etc., etc.

And so it went on with the same alternation of the voices through seven or eight verses; and it was curious to feel how much was gained by this simple variation of the voices.

When I passed back to the fair-green, I met the men I am staying with, and went off with them under an archway, and into a back-yard, to look at a little two-year-old filly that they had bought, and left for the moment in a loose-box with three or four young horses. She was prettily and daintily shaped, but looked too light, I thought, for the work she will be expected to do. As we came out again into the road, an old man was singing an out-spoken ballad on women in the middle of the usual crowd. Just as we passed, it came to a slightly scandalous conclusion; and the women scattered in every direction, shrieking with laughter, and holding shawls over their mouths.

---

177. The Russo-Japanese War (1904–5), over the control of Manchuria, was in progress at this time.

At the corner we turned into a public-house where there were men we knew, who had done their business also; and we went into the little alcove to sit down quietly for a moment. 'What will you take, sir?' said the man I lodge with. 'A glass of wine?'

I took beer, and the others took porter; but we were only served after some little time, as the house was thronged with people.

The men were too much taken up with their bargains and losses to talk much of other matters; and before long we came out again and the son of the house started homewards, leading the new filly by a little halter of rope.

Not long afterwards I started also. Outside Killorglin rain was coming up over the hills of Glen Car,[178] so that there was a strained hush in the air, and a rich aromatic smell coming from the bog-myrtle, or some other boggy shrub, that grows thickly in this place. The strings of horses and jennets scattered over the road did not keep away a strange feeling of loneliness that seems to hang in the evening over this brown plain of bog that stretches from Carrantuohill to Cuchulain's House.[179]

Before I reached the cottage dense torrents of rain were closing down through the glens, and driving in white sheets between the little hills that are on each side of the way.

One morning in autumn some weeks later I started in a local train for the first stage of my journey to Dublin, seeing the last of Magillicuddy's Reeks, that were touched with snow in places, Dingle Bay, and the islands beyond it. At a little station[180] where I changed trains I got into a carriage where there was a woman with her daughter, a girl of about twenty, who

---

178. Glencar, the valley of the Caragh River that empties into Lough Caragh, south of Kilorglin.

179. Mountains in the McGillicuddy Reeks range, Carrantuohil being the highest mountain in Ireland.

180. Most likely Faranfore, where the branch line to Valentia met the main Tralee to Killarney line.

seemed uneasy and distressed. Soon afterwards when a collector was looking at our tickets, I called out that mine was for Dublin; and as soon as he got out the woman came over to me.

'Are you going to Dublin?' she said.

I told her I was.

'Well,' she went on, 'here is my daughter going there too; and maybe you'd look after her, for I'm getting down at the next station. She is going up to an hospital for some little complaint in her ear, and she has never travelled before, so that she's lonesome in her mind.'

I told her I would do what I could, and at the next station I was left alone with my charge, and one other passenger, a returned American girl, who was on her way to Mallow to get the train for Queenstown.[181] When her mother was lost sight of, the young girl broke out into tears; and the returned American and myself had much trouble to quiet her.

'Look at me,' said the American; 'I'm going off for ten years to America, all by myself, and I don't care a rap.'

When the girl got quiet again, the returned American talked to me about scenery and politics and the arts – she had been seen off by her sisters in bare feet, with shawls over their heads – and the life of women in America.

At several stations girls and boys thronged in to get their places for Queenstown, leaving parties of old men and women wailing with anguish on the platform. At one place an old woman was seized with such a passion of regret, when she saw her daughters moving away from her for ever, that she made a wild rush after the train; and when I looked out for a moment I could see her writhing and struggling on the platform, with her hair over her face, and two men holding her by the arms.

Some young men had got into our compartment for a few stations only, and they looked on with the greatest satisfaction.

'Ah,' said one of them, 'we do have great sport every Friday and Saturday, seeing the old women crying and howling in the stations.'

---

181. Queenstown, now Cóbh, was at this time the main port in Ireland for transatlantic passenger liners.

At a junction[182] I moved into a Dublin train with my companion; and I could see that our unusual fellowship made great curiosity in the crowd of tourists and others who filled the carriage.

When we reached Dublin, I left my charge for a moment to see after my baggage; and when I came back I found her sitting on a luggage-barrow with her package in her hand, crying with despair because several cabmen in succession had turned her out of their cabs when she told them she was going to an hospital, on the pretext that they dreaded infection.

I could see they were looking out for some rich tourist with his trunks as a more lucrative fare; so I sent for the head-porter who had charge of the platform, and in a moment the cabmen changed their tone. When the porter arrived, we chose a comfortable cab; and I saw my charge driven off, sitting on the front seat of the cab, with her handkerchief to her eyes.

The Shanachie (Winter 1907)

---

182. Probably Killarney.

['In West Kerry': At the Races'][183]

For the last few days – I am staying in the Kerry cottage I have spoken of already[184] – the people have been talking of horse-races that were to be held on the sand,[185] not far off, and this morning I set out to see them with the man and woman of the house and two of their neighbours. Our way led through a steep boreen for a quarter of a mile to the edge of the sea, and then along a pathway between the cliffs and a straight grassy hill. When we had gone some distance the old man pointed out a slope in front of us, where, he said, Diarmuid had done his tricks of rolling the barrel and jumping over his spear, and had killed many of his enemies. He told me the whole story, slightly familiarised in detail, but not very different from the version everyone knows.[186] A little further on he pointed across the sea to our left – just beyond the strand where the

---

183. Though Synge did not live to publish this final essay in his West Kerry series, a more or less complete draft under this title is to be found in MS 4344, ff. 156r–172r. The essay is based on his last visit to the Harrises of Mountain Stage, 25 August–12 September 1906, and his brief return to the Dingle peninsula 12–16 October 1907.

184. The Harrises.

185. On Rossbeigh Strand, near Glenbeigh.

186. For Lady Gregory's popular version of these stories from the Fianna cycle of how Diarmuid, pursued by Fionn mac Cumhail after he eloped with Grania, defeated his pursuers, see *Gods and Fighting Men* (London: John Murray, 1913 [1904]), pp. 358–9.

races were to be run – to a neck of sand where, he said, Oisin was called away to the Tir-na-nOg.[187]

'The Tir-na-nOg[188] itself', he said, 'is below that sea, and a while since there were two men out in a boat in the night-time, and they got stuck outside some way or another. They went to sleep then, and when one of them wakened up he looked down into the sea, and he saw the Tir-na-nOg and people walking about, and sidecars driving in the squares.'

Then he began telling me stories of mermaids – a common subject in this neighbourhood.

'There was one time a man beyond of the name of Shee,' he said, 'and his master seen a mermaid on the sand beyond combing her hair, and he told Shee to get her. "I will," said Shee, "if you'll give me the best horse you have in your stable." "I'll do that," said the master. Then Shee got the horse, and when he saw the mermaid on the sand combing her hair, with her covering laid away from her, he galloped up, when she wasn't looking, and he picked up the covering and away he went with it. Then the waves rose up behind him and he galloped his best, and just as he was coming out at the top of the tide the ninth wave cut off his horse behind his back, and left himself and the half of his horse and the covering on the dry land. Then the mermaid came in after her covering, and the master got married to her, and she lived with him a long time, and had children – three or four of them. Well, in the wind-up, the master built a fine new house, and when he was moving into it, and clearing the things out, he brought down an old hamper out of the loft and put it in the yard. The woman was going about, and she looked into the hamper, and she saw her covering hidden away in the bottom of it. She took it out then and put it upon her and went back into the sea, and her children used to be on the shore crying after her. I'm told from that day there isn't one of the Shees can go out in a boat in that bay and not be drowned.'

We were now near the sandhills, where a crowd was beginning to come together, and booths were being put up for the sale of apples and

---

187. The subject of Yeats' first long narrative poem, *The Wanderings of Oisin*.
188. Tír na nÓg, literally 'the country of the young', Irish land of the fairies.

porter and cakes. A train had come in a little before at a station a mile or so away,[189] and a number of the usual trick-characters, with their stock-in-trade, were hurrying down to the sea. The roulette-man passed us first, unfolding his table and calling out at the top of his voice:

> Come play me a game of timmun and tup,
> The more you puts down the more you takes up.

'Take notice, gentlemen, I come here to spend a fortune, not to make one. Is there any sportsman in a hat or a cap, or a wig or a waistcoat, will play a go with me now? Take notice, gentlemen, the luck is on the green.'

The races had to be run between two tides while the sand was dry, so there was not much time to be lost, and before we reached the strand the horses had been brought together, ridden by young men in many variations of jockey dress. For the first race there was one genuine race-horse, very old and bony, and two or three young horses belonging to farmers in the neighbourhood. The start was made from the middle of the crowd at the near end of the strand, and the course led out along the edge of the sea to a post some distance away, back again to the starting-point, round a post and out and back once more.

When the word was given the horses set off in a wild helter-skelter along the edge of the sea, with crowds cheering them on from the sandhills. As they got small in the distance it was not easy to see which horse was leading, but after a sort of check, as they turned the post, they began nearing again a few yards from the waves, with the old race-horse, heavily pressed, a good length ahead. The stewards made a sort of effort to clear the post that was to be circled, but without much success, as the people were wild with excitement. A moment later, the old race-horse galloped into the crowd, twisted too suddenly, something cracked and jolted, and it limped out on three legs, gasping with pain. The next horse could not be stopped, and galloped out at the wrong end of the crowd for some little way before it could be brought back, so the last horses set off in front for the final lap.

---

189. Glenbeigh.

The lame race-horse was now mobbed by the onlookers and advisers, talking incoherently.

'Was it the fault of the jock?' said one man.

'It was not,' said another, 'for Michael (the owner) didn't strike him, and if it had been his fault, wouldn't he have broken his bones?'

'He was striving to spare a young girl had run out in his way,' said another. 'It was for that he twisted him.'

'Little slut!' said a woman; 'what did she want beyond on the sand?'

Many remedies were suggested that didn't sound reassuring, and in the end the horse was led off in a hopeless condition. A little later the race ended with an easy win for the wildest of the young horses. Afterwards I wandered up among the people, and looked at the sports. At one place a man, with his face heavily blackened, except one cheek and eye – an extraordinary effect – was standing shots of a wooden ball behind a board with a large hole in the middle, at three shots a penny. When I came past half an hour afterwards he had been hit in the mouth – by a girl someone told me – but seemed as cheerful as ever.

On the road, some little distance away, a party of girls and young men were dancing polkas to the music of a melodeon,[190] in a cloud of dust. When I had looked on for a little while I met some girls I knew, and asked them how they were getting on.

'We're not getting on at all,' said one of them, 'for we've been at the races for two hours, and we've found no beaux to go along with us.'

When the horses had all run, a jennet race was run and greatly delighted the people, as the jennets – there were a number of them – got scared by the cheering and ran wild in every direction. In the end it was not easy to say which was the winner, and a dispute began which nearly ended in blows. It was decided at last to run the race over again the following Sunday after Mass, so everyone was satisfied.

The day was magnificently bright, and the ten miles of Dingle Bay were wonderfully brilliant behind the masses of people and the canvas booths, and the scores of upturned shafts. Towards evening I got tired

---

190. A button accordion.

taking or refusing the porter my friends pressed on me continually, so I wandered off from the racecourse along the path where Diarmuid had tricked the Fenians.

Later in the evening news had been coming in of the doings in the sandhills, after the porter had begun to take effect and the darkness had come on.

'There was great sport after you left,' a man said to me in the cottage this evening. 'There were all beating and cutting each other on the shore of the sea. Four men fought together in one place till the tide came up on them, and was like to drown them; but the priest waded out up to his middle and drove them asunder. Another man was left for dead on the road outside the lodges, and some gentleman found him and had him carried into his house, and got the doctor to put plasters on his head. Then there was a red-headed fellow had his finger bitten through, and the postman was destroyed for ever.'

'He should be,' said the man of the house, 'for Michael Patch broke the seat of his car into three halves on his head.'

'It was this was the cause of it all,' said Danny-boy: 'they brought in porter east and west from the two towns you know of, and the two porters didn't agree together, and it's for that the people went raging at the fall of night.'

I have been out to Bolus Head,[191] one of the finest places I have met with. A little beyond Ballinskelligs the road turns up the side of a steep mountainy hill where one sees a brilliant stretch of sea with many rocks and islands – Deenish, Scariff, the Hog's Head and Dursey far away. As I was sitting on the edge of the road an old man came along and we began to talk. He had little English, but when I tried him in Irish we got on well, though he didn't follow any Connaught forms I let slip by accident.[192]

---

191. On the entrance to Ballinskelligs Bay, a long cycle, or train and cycle ride to the south of Mountain Stage where Synge was staying.

192. 'I am making great strides with the Munster dialect,' Synge wrote to Lady Gregory in a letter of 4 August 1905, during his visit to Ballyferriter: *CL* I 119.

We went on together, after a while, to an extraordinary straggling village along the edge of a hill. At one of the cottages he stopped and asked me to come in and take a drink and rest myself. I did not like to refuse him, we had got so friendly, so I followed him in, and sat down on a stool while his wife – a much younger woman – went into the bedroom and brought me a large mug of milk. As I was drinking it and talking to the couple, a sack that was beside the fire began to move slowly and the head of a yellow, feverish-looking child came out from beneath it, and began looking at me with a heavy stare. I asked the woman what ailed it, and she told me it had sickened a night or two before with headache and pains all through it; but she had not had the doctor, and did not know what was the matter. I finished the milk without much enjoyment, and went on my way up Bolus Head and then back to this cottage, wondering all the time if I had the germs of typhus in my blood.

Last night, when I got back to the cottage, I found that another 'travelling man' had arrived to stay for a day or two; but he was hard of hearing and a little simple in his head, so that we had not much talk. I went to bed soon after dark and slept until about two o'clock in the morning, when I was awakened by fearful screams in the kitchen. For a moment I didn't know where I was; then I remembered the old man, and I jumped up and went to the door of my room. As I opened it I heard the door of the family room across the kitchen opening also, and the frightened whispers of the people. In a moment we could hear the old man, who was sleeping on the settle, pulling himself out of a nightmare, so we went back to our beds.

In the morning the woman told me his story:

'He was living above on a little hillside,' she said, 'in a little bit of a cabin, with his sister along with him. Then, after a while, she got ailing in her heart, and he got a bottle for her from the doctor, and he'd rise up every morning before the dawn to give her a sup of it. She got better then, till one night he got up and measured out the spoonful, or whatever it was, and went to give it to her, and he found her stretched out dead before him. Since that night he wakes up one time and another, and begins crying out for Maurya – that was his sister – and he half in his dreams. It was that you heard in the night, and indeed it would frighten any person to hear him screaming as if he was getting his death.'

When the little man came back after a while, they began asking him questions till he told his whole story, weeping pitiably. Then they got him to tell me about the other great event of his life also, in the rather childish Gaelic he uses.

He had once a little cur-dog, he said, and he knew nothing of the dog-licence; then one day the peelers – the boys with the little caps – asked him into the barracks for a cup of tea. He went in cheerfully, and then they put him and his little dog into the lock-up till someone paid a shilling for him and got him out.

He has a stick he is proud of bound with pieces of leather every few inches – like one I've seen with a beggar in Belmullet. Since that first night he has not had nightmare again, and he lies most of the evening sleeping on the settle, and in the morning he goes round among the houses, getting his share of meal and potatoes.

I do not think a beggar is ever refused in Kerry. Sometimes, while we are talking or doing something in the kitchen, a man walks in without saying anything and stands just inside the door, with his bag on the floor beside him. In five or ten minutes, when the woman of the house has finished what she is doing, she goes up to him and asks: 'Is it meal or flour?'[193] 'Flour,' says the man. She goes into the inner room, opens her sack, and comes back with two handfuls. He opens his bag and takes out a bundle carefully tied up in a cloth or handkerchief; he opens this again, and usually there is another cloth inside, into which the woman puts her flour. Then the cloths are carefully knotted together by the corners, put back in the bag, and the man mutters a 'God bless you,' and goes on his way.

The meal, flour and potatoes that are thus gathered up are always sold by the beggar, and the money is spent on porter or second-hand clothes, or very occasionally on food when he is in a neighbourhood that is not hospitable. The buyers are usually found among the coastguards' wives, or in the little public-houses on the roadside.

---

193. Oatmeal or wheaten flour.

'Some of these men', said the woman of the house, when I asked her about them, 'will take their flour nicely and tastily and cleanly, and others will throw it anyway, and you'd be sorry to eat it afterwards.'

The talk of these people is almost bewildering. I have come to this cottage again and again, and I often think I have heard all they have to say, and then someone makes a remark that leads to a whole new bundle of folk-tales, or stories or wonderful events that have happened in the barony in the last hundred years. Tonight the people were unusually silent, although several neighbours had come in, and to make conversation I said something about the bull-fights in Spain that I had been reading of in the newspapers. Immediately they started off with stories of wicked or powerful bulls, and then they branched off to clever dogs and all the things they have done in West Kerry, and then to mad dogs and mad cattle and pigs – one incident after another, but always detailed and picturesque and interesting.

I have come back to the north of Dingle, leaving Tralee late in the afternoon.[194] At the station there was a more than usually great crowd, as there had been a fair in the town and many people had come in to make their Saturday purchases. A number of messenger boys with parcels from the shops in the town were shouting for the owners, using many familiar names, Justin McCarthy, Hannah Lynch and the like. I managed to get a seat on a sack of flour beside the owner, who had other packages scattered under our feet. When the train had started and the women and girls – the carriage was filled with them – had settled down into their places, I could see I caused great curiosity, as it was too late in the year for even an odd tourist, and on this line everyone is known by sight.

Before long I got into talk with the old man next me, and as soon as I did so the women and girls stopped their talk and leaned out to hear what we were saying.

He asked first if I belonged to Dingle and I told him I did not.

---

194. This was Synge's last visit to Kerry, 12–16 October 1907, when he stayed in Ventry on the Dingle peninsula, curtailed by the onset of asthma.

'Well,' he said, 'you speak like a Kerryman, and you're dressed like a Kerryman, so you belong to Kerry surely.'

I told him I was born and bred in Dublin and that I had travelled in many places in Ireland and beyond it.

'That's easy said,' he answered, 'but I'd take an oath you were never beyond Kerry to this day.'

Then he asked sharply: 'What do you do?'

I answered something about my wanderings in Europe, and suddenly he sat up, as if a new thought had come to him.

'Maybe you're a wealthy man?' he said.

I smiled complacently.

'And not married?'

'No.'

'Well then,' he said, 'you're a damn lucky fellow to be travelling the world with no one to impede you.'

Then he went on to discuss the expenses of travelling.

'You'll likely be paying twenty pounds for this trip', he said, 'with getting your lodging and buying your tickets, till you're back in the city of Dublin?'

I told him my expenses were not so heavy.

'Maybe you don't drink so,' said his wife, who was near us, 'and that way your living wouldn't be so costly at all.'

An interruption was made by a stop at a small station and the entrance of a ragged ballad-singer, who sang a long ballad about the sorrows of mothers who see all their children going away from them to America.

Further on, when the carriage was much emptier, a middle-aged man got in, and we began discussing the fishing season, Aran fishing, hookers, nobbies and mackerel. I could see, while we were talking, that he, in his turn, was examining me with curiosity. At last he seemed satisfied.

'Begob,' he said, 'I see what you are; you're a fish-dealer.'

It turned out that he was the skipper of a trawler, and we had a long talk, the two of us and a local man who was going to Dingle also.

'There was one time a French man below,' said the skipper, 'who got married here and settled down and worked with the rest of us. One day we were outside in the trawler, and there was a French boat anchored a bit of a way off. "Come on", says Charley – that was his name – "and see can we get some brandy from that boat beyond." "How would we get brandy?" says I, "when we've no fish, or meat, or cabbages or a thing at all to offer them?" He went down below then to see what he could get. At that time there were four men only working the trawler, and in the heavy season there were eight. Well, up he comes again and eight plates under his arm. "There are eight plates," says he, "and four will do us; so we'll take out the other four and make a swap with them for brandy." With that he set the eight plates on the deck and began walking up and down and looking on them.

"The devil mend you," says I. "Will you take them up and come on, if you're coming?"

"I will," says he, "surely. I'm choicing out the ones that have pictures on them, for it's that kind they do set store on."'

Afterwards we began talking of boats that had been upset during the winter, and lives that had been lost in the neighbourhood.

'A while since,' said the local man, 'there were three men out in a canoe, and the sea rose on them. They tried to come in under the cliff, but they couldn't come to land with the greatness of the waves that were breaking. There were two young men in the canoe, and another man was sixty, or near it. When the young men saw they couldn't bring in the canoe, they said they'd make a jump for the rocks and let her go without them, if she must go. Then they pulled in on the next wave, and when they were close in the two young men jumped on to a rock, but the old man was too stiff, and he was washed back again in the canoe. It came on dark after that, and all thought he was drowned, and they held his wake in Dunquin. At that time there used to be a steamer going in and out trading in Valencia and Dingle and Cahirciveen, and when she came into Dingle, two or three days after, there was my man on board her, as hearty as a salmon. When he was washed back he got one of the oars, and kept her head to the wind; then the tide took him one bit and the wind took him another, and he wrought and he wrought till he was safe beyond in Valencia. Wasn't that a great wonder?' Then as he was ending his story we ran down into Dingle.

['IN WEST KERRY': AT THE RACES']

Often, when one comes back to a place that one's memory and imagination have been busy with, there is a feeling of smallness and disappointment, and it is a day or two before one can renew all one's enjoyment. This morning, however, when I went up the gap between Croagh Martin and then back to Slea Head,[195] and saw Innishtooskert and Inishvickillaun and the Great Blasket Island itself, they seemed ten times more grey and wild and magnificent than anything I had kept in my memory. The cold sea and surf, and the feeling of winter in the clouds, and the blackness of the rocks, and the red fern everywhere, were a continual surprise and excitement.

Here and there on my way I met old men with tailcoats of frieze, that are becoming so uncommon. When I spoke to them in English they shook their heads and muttered something I could not hear; but when I tried Irish they made me long speeches about the weather and the clearness of the day.

In the evening as I was coming home, I got a glimpse that seemed to have the whole character of Corkaguiney – a little line of low cottages with low roofs, and an elder tree without leaves beside them, standing out against a high mountain that seemed far away, yet was near enough to be dense and rich and wonderful in its colour.

Then I wandered round the wonderful forts of Fahan.[196] The blueness of the sea and the hills from Carrantuohill to the Skelligs, and the singular loneliness of the hillside I was on, with the few choughs and gulls in sight only, had a splendour that was almost a grief to the mind.

I turned into a little public-house this evening, where Maurice – the fisherman I have spoken about before – and some of his friends often sit when it is too wild for fishing. While we were talking a man came in, and joined rather busily in what was being said, though I could see he was not belonging to the place. He moved his position several times till he was quite close to

---

195. The south-western point of the Dingle peninsula, with the mountain Croagh Martin close by.

196. Just above the coast of Dingle Bay between Slea Head and Ventry.

me, then he whispered, 'Will you stand me a medium, mister? I'm hard set for money this while past.' When he had got his medium he began to give me his history. He was a journeyman tailor who had been a year or more in the place, and was beginning to pick up a little Irish to get along with. When he had gone we had a long talk about the making of canoes and the difference between those used in Connaught and Munster.

'They have been in the country', said Maurice, 'for twenty or twenty-five years only, and before that we had boats; a canoe will cost twelve pounds, or maybe thirteen pounds, and there is one old man beyond who charges fifteen pounds. If it is well done a canoe will stand for eight years, and you can get a new skin on it when the first one is gone.'

I told him I thought canoes had been in Connemara since the beginning of the world.

'That may well be,' he went on, 'for there was a certain man going out as a pilot, up and down into Clare, and it was he made them first in this place. It is a trade few can learn for it is all done within the head; you will have to sit down and think it out, and then make up when it is all ready in your mind.'

I described the fixed thole-pins that are used in Connaught – here they use two freely moving thole-pins, with the oar loose between them, and they jeered at the simplicity of the Connaught system. Then we got on the relative value of canoes and boats.

'They are not better than boats,' said Maurice, 'but they are more useful. Before you get a heavy boat swimming you will be wet up to your waist, and then you will be sitting the whole night like that; but a canoe will swim in a handful of water, so that you can get in dry and be dry and warm the whole night. Then there will be seven men in a big boat and seven shares of the fish; but in a canoe there will be three men only and three shares of the fish, though the nets are the same in the two.'

After a while a man sang a song, and then we began talking of tunes and playing the fiddle, and I told them how hard it was to get any sound out of one in a cottage with a floor of earth and a thatched roof over you.

'I can believe that,' said one of the men. 'There was a man a while since went into Tralee to buy a fiddle; and when he went into the shop an old fiddler followed him into it, thinking maybe he'd get the price of a pint. Well, the man was within choicing the fiddles, maybe forty of them, and the old fiddler whispered to him to take them out into the air, "for there's many a fiddle would sound well in here wouldn't be worth a curse outside", says he; so he was bringing them out and bringing them out till he found a good one among them.'

This evening, after a day of teeming rain, it cleared for an hour, and I went out while the sun was setting to a little cove where a high sea was running. As I was coming back the darkness began to close in except in the west, where there was a red light under the clouds. Against this light I could see patches of open wall and little fields of stooks, and a bit of laneway with an old man driving white cows before him. These seemed transfigured beyond any description.

Then I passed two men riding bare-backed towards the west, who spoke to me in Irish, and a little further on I came to the only village on my way. The ground rose towards it, and as I came near there was a grey bar of smoke from every cottage going up to the low clouds overhead, and standing out strangely against the blackness of the mountain beyond the village.

Beyond the patch of wet cottages I had another stretch of lonely roadway, and a heron kept flapping in front of me, rising and lighting again with many lonely cries that made me glad to reach the little public-house near Smerwick.

> First published in *Works*, Vol. IV (Dublin: Maunsel, 1910)

'In Wicklow: On the Road'

One evening after heavy rains I set off to walk to a village at the other side of some hills, part of my way lying along a steep, heathery track. The valleys that I passed through were filled with the strange splendour that comes after wet weather in Ireland, and on the tops of the mountains masses of fog were lying in white even banks. Once or twice I went by a lonely cottage with a smell of earthy turf coming from the chimney, weeds or oats sprouting on the thatch, and a broken cart before the door, with many straggling hens going to roost on the shafts. Near these cottages little bands of half-naked children, filled with the excitement of evening, were running and screaming over the bogs, where the heather was purple already, giving me the strained feeling of regret one has so often in these places when there is rain in the air.

Further on, as I was going up a long hill, an old man with a white pointed face and heavy beard pulled himself up out of the ditch and joined me. We spoke first about the broken weather, and then he began talking in a mournful voice of the famines and misfortunes that have been in Ireland.

'There have been three cruel plagues,' he said, 'out through the country since I was born in the West. First there was the big wind in 1839 that tore away the grass and green things from the earth. Then there was the blight that came on the ninth of June in the year 1846. Up to then the potatoes were clean and good, but that morning a mist rose up out of the sea, and you could hear a voice talking near a mile off across the stillness of the earth. It was the same the next day and the day after, and so on for three days or more, and then you could begin to see the tops of the stalks lying over as if the life was gone out of them. And that was the beginning of the great trouble and famine that destroyed Ireland. Then the people went on, I suppose, in their wickedness and their animosity of one against the other, and the Almighty God sent down the third plague, and that was the sickness called the choler. Then all the people left the town of Sligo – it's in Sligo I was reared – and you could walk through the streets at the noon of day and not see a person, and you could knock at one door and another door and find no one to answer you. The people were travelling out north and south and east, with the terror that was on them, and the country people were digging ditches across the roads and driving them back where they could, for they had a great dread of the disease.

'It was the law at that time that if there was sickness on any person in the town of Sligo you should notice it to the Governors, or you'd be put up in the gaol. Well, a man's wife took sick, and he went and noticed it. They came down then, with bands of men they had, and took her away to the sick-house, and he heard nothing more till he heard she was dead and was to be buried in the morning. At that time, there was such fear and hurry and dread on every person, they were burying people they had no hope of, and they with life within them. My man was uneasy a while thinking on that, and then what did he do but slip down in the darkness of the night and into the dead-house, where they were after putting his wife. There were beyond two score bodies, and he went feeling from one to the other. Then I suppose his wife heard him coming – she wasn't dead at all – and "Is that Michael?" says she. "It is then," says he; "and, oh, my poor woman, have you your last gasps in you still?" "I have, Michael," says she, "and they're after setting me out here with fifty bodies the way they'll put me down into my grave at the dawn of day." "Oh my poor woman," says he; "have you the strength left in you to hold on my back?" "Oh, Micky," says she, "I have surely." He took her up then on his back, and he carried her out by lanes and tracks till he got to his house. Then he never let on a word about it, and at the end of three days she began to pick up, and in a month's time she came out and began walking about like yourself or me. And there were many people were afeard to speak to her, for they thought she was after coming back from the grave.'

Soon afterwards we passed into a little village, and he turned down a lane and left me. It was not long, however, till another old man that I could see a few paces ahead stopped and waited for me, as is the custom of the place.

'I've been down in Kilpeddar[197] buying a scythe-stone,' he began when I came up to him, 'and, indeed, Kilpeddar is a dear place, for it's threepence they charged me for it; but I suppose there must be a profit from every trade, and we must all live and let live.'

When we had talked a little more, I asked him if he had been often in Dublin.

'I was living in Dublin near ten years,' he said, 'and, indeed, I don't know what way I lived that length in it, for there is no place with smells like the city of Dublin. One time I went up with my wife into those lanes where they sell old clothing, Hanover Lane and Plunket's Lane, and when my wife – she's dead now, God forgive her! – when my wife smelt the dirty air she put her apron up to her nose, and "For the love of God", says she, "get me away out of this place." And now may I ask if it's from there you are yourself, for I think by your speaking it wasn't in these parts you were reared?'

I told him I was born in Dublin, but that I had travelled afterwards and been in Paris and Rome, and seen the Pope Leo XIII.[198] 'And will you tell me,' he said, 'is it true that anyone at all can see the Pope?'

I described the festivals in the Vatican, and how I had seen the Pope carried through long halls on a sort of throne. 'Well, now,' he said, 'can you tell me who was the first Pope that sat upon that throne?'

I hesitated for a moment, and he went on:

---

197. A small village on the road from Wicklow to Dublin, normally spelled Kilpedder.
198. Synge lived in Rome from February to April 1896, and saw Leo XIII (1810–1903) on 6 March.

'I'm only a poor, ignorant man, but I can tell you that myself, if you don't know it with all your travels. Saint Peter was the first Pope, and he was crucified with his head down, and since that time there have been Popes upon the throne of Rome.'

Then he began telling me about himself.

'I was twice a married man,' he said 'my first wife died at her second child, and then I reared it up till it was as tall as myself – a girl it was – and she went off and got married and left me. After that I was married a second time to an aged woman, and she lived with me ten years, and then she died herself. There is nothing I can make now but tea, and tea is killing me, and I'm living alone in a little hut beyond, where four baronies, four parishes, and four townlands meet.'

By this time we had reached the village inn where I was lodging for the night, so I stood him a drink, and he went on to his cottage along a narrow pathway through the bogs.

Manchester Guardian (10 December 1908)

Bibliography

WORKS BY SYNGE

The Aran Islands (London: Elkin Matthews; Dublin: Maunsel, 1907)
The Aran Islands, ed. Tim Robinson (Harmondsworth: Penguin, 1992)
Collected Letters, ed. Ann Saddlemyer (Oxford: Clarendon Press, 1983), 2 vols.
Collected Works, general editor Robin Skelton (London: Oxford University Press, 1962–8) 4 vols:
    I *Poems*, ed. Robin Skelton (1962)
    II *Prose*, ed. Alan Price (1966)
    III *Plays*: Book 1, ed. Ann Saddlemyer (1968)
    IV *Plays*: Book 2, ed. Ann Saddlemyer (1968)
In Wicklow, West Kerry and Connemara (Dublin: Maunsel, 1911)
My Wallet of Photographs (Dublin: Dolmen, 1971)
Travels in Wicklow, West Kerry and Connemara (London: Serif, 2005)
Works (Dublin: Maunsel, 1910), 4 vols.

OTHER WORKS CITED

Arnold, Bruce, *Jack Yeats* (New Haven and London: Yale University Press, 1998)
Breathnach, Ciara, *The Congested District Board of Ireland, 1891–1923* (Dublin: Four Courts, 2005)
Campbell, J.F., *Popular Tales of the West Highlands* (Edinburgh: Birlinn, 1994 [1860])
Carpenter, Andrew (ed.), *My Uncle John: Edward Stephens's Life of J.M. Synge* (London: Oxford University Press, 1974)

Dunlop, John Colin, *History of Fiction*, revised H. Wilson, 2 vols. (London: Bell, 1888)
Flower, Robin, *The Western Island, or The Great Blasket* (Oxford: Clarendon Press, 1944)
Greene, David H. and Edward M. Stephens, *J.M. Synge 1871–1909* (New York: Collier, 1961 [1959])
Gregory, Lady, *Gods and Fighting Men* (London: John Murray, 1913 [1904])
Grene, Nicholas (ed.), *Interpreting Synge: Essays from the Synge Summer School 1991–2000* (Dublin: Lilliput, 2000)
Grene, Nicholas, 'Synge's Creative Development in *The Aran Islands*', *Long Room*, 10 (1974), 30–36
Hammond, J.L., *C.P. Scott of the Manchester Guardian* (London: Bell, 1934)
Hannigan, Ken and William Nolan (eds), *Wicklow: History and Society* (Dublin: Geography Publications, 1994)
The Last County: the Emergence of Wicklow as a County 1606–1845 (County Wicklow Heritage Project, 1993)
Mac Conghail, Muiris, *The Blaskets* (Dublin: Town House, 1987)
Mc Cormack, W.J., *Fool of the Family: A Life of J.M. Synge* (London: Weidenfeld & Nicolson, 2000)
McDonough, Steve, *The Dingle Peninsula: History, Folklore, Archaeology* (Dingle: Brandon Books, 1993), cited at http://www.dingle-peninsula.ie/ballyferriter/bf-history.html
Maxwell, Constantia, 'Bianconi and his Irish cars', *Country Life*, 16 April 1948, 776–7
Micks, W.L., *An Account of the Constitution, Administration and Dissolution of the Congested Districts Board for Ireland from 1891 to 1923* (Dublin: Easons, 1925)
O'Crohan, Tomás, *The Islandman*, trans. Robin Flower (Oxford: Oxford University Press, 1951 [1937])
O'Donoghue, John, *The Sunny Side of Ireland* (Dublin: Alex Thom, n.d. [1898])
Ó Muirithe, Diarmaid, *A Dictionary of Anglo-Irish* (Dublin: Four Courts, 1996)
Munch-Pedersen, Ole (ed.), *Scéalta Mháirtín Neile* (Baile Átha Cliath: Comhairle Bhéaloideas Éireann An Coláiste Ollscoile, 1994)
Pyle, Hilary, *The Different Worlds of Jack B. Yeats* (Dublin: Irish Academic Press, 1994)
Robinson, Tim, *Stones of Aran: Pilgrimage* (The Lilliput Press: Mullingar, 1986)
Schafer, Joseph (ed.), *Memoirs of Jeremiah Curtin* (Milwaukee: State Historical Society of Wisconsin, 1940)
Spenser, Edmund, *A View of the State of Ireland*, ed. Andrew Hadfield and Willy Maley (Oxford: Blackwell, 1997)

Stephens, E.M., *Life of J.M. Synge* (unpublished manuscript in Trinity College Dublin Library)

The Synge Manuscripts in the Library of Trinity College Dublin (Dublin: Dolmen, 1971)

Yeats, W.B., *Collected Letters*, II, *1896–1900*, ed. Warwick Gould, John Kelly, and Deirdre Toomey (Oxford: Clarendon Press, 1997)

Traynor, Michael, *The English Dialect of Donegal* (Dublin: Royal Irish Academy, 1953)

Yeats, W.B., *Essays and Introductions* (London: Macmillan, 1961)

Yeats, W.B., *Synge and the Ireland of His Time* (Dundrum: Cuala, 1911)